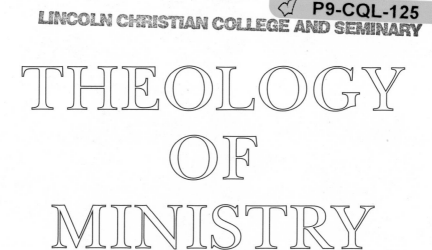

THEOLOGY OF MINISTRY

Completely Revised Edition

Thomas F. O'Meara, O.P.

PAULIST PRESS
New York/ Mahwah, N.J.

Cover design by John Petersen, JP Graphics

Book design by Theresa M. Sparacio

Library of Congress Cataloging-in-Publication Data

    O'Meara, Thomas F., 1935–
    Theology of Ministry / Thomas F. O'Meara.—Rev. ed.
      p. cm.
    Includes bibliographical references and index.
    ISBN 0-8091-3856-5 (alk. paper)
    1. Pastoral theology—Catholic Church. 2. Catholic Church—Doctrines.
I. Title.
BX1913.045   1999
253–dc21   99–13339
                                           CIP

Published by Paulist Press
997 Macarthur Boulevard
Mahwah, New Jersey 07430

www.paulistpress.com

Printed and bound in the
United States of America

CONTENTS

PREFACE   1

1. MINISTRY: BETWEEN CULTURE AND GRACE   5
   The Explosion of Ministry in the Changing
      Parish Model   6
   The Sources of Change   12
   Between Culture and Grace: The Challenges
      to a Theology of Ministry   22
   Church and Ministers: Trajectories of History   27
   A Ministering Church   33

2. PRIMAL MINISTRY: SPIRIT, FREEDOM,
   CHARISM, AND MINISTRY   35
   Jesus' Preaching of the Kingdom of God   35
   From Religion to the Sacrament of the Spirit   41
   Primal Ministry   45
   Beyond Religion: Spirit, Freedom, Charism,
      and Ministry   49
   Diaconal Charisms   62
   A Realm of Ministries   65
   Primal Ministry: Three Characteristics   74
   Communities of Ministers   76

3. THE METAMORPHOSES OF MINISTRY   80
   The Church in History   82
   Ministry and History   135

4. A MINISTERING CHURCH   139
   Characteristics of Ministry   141
   A Definition of Ministry   150
   Language and Ministry   151

Circles of Ministries   157
Reversals in Ministry   164

5. MINISTERS IN THE CHURCH   167
    One Body, Many Activities   167
    Diversity in Ministry   168
    The Clergy-Laity Distinction: History and Reality   172
    Kinds of Ministries   182
    Ministry and Life   186
    Ministers for the Church   192

6. SOURCES OF MINISTRY   199
    The Spirit's Gifts   200
    The Activity of God and the
        Vocation of the Individual   207
    First Entry into Ministry: Baptism   210
    Further Liturgical Entries into Ministry   212

7. THE SPIRITUALITY OF MINISTRY   225
    Disciples of Jesus, Servants of the Reign of God   225
    Spirituality as a Source of Ministry   231
    Spiritualities for Ministry   233
    Ministerial Spirituality: Facets and Dangers   239
    Doing and Being: Ministerial Modes of Life   252

CONCLUSION   259

NOTES   263

INDEX OF NAMES   298

PREFACE

My book *Theology of Ministry* was published in 1983. The following chapters are more than a revision of the first book: retaining much of the material, they are a rearrangement that is both reduction and expansion.

Theology of Ministry had a certain success in the United States, Canada, and abroad. It was written after a decade in which thousands of Catholics sought education and positions in church ministry. It was not a prescription for what should be done in the church nor an insistent prediction of the future, but a reflection on diocese and parish as they were changing after 1968. It tried to explain why the ministry in the Catholic Church had been expanding since Vatican II, and how this new ecclesiology was related to the New Testament's views of ministry and to the historical metamorphoses of church forms. It did not at all challenge the ministries of bishop and presbyter but located them centrally in churches where other ministries were now present. My book, however, did not accept passivity and secularization, an absence of ministry, as the basic condition of the baptized citizens of the reign of God; it also did not encourage competition among ministries. Many found the book realistic and practical. Both advocates and critics cited its definition of ministry: not all agreed fully with that definition but apparently approved of the attempt to clarify, apart from academic trends and ecclesiastical ghosts, just what Christian ministry is.

This book retains much of the material of the earlier one, mainly because those ideas are basic and, for any theology of ministry, still important. Theologies of some important area of Christianity do not appear in rapid succession, and a writer is given only a few insights. One of the reasons why *Theology of*

1

Ministry retained a relevance over fifteen years is because some ecclesiastical leadership during that time offered few helpful theological and practical directives; on the other hand, around the world, many bishops encouraged and permitted the expansion of ministry in their dioceses—in recent years, offering guidelines and local education programs.

This new version—more than a slightly revised edition—of *Theology of Ministry* has its own order and arrangement: there are new sections, some large and some small; there is also some combination of the biblical sections, while the historical, theological, and pastoral areas have been modestly enlarged. Large, important sections have been retained, but with some very slightly rewritten text.

Friends and critics have helped me to see the sources and limits of this theology. It is drawn from St. Paul, from the theology (but not always from the ecclesiology) of Thomas Aquinas, and from the fundamental theology of grace in Christ and the church as the sacramental center of a world marked by circles of God's gift of eschatological life developed by Karl Rahner.[1]

Parishes have, since the 1960s, fashioned a new model of *parish:* no longer that of pastor and assistants, with sisters in the school, but a model of circles of ministry around the pastor. This book is simply an attempt to respond to that shift from biblical, historical, and theological perspectives. The following chapters sketch a fundamental theology of ministry to explain that new model. Fundamental theology is about revelation, grace, and life in the church, and so, about the presence of the Holy Spirit. This book is also a cultural theology of ministry, because it looks at how different cultures and historical periods modify or enhance church ministry. It is not based on recent church documents nor does it not give a model diocesan plan: its principles and vision lie deeper in the New Testament, although it does not claim to resolve precise exegetical and historical questions that ministry past and present raises. In the last analysis, one's view of men and women active in the church reflects a particular theology of grace: an understanding of how the reign of God that Jesus preached continues on in the lives of the faithful touched by the Spirit.

The first chapter describes the context of ministry, the new situation of recent decades, in which ministry has expanded and during which new and old theological issues have emerged; the second chapter looks at the origins of ministry in the work of Jesus and in the experiences and ecclesiologies of the first communities; the third chapter discloses the metamorphoses of ministry through the centuries; the fourth and fifth chapters look at ministry and ministers today, while the next two chapters present ideas on the sources and spirituality of ministry.

For anyone who writes on ministry, experience as well as research should be a mentor. One must learn from the variety of local churches in North America and, at the same time, seek information about churches in other continents facing the challenge of increasing numbers. Catholics are still, thirty years after Vatican II, experiencing one of the deepest upheavals in church structure in Christian history. The following pages try to be faithful to the revelation of ministry and also to explain lucidly why ministry has been changing—indeed, why under the aegis of the Holy Spirit, it must change. This book's world, audience, and examples are primarily Catholic, but its ideas have been shown to have some value for other Christian churches undergoing similar alterations.

Where should we find today's church? In the past or in the present? Where to look for the church? At the multiplicity of old ethnic churches in decaying cities or at the diversity of people in growing archdioceses? When we look at the large numbers of the baptized and at the age of presbyters, the church seems to be moving into a difficult situation. If, however, we look at one of the greatest expansions of church ministers in history taking place over the past thirty years, we have a different picture. To the extent that one focuses upon the church of the Baroque and the nineteenth century, upon curious rituals and a cafeteria of quick sacramentals, a myopic and fearful mentality may rule. But if one looks at the ever growing churches with many languages and cultures, with more and more women and men eager to volunteer their baptismal charisms and service (which are prior to every ecclesial ministry and office), one understands why the Spirit,

which is the life-principle of a diverse community with its potentialities and responsibilities seeks to find forms which enable the
expansion of Church and Gospel. Supporting this vision is St.
Paul's metaphor and theology of the Body of Christ in which "the
Spirit living in you" (Rom 8:11) brings "all sorts of services" for
the church (1 Cor 12:5).

1

MINISTRY: BETWEEN CULTURE AND GRACE

The following pages have one goal: to reflect on the expansion and reconfiguration of ministry in the church. Ministry has moved from being a vocation for the few to being a gift and work of many, a facet of baptized life. Who are doing ministry in the local church? How are they employed and designated? How do these ministers relate to the ordained ministries?[1]

Ministry is a horizon within the life of the Christian community. A woman, a man is baptized not into an audience or a club but into a community which, accepting a vision of humanity and a faith in unseen divine presence, is essentially and unavoidably ministerial. Just as Christian faith is communal, so Christian community is ministerial. Churches are clusters of people with a world to serve.

Christians, however, have been repeatedly tempted to reduce ministry to one office and to turn a ministerial community into a passive attending of a sacral cult. In places and periods, the organic Body of Christ changed back into a caste system, and baptism was understood as insurance rather than as commission. In the New Testament, Jesus (and his Spirit) does not invite his followers to passive life but to a life serving the kingdom of God. This is not to claim that everything done justly, neatly, or soberly in the world is Christian ministry, or that charism and public service refer solely to inner realms of the soul or to the sublimity of heaven. Not all human activity is ministry, but all baptized men and women are called at times to some precise ministry for the reign of God. That call comes with baptism, and then it comes, too, throughout life, from the Spirit.

5

I. The Explosion of Ministry in the Changing Parish Model

A burst of ministry followed upon the ecclesial event of Vatican II and the social upheavals of the 1960s. It was not dictated by the Council or even by the churches. Steadily growing over decades, it is both a wave of expansion in ministry and a question for church structure, part of a cultural upheaval whose roots lie in a search for freedom, ministerial efficacy, maturity, and social responsibility within the church.

Very rapidly, within the years after the Council, the patterns of parish and diocesan ministry changed. They changed because of the increase in the numbers of Catholics, and they changed by expanding into ministries of education, liturgy, and social justice. The ministries of peace, justice, and social service emerged in a new variety and frequency while campus ministry and health care ministry changed in their format and breadth; finally, there was a development of diocesan offices directing ministries. If we focus on the basic place of ministry, the parish, from 1965 to 1975, parishes changed in terms of which ministries were done and in terms of who did them: the "parish plant" was no longer an accurate architectural symbol for the community—church, school, rectory, convent. The ministerial staff, like the ministry itself, worked beyond the buildings. The priests were joined not only by principals and teachers in schools but by colleagues working in adult education, liturgy, family care, and social action. The liturgy of deacons, lectors, cantors, and communion bearers illustrated the expansion of the ministry outside of Sunday morning. The early church understood that the liturgical array of ministers existed to nourish the external, evangelistic array of ministers. Now that dual interplay of liturgy and public ministry had returned—in directors of different levels of education, ministers involved in worship or social justice, ministers to families, to the aging or to the young, and permanent deacons—churches again lived in the pattern of concentric circles of ministry, moving from the leaders to all full-time and professionally trained ministers out through levels of part-time ministers to all of the baptized. In the acceptance of the team or staff model of ministry, an expansion beyond the monoform, monastic, and sacerdotal ministry was clearly visible.

Inevitably the appearance and activity of the Catholic parish and diocese in North America and in other parts of the world had changed. For indeed, *the very model of ministry* had changed. The parishes had changed in their patterns—theological, ecclesiological, and professional—regarding what was done and who did it.[2]

What we call an "explosion" of ministry is a worldwide phenomenon; it affects cultures and churches differently. Special church councils are "ecumenical" because they are somehow worldwide. Vatican II was ecumenical because it represented the entire church and not just some countries; its ecumenicity was present also in its positive attitude toward its present and the future and, finally, in the breadth of the issues it treated. It was a silent change: beginning unperceived and soon appearing throughout the world (I saw its transformation of the Midwest and experienced in Nigeria and New Zealand the same dynamics at work; I wrote my book, *Theology of Ministry,* not to prescribe a program but to explain what was in fact happening.)

The postconciliar period touched the ministry in four ways. First, the parish and diocese did much more, and all forms of education reappeared, most in more theological and extensive forms. Second, what seemed to be new ministries appeared, for instance, in health care institutions and penal institutions. Third, new paths (other than those of pastor, priest, sister) led to ministry, and thousands of Christians—without vows or orders—entered the ministry. Fourth, the permanent diaconate and later the creation of the office of pastoral administrator brought people to public ministry and leadership who were not priests. Two areas that occupied local churches more were education and liturgy. Before the 1960s, the church had concentrated upon educating children. Suddenly, something rather obvious was pointed out. People live most of their lives as adults, and Christianity is very much a faith for adults, for it exists within life and death, hope and tragedy, cross and resurrection. The community needed to maintain Christian education for children and develop better programs for adults. At the same time, Vatican II, through a never-ending panoply of liturgical changes, introduced diversity and personal meaning into the liturgy. Elements of creativity *should* enter the liturgical celebration of baptism, marriage, and the Eucharist. No longer was liturgy a sacral routine, distant and monolithic. There were eucharistic canons for children, frequent anointings for the sick, charismatic meetings, and a variety of ceremonies for marriage and anniversaries.

Before Vatican II, the "position" of the laity in the church was to sit at the sermon, kneel for communion, and reach into their pockets for the collection: in short, "to pray, pay, and obey." There were extraordinary initiatives by Dorothy Day in New York or by Pier Giorgio Frassati in Turin, but they were very rare. At mass, Catholics' responses were said by the altar boys, and often they prayed another prayer during the liturgy, since it was removed, silent, and unintelligible. Theology books held nothing on the laity, and the code of canon law said they had one right—to receive from the clergy spiritual aids for their salvation; thus, they were defined negatively. Before the 1960s, the parish offered masses and sacraments in Latin, and little more. Converts were quickly instructed; marriages needed brief, mainly legal, preparations; baptisms, except for the careful pouring of water, were automatic. The unordained did not enter the sanctuary (the prepubescent altar boys were more angelic than human), and no ministry, that is, no ministry essentially, formally, and publicly connected to the church's life (as education, liturgy, and the director of the RCIA are), took place outside of the sanctuary (the laudable collecting of canned goods or coaching of basketball teams are not what St. Paul had in mind with *diakonia*). In short, the parish of 1962 was little different from a parish in 962 (in 962 the Norman Vikings were settling down in northern France; that was three hundred years before the completion of the cathedral of Notre Dame in Paris and seven hundred years before the Puritans were founding towns in New England).

A second reflection on ministry-in-transition, past and present, touches the New Testament. In the years just before the Council, the American parish was full of repressed vitality, but Sunday morning had little connection with the descriptions of church and ministry that were read at mass in the letters of the New Testament. What did it mean to say that all Christians were to be active in the Body of Christ, when they sat passively facing forward in church pews? What did Paul intend with ideas about a public liturgy of preaching and life and all kinds of services, when the activities of the sole minister were silent and isolated? Why read a list of ministries in Paul's letters to the Romans and Corinthians, when there was only one active role in a church, that of the priest? What did the mention of ministries of *evangelist* or *apostle* mean when no formal outreach in American society took place? The word *ministry* was a Protestant term not used by Catholics,[3] and *charism* was a term intended to give some respectability to a dangerous figure like Catherine of Siena or Dorothy Day.

The concrete form of the parish of 1962 or of 962, however, does not, by and large, resemble parishes in most of the United States flourishing in a postconciliar style. Now, one can easily apply those passages on charisms and ministries to the church that we know. Any parish in which the liturgy is done well and is continued in the ministry of education, care, and social service, does not consist exclusively of a pastor and one or two assistants, with sisters nearby running a grade school. The new model involves a staff of full-time ministers, a community of ministers, led by the pastor, with their own education, expertise, natural gifts, and commission.

The entry of those not ordained to the priesthood into public ministry is a remarkable phenomenon and has largely escaped the analysis of religious sociologists. It was unusual in that church structure changed at the same time that people sought out new ministries. It was not the movement of a lay elite but of large numbers whose desire for theological education and effective ministry had to overcome ecclesiastical and financial obstacles; it took place not through a new religious order, a sodality, a third order, a center for need, but through thousands, tens of thousands, of men and women, religious and married, who were welcomed into the council-inspired expansion of the parish and diocese. The emergence of lay ministry was unique in the past millennium.

The world and the church are foci around which the streams of creation, sin, and grace swirl. Thinking about ministry is no secondary, merely pragmatic assignment. Nor is the theology of ministry only the latest program for the parish. Ministry has become the normal and forceful way to ponder and confront that aspect of Christianity that has absorbed almost all theological attention over the past four centuries: the church itself. For thirty years, a new praxis and a new theology have challenged the church to appear and to act differently: that is, in the words of Paul VI, to become itself. "At the Council, *the church is looking for itself.* It is trying, with great trust and with a great effort, to define itself more precisely and to understand what it is."[4] The first theological study on the laity, by Yves Congar, appeared in 1953. "It is not just a matter," he wrote, "of adding a paragraph or a chapter to an ecclesiological exposition which from beginning to end ignores the principles on which a 'laicology' really depends. Without these [new] principles we should have, confronting a laicised world, only a clerical Church which would not be the people of God in the fullness of its truth. At bottom there can be only one sound and sufficient theology of laity, and that is a 'total ecclesiology.' "[5] Twenty years later, after the Council, reexamining his previous work, Congar concluded: "I have not written that ecclesiology," and that essay of 1972 intended to correct a vision "which at first was principally and unthinkingly clerical....The church of God is not built up solely by the actions of the official presbyteral ministry but by a multitude of diverse modes of service, stable or occasional, spontaneous or recognized, and, when the occasion arises consecrated, while falling short of sacramental ordination. These modes of service do exist....mothers at home, the person who coordinates liturgical celebrations or reads the sacred text, the woman visiting the sick or prisoners, adult catechists....They exist now, but up to now were not called by their true name, ministries, nor were their place and status in ecclesiology recognized."[6] A new—that is, an older—model was needed. "It is worth noticing that the decisive coupling is not 'priesthood/ laity,' as I used it in *Jalons [Lay People in the Church],* but rather 'ministries/modes of community service'," and Congar sketched a model which would replace the bipolar division of clergy and laity: a circle with Christ and Spirit as ground or power animating ministries in community. He continued: "It is necessary to substitute for the linear scheme a scheme where the community appears as the enveloping reality *within which* the ministries, eventually the instituted sacramental ministries, are placed as *modes of service* of what the community is called to be and do."[7]

These changes in ministry, theological and epoch-making,

took place under the impetus of the Council. That theological renewal was put in place, was realized and experienced in a particularly expansive way in the American parish. Today, the Council's documents look rather ordinary—but they set in motion much more than they expressed.[8] Their impetus was such that it continued and intensified in the following years. It is as though the Spirit draws out of the conciliar event more profound and complex issues. The work of Vatican II was to "translate," to "accommodate," to bring up to date *(aggiornamento)*. Was the expansion of ministry a "translation"? It was certainly a momentous shift, occurring rapidly and enthusiastically in the United States. Regardless, this translation, this inculturation drew on American characteristics: a delight in belonging to groups, a tradition of helping and service, a natural activism. Parish ministry became a celebration of belonging-through-active-service, typical of an American mentality.

What a coincidence: as the needs of the church and society pointed to a wider ministry, there have emerged so many thousands of people intent upon ministry. Men and women, sisters and priests, teachers and activists prepared themselves at professional and graduate schools for a specific ministry. Thousands of religious women—Benedictines, Sisters of Mercy, Dominicans, Franciscans—moved into new ministries in education, social care, justice, and health care. In some communities, over a third of the members sought activities closer to the center of the kingdom of God. Clearly, the single ministry of priest and pastor could not meet all the needs of being-a-church in today's society. Without leaving the traditional roles of liturgical presider, preacher, and administrator, could the pastor be involved also in teaching, musical direction, social issues, community building, family and individual counseling? The legitimate and healthy needs of the community would dismay and destroy a minister who assumed them all. There were only two options: for the pastor to be the leader of ministries or to withdraw in fear.

While this was taking place, the recent era of numerous candidates for priesthood and vowed life came to an end. That time of great abundance was not as normal or as lengthy as first appeared. Apart from the world around Boston, Philadelphia, and New York, it had lasted little more than a dozen years. The increase in population and the decline in the number of priests also indicated a need for new approaches to ministry. The new model of the parish came from the stimulus of Vatican II; however, it was providentially in place to supply for the expanding ministries and growing churches.

The present "expansion," "alteration," or "explosion" in ministry is a worldwide movement begun by conciliar suggestions, sustained by biblical and theological perspectives, and realized and confirmed by praxis. In the United States its appearance was complicated by shifts in the Catholic population. There was a constant increase of numbers: the immigration of large Hispanic populations into the United States; the movement of Catholics from the Northeast to the South and Southwest, where Catholic parishes and institutions were few; the escalation of education among Catholics; and the immigration of Europeans, particularly from Central Europe. Over the last third of the century, in the midst of this swirl of populations, the bishops, pastors, and ministers succeeded in adapting and expanding the church.

II. The Sources of Change

What caused this explosion of ministry? It was not mandated by universal or local churches, nor by bishops or curia in Rome. Change in the form of parish and diocesan offices did not come from bishops, nor from plans drawn up by chancery officials; nor did it come from the methodologies of theologians or from sociological surveys of the Catholic Church or academic observers of American religion. New theologies of the church and liturgy prepared the way, but new perceptions and forms of ministry quickly passed beyond the ideas of theologians. Church ministry expanding throughout the world suggests that the Holy Spirit is intent upon a wider service, a more diverse ministry for church life. It did not come about because of a decline in priests. Although it was not to become evident until the late 1960s, decline in vocations to the diocesan priesthood and to religious orders of men and women had begun before the Council and was likely tied to changes in the aspirations of Catholics who were no longer of an immigrant world.[9] Healthy and grand theological movements can come from the grass roots, from changes in the activity of movements, and from dedicated individuals. Someone sees and lives differently, and others find this approach helpful.

Ministry has changed and will be changed. We should first observe that history indicates that the forms of the church can and do change—the names of ministries and their vestments were not given by Jesus or Peter. Nothing is more obvious about the church than that it lives in history, that is, it grows, adapts, changes, remains too static and suffers deformity, reforms, renews, and is renewed. Only a true church can change: only a church with inner resources of creativity and diversity can adapt itself to new—in space and time—cultures. On the other hand, some sects divide into further sects, a process which in fact lacks pluralism and diversity although it appears to have such, because the reproduction of independent churches is not the result of inner diversity but the effect of a lack of an inner pluralistic dynamic.

A. From within Society

The world's population grows. The number of people living on this planet expands geometrically. Moreover, people are not content merely to subsist in a changeless life punctuated with rare moments of contentment but search for a fuller life summed up in some kind of freedom. In the Catholic Church there are almost a billion members, and the idea of a parish that is simply a station for the rapid reception of sacraments lies thirty years in the past. The desire for quality in Christian life as well as the increase in population and a search for maturity have led Christians to expect wider ministry in their churches. The church itself is a ministry, a collective ministry serving the multiform presence of grace in the diverse social consciousness of the world and addressing the cultures and organizations that represent the aspirations of the world.

The new realization of ministry and its expansion is proceeding through different stages. In the ten or fifteen years after the Council, after having ministered successfully to immigrants and neighborhoods, the Catholic Church, in danger after World War II of becoming merely an impersonal organization for millions of nameless people, sought the new directions sketched above. Numbers made this necessary, as did a process of education and maturity. As the 1970s yielded to the 1980s, the American church became increasingly educated. If the church had remained in its simple devotional format of the 1930s, would it have withstood the forces of society, whether those be education and secularity, or heeded the call to be a prophetic minister among social ills? Parishes needed and were searching for community and religious activity, life beyond the impersonality of many parishes, the automatic rituals and the irrelevant preaching. Catholics would need their parish to address their lives and to educate them somewhat in the Bible, Christianity, and ethics. Could the ministry be come less aristocratic, less distant, less automatic? Could it develop a variety of services to an educated, adult church? A church membership grown in quantity and concerned over the quality of life could only lead to an expansion of the ministry—or to a paranoid withdrawal of the clergy and a slow apostasy of the members.

As the Council suggested that the local church, passing beyond the spirituality of the soul and the dark church, undertake more ministry and education in the United States, the 1960s brought an awareness of social problems: of racism, of poverty, of industries of war. When the church theologically accepted the aspirations and forms of contemporary peoples at the Council, it also agreed to live within the world of their problems and misdirections, to counter and heal and not just judge social sinfulness and inhumanity. This entire span of ecclesial life—the church for three centuries had been partly reduced and sublimated into the spiritual journey of a soul—needed ministers and ministries because the world needed them.

B. From within the Church

The impetus for change came first from the Council's documents—but not just from Latin texts. Vatican II was an event. Its members and their theology initiated the new dynamic of becoming a world-church; its pastoral focus set in motion aspects of pastoral renewal that occasioned this book and books in many other areas. Vatican II is a "tradition-event." If Jesus Christ is the act and content of tradition, still the church's life precisely as contemporary is the recipient and bearer of the act of the tradition. The recollection, mediation, and interpretation that compose tradition are very much focused on the present. For tradition does not look only at distant rites, but in the very event of tradition succeeds in bringing into existence new groups and new forms, new architecture and new liturgy. Yves Congar viewed the implications of Vatican II involving communion, the contributions of local churches, the activity of the Spirit, tradition, and conciliarity,[10] while Hervé Legrand sees a new empiricism coming from the Council, that is, a new attention to what is real and local. The local church is "the subject of the church." Consultative bodies like pastoral councils and episcopal conferences as well as the baptized and the bishops are part of the restoration of the active personality of each local church.[11] The various documents of the Council implied, that there was more to be done in a parish than saying a routine mass or organizing a Halloween dance. But the Spirit of the Council determined that new theological impetuses (which were often in fact venerable traditions or early theologies) would gain an influential freedom. They were the theology of the people of God over against hierarchy alone; baptism as ordination; grace as empowerment rather than insurance policy; liturgy as the ritual for ministry; a theology of charism flowing into ministry. "Pastors also know that they themselves were not meant by Christ to shoulder alone the entire saving mission of the Church toward the world. On the contrary, they understand that it is their noble duty so to shepherd the faithful and recognize their services and charismatic gifts that all according to their proper roles may cooperate in this common undertaking with one heart."[12] Hermann Pottmeyer describes well the event of Vatican II: "...like any other council, not only a Pentecostal event but also an event of its own time." Statements of the Council were understood well only when they were understood as something beyond previous councils and their times, but also in light of the modern, European culture that the Council addressed, not just as critic but as friend. "The reception of Vatican II is not yet complete. All attempts to break off the process of reception—whether through overly restrictive legislation or through a 'progressive interpretation'—are incompatible with a professed fidelity to the Council. A new phase in the process of reception is certainly due, one that will end the conflict of selective interpretations and explain the letter of the conciliar texts in accordance with the 'spirit' of the Council, aided by a hermeneutic that does justice to the character of Vatican II as a transitional council."[13] Thus the Council itself encourages a reception that is more than ideas and rules, not the trends of religious phenomenologies but the developments of its dynamic principles as reception.

Richard McBrien presents the ecclesiology of Vatican II in a synthesis of theological and pastoral principles: the church as sacrament; the church as the whole people of God; the mission of that people, including service to the social order as well as within liturgy; an emphasis upon the local church; an expanded and more traditional understanding of the mission of the entire church; an appreciation of those many services in subordination to the kingdom of God; and authority exercised in a collegial manner.[14] The key ideas of the Council for understanding the church are "People of God" and "Universal Sacrament of Grace and Revelation for the World." These have considerable import for ministry: the first, unlike so much ecclesiology written from 1860 to 1960, does not identify the active church with the clergy but implies that in this society all have a quest for vitality and service.[15] The second, while including previous liturgies and devotions, expands anew the activity of the church outwards—parish and diocese must view the struggles of the world positively, seeking some word and presence in evangelization and social justice. The Council gave an emphasis to national and local churches, to the universal church as a communion of churches, and to a single church as a communion of different ministries.[16] So the church has a dual sacramentality: one for its members, through a vitalization of the ancient rites and theologies of sacraments now enhanced by attention being given to the liturgy being done well; and one to the world, which it affirms in its humane quests and draws to the confessed center of all degrees of grace, Jesus Christ. The parish is the sacramental realization of the kingdom of God preached by Jesus, but it is also the Christian mirror and minister of an invitation to see how the complexities of contemporary society may need and intimate the workings of grace, and how the Gospel forecasts, interprets, and empowers the church serving the Spirit at work in the world.[17] The renewal of the local church, priesthood, episcopacy, and life in vows initiated by Vatican II led to practical consequences like the shift of many men and women from one ministry to another, and renewal opened the church's life to evaluation and change in areas that had remained unaltered for centuries.

Vatican II was a council intent upon pastoral improvement, and it prepared in various ways for a new theology and structure of ministry. First, it returned the basic Christian ecclesial emphasis to the local church; the local church not only had an identity and vigor but, in diocese, region, and nation, it should respond to its needs. Second, both the bishop and the laity (but not the priest and the parish) were highlighted. After a long period of overemphasis upon sacrificial Eucharist and sacral priesthood, baptism was given a new appreciation. Baptism made the Christian, but baptism raised the issue of a universal ministry incumbent upon all the baptized.

Of particular importance was the Council's new look at its traditional ministries. Contrary to the medieval position, the ministries of bishop, presbyter, and deacon were affirmed as distinct. They were not simply a step up or a step aside from a sacral priesthood imitating Christ's. Each had its own identity, its own ordination, its own purpose. The bishop ceased to be defined as a venerable or glorious version of a priest. Official documents referred to the priest by his more accurate designation as *presbyter*. The ministry of diaconate was restored. Deacons were no longer seminarians in their final year of study who functioned at liturgies, but were men, frequently married and holding other jobs, who shared in the official ministry of the church (these fathers and husbands, plumbers and teachers were ordained, and ordained to a ministry that was not the priesthood). The restoration of the diaconate, the view of priest as presbyter and therefore representative of the bishop, and the restoration of the bishop, not as papal vicar or high priest, but as leader of a local church—these were practical statements that the church had more than one ministry, that not all ministry was priesthood, and that ministry was not necessarily joined to celibacy. The ministry of the local church had changed from being a group of priests led by a "superpriest" to a bishop with assisting, distinct ministers called presbyters and deacons. Could there be other assistants in the ministry? Other ministers and other ordinations?

Today, we often hear of a decline in the number of diocesan clergy, a decline in the number of priests at work in Europe and in Latin and North America. The expansion of ministry did not come from the decline in the number of priests: the ministries of baptized men and women were often ministries that had not existed for some centuries. A diminishing diocesan clergy is not the problem, however, and pessimistic statistics may be camouflage for much larger theological issues—those of an expanding ministry. Even if the number of priests in large, urban dioceses were to triple, or return to earlier larger numbers, in view of the new demands upon ministry by quantity and quality, this would still not give the church enough ministers. As we have pointed out, the number of Roman Catholics has grown, and the expectation of church life has expanded. The crisis in the number of priests could not be solved by a greater number of clergy; it touches upon a change within the life of healthy Christian communities. The ministry is both declining and expanding—it all depended upon how you looked at it. There are fewer seminarians but thousands in theological schools; fewer men and women active in parochial schools but many more in social action. The expansion of the ministry is not, then, a random or annoying occurrence but an aspect of a new church that is comprehending itself anew in its biblical sources and in its commission to be not just Italian or French but worldwide. Size, expansion, and potential must begin every discussion of ministry, theoretical and pastoral, for they are the immediate context and point out the limitations of the past and the possibilities for the future.

The documents of the Council did not fully cause the expansion of ministry that was due to increasing numbers of Catholics and increased expectations of what a church and its ministry and liturgy should be. Congar did not think that the upheavals in the postconciliar era had their roots in Vatican II but, rather, in the constrictive decades or centuries before it.

> The years after the Council are a global phenomenon with worldwide dimensions. A crisis would have come anyway. The Council assisted its entry into the church by ending the isolation of the church, by giving a wider audience to the church, and by ending a monolithic institution protected by fictions. The present time is linked to the gigantic change which touches culture, the ways of life in society and the 'cohumanity' around the world....I do not believe that the present crisis in the church is the result of Vatican II...the realities that preoccupy us today were already present or beginning to appear in the 1950s and even in the 1930s.[18]

Guy Lafont sees the following process as helpful for reflecting on the Catholic church today: examine with loyalty but also with a critical realism the conflict between modernity and the hierarchy; define more closely the underlying inspiration in the institutional forms of the church that have been preserved during the last millennium; show how Vatican II has, for the first time in many centuries, begun, sometimes with audacity, sometimes with timidity, to look at the conflict and to reform institutions; fashion a work of theological imagination which ends in quite concrete propositions.[19]

The expansion of the ministry cannot go backwards ("All the work of the Council is a half-way station"[20]). The growth of the church and the diminishment of the diocesan priesthood insure that. It is interesting to ponder how the influx of large numbers of vocations into the preconciliar church was to be a factor in the alteration of religious life and ministry, for they, members of the postconciliar generation who avidly sought to work in a more challenging and more demanding pastoral atmosphere, furthered the ministry of the baptized beyond diocese and religious order.

The expansion of the ministry has gone through two stages in the past twenty-five years in terms of the ministries themselves and preparation for them.

In the first stage the new ministries were clear and rather few: a director of religious education, perhaps a minister connected with youth, or the elderly, or the liturgy. Education took place in masters' programs at seminaries, which had become theological schools educating priests, deacons, and lay ministers, and at Catholic colleges and universities (often this education took place during the summers). Those entering these ministries were from all areas of the church, but a large number were religious women and men moving into direct ecclesial ministry.

A second stage followed. Churches did not retreat from this new situation but tried to take it seriously at both the parish and diocesan levels. There was a realization that the Gospel now must address many needs, and the time of the pastor could no longer be monopolized by sermon or sacrament. Marriage and family were embattled; people live longer today; the ministry could hardly neglect the large number of Christians who were retired, sick, elderly, and dying. The 1960s had spotlighted the poor and disenfranchised—these were not a few needy cases but entire segments of the population of American cities. Family, justice, education—even slight involvement in any of these would lead to advocacy in the political arena and to a critical look at liturgy and preaching within the local church.

This same desire to prepare for a new and diverse ministry is evident at the level of an individual church, a parish, a campus, a diocese. The student of ecclesial structures can find examples of all of these "churches" engaged in running their own schools for ministry. There are dioceses who do not see themselves as running primarily a Tridentine seminary but as developing a program of education for the full ministerial potential of the Christian ministry. Finally, we can view the large theological educational programs of universities and retreat centers as schools for ministry; ultimately the people they educate have come from and will return to direct, explicit Christian ministry.

Why did this change come about? As we have said, it came, above all, from a deep encounter between the Spirit of the risen Jesus and the people of God. This meeting, commissioned by and filled with renewal, was prepared for and interpreted by the studies in the Bible and of early church accomplished by European theologians whose works reemphasized the sacerdotal character of baptism, and the dignity of being a Christian (which was more than being a "layperson"). Apparently the Holy Spirit wanted to alter, to broaden the way the church's members understood themselves and the church's mission. A restored theology of baptism called people to a Spirit-infused life whose ministries and charisms were present and inviting, a local church which, largely abandoning the very circumscribed and inevitably faint efforts of the privately dedicated layperson or the priest who had become a scientist, found opportunities for ministry all around.

It is important to understand the themes of this first chapter: That the church is growing enormously, even if in some urban centers or European countries it is declining; that the age of the parish as a service station dispensing a few rapid liturgies is remembered by few people; that the model of the parish implies circles of ministry, and this brings the requirements of educational, spiritual, and financial support for ministers. And it is important to ponder the change in ministry and its expressions through community, people, and history, and not to think that words determine realities, or that rearranging words, canonical or not, removes one from fashioning a theology of the church-in-service. Ministry is part of the continuing incarnation of the Word, and Jesus the incarnate Word, the central event of Christianity, is not just a teaching but a reality. A theology of ministry is first and foremost a study of history: forms of ministry come from certain periods in history. The incarnation of the Word of God took place in Jesus ben Joseph. This incarnation continues in the church, the Body of Christ. When a theology is grounded in history, it has some hope of touching reality. The following pages attempt to explain through words but not to explain words. Even holy and ancient words do not ultimately explain anything as active and personal as one human being serving the presence of God in another man or woman. In charting ministry, we cannot be content with verbal justifications, whether they are the gift of hierarchies or of theologians; but, like the New Testament with its fresh metaphors and concrete proclamations, we must push our discussion of priesthood and charism until we have reached their reality in psyche and society.

III. Between Culture and Grace:
The Challenges to a Theology of Ministry

For a theology of ministry, four challenges come to mind:

The *first* challenge is to explain why passing decades bring more ministers in the church, many of whom are not priests. We need a theological interpretation of these ministers: some have full seminary educations, some have had weekend courses; some are shaping their ministerial fields and their ministerial identities while others are reviving traditional church forms. Some are married, some are not; some serve within liturgy, others in urban streets and rural areas. This diversification of the ministry inviting the theologically educated and the committed parishioner to full-time and part-time ministry is integral to healthy church life.

The *second* challenge is to underline and enhance the importance of leadership in presbyter and bishop even as they are complemented by other full-time services. A theology of ministry takes nothing from the identity of the ordained but locates them realistically amid other diverse and parallel ministries, that is, within the church. This wider view of ministry does not remove or dilute the ministries of leadership but rather outlines their responsibilities and etches their limits. For to be a leader of an adult community committed to prayer, service, and evangelization is quite different from being the solitary, sacral mediator for an audience. And yet we are moving beyond the medieval and Baroque conclusion that there is only one ministry, that of priesthood.

The *third* challenge is that of history. Congar said that Vatican II marked the church's acceptance of history. "The vision of the Council," Congar wrote retrospectively, "has been resolutely that of the history of salvation completed by eschatology."[21] Historical moments can be violent and negative, but change is not always oppressive, although it may be unnerving. In terms of the church, in one parish or around the world, there must be a sense of history: of rediscovering an earlier time in the church, of letting go of the nineteenth century, of understanding that the opportunities and size of the church today are vastly different than they were forty years ago. A look at the fragmentary records of ministry in the first churches leads on further to seeing the variety in church structure over almost two millennia; then we grasp the incomplete but expanding ministry today. We have gained not a historical record but rather an insight into the variety and unity in ministry. History shows the inner nature and the inner creativity of what Jesus and his Spirit gave to the world as service to the kingdom of God. To know history is to be set free. The New Testament's theologies of ministry are richer, more demanding and varied than we expect. The history of ministry offers not a set of norms of limited successful realizations but forms of cultural history, principles of church life and self interpretation.

The situation of the church is history. Must the church like all the institutions of civilization become an antique? Faith holds that the church will not end, but will it spend, as it has in the past, decades in antiquarianism or self-parody? History shows the wounds and failings of the church but also attests to its survival. Precisely when the church pretends to be eternal, it is vulnerable to the ravages of time; for nature and human life are shot through with change. When the church tries to hold back history and neurotically assumes the mask of an age that is dead or dying, history appears harsh. The church wants to stay with this or that civilization and will not admit the evils that history might in its course correct. In short, the church will not live by faith and hope, and its leaders plan not a mission but a museum.

If the blood of the church is history, the flesh of the community of Christ is culture. The forms through which the church acts on behalf of the kingdom of God come from the culture of a time and a place. The Word of God assumed the culture of a particular tradition, selecting a language and its way of expressing reality, a landscape and a poetry with its limitations. The church lives within cultures, because human beings are effectively addressed and personally touched within their psychic and cultural worlds. All that was said above of history is true of culture as it touches the church. The verbal system of a language expresses something new about the past and future of Christ; one mythology prepares for the Crucifixion and Resurrection differently than does another. The sacred space and holy symbols of this architecture will invite, even enclose, the Spirit in their own way.

Ministry, then, is a fullness, a pleroma, a mine awaiting new excavations. Just as there is an essence of the church in history, however, so too there is a fullness of ministry in and through cultures. But we human beings—limited in time and church never meet all the ways and depths of ministry. We fall again and again into the ethereal theory that our ministry alone is God's elected form. What we call a perfect priesthood, above history and time, may be, of course, only an imperfect mixture of elements from Rome in the fifth century or from France in the Baroque era. Looking at the sociological images, the cultural realizations in classes and clothes and ecclesiastical powers, Hans Küng describes a pageant of length and variety:

> Pastoral ministries have undergone several changes as we can see if we think of the varied forms they have assumed in the course of the centuries...the Corinthian pastors...the ascetics and monks and the basilical clergy and court bishops...medieval simple priests, canonists, court chaplains, spiritual princes, curial officials and warring popes to the clergy and missionaries and the worker priests of modern times. A long and highly varied procession comes to our eyes as we look back down the centuries; it reminds us not only of the relativity of clothes and social symbols but also of the external and internal forms of the ministry as such. The different forms it took were not dictated by the special commission given to the clergy, nor by the original Christian message, but by all kinds of cultural, social, political and psychological factors.[22]

The *fourth* challenge is to see the theology of ministry as a theology of grace. If the following pages are a fundamental theology of ministry, they are also "a cultural ecclesiology of grace." It is grace and history that bring limits and unity to the following interpretation of ministry: the principle by which life and service in the Christian community are viewed is the development of charisms of life and ministry in different eras of cultural history. A fundamental theology of ministry is ultimately a theology of grace, because it is a new divine presence that calls and enables service in men and women to itself. Grace, the presence of the Triune God,[23] is the source of our attempt at a coherent theology of ministry. Ministry begins with the Spirit's charism; the goal of ministry is to serve the kingdom of God, which theologians have called "grace." The promptings that lead the worldwide church toward an expansion of ministry are charisms of the Spirit. In a Thomist perspective, grace for ministry will enable and lead a person suited for a particular ministry; nature and grace are not in conflict, nor can grace be counted on to overcome unsuitable orientations and limits of this man or woman.

Grace is the presence of Jesus and his Spirit. The following chapters spend some time in seeing how the New Testament and tradition depict the impetus of the Spirit active in the life of the church and how such a perspective of grace within culture might be guiding the developments of ministry in these decades. The Spirit is a divine person with loving plans, and each man and woman is an individual bestowed with subjectivity, freedom, and existence. A fundamental theology of ministry begins with the Spirit as the inspiring force within the Body of Christ and with the dignity of the baptized. Such a theology is existential in that it takes the conditions of local churches seriously as well as the individual gifts and aspirations of people and peoples; it is transcendental because it describes the history of the collective consciousness of the church precisely as endowed with charisms and services of nurture, growth, and enrichment; it is correlative because its method is to relate the ministerial charisms of the Spirit to cultural history, in the first century, in key subsequent cultural periods, and in our present time.

What would hold it back? It might be the barrier of the sacral figure whose monopoly of ministry is inadequate. It might be the barrier, worn and collapsing between Christians, those sacred and those secular. It might be a failure of nerve to follow the Council, gift of the Spirit, into new ways and to retreat into small corners of the past. Ultimately, uncertainty and anxiety come not from profound theological questions but from the ethos, the fading or shaking ethos, of the church that has come from the recent past. Churches throughout the world have great opportunities for growth and service that they now glimpse, If the priesthood in a solipsistic victory alienates itself from the rest of the church, devoid of challenge and isolated from its fellow Christians from whom it has withheld the grace of ministry, mediocre and passive men interested not in service but in performance will be the resulting remnant. The worst situation would be a division among parishes and reactionary church leaders and small groups incapable of imagining a church different and broader than that of American Catholicism in 1950 or German Catholicism in 1750. The church's next age, beyond the postconciliar era, would then be characterized by ecclesial illnesses, by a reawakened split between the sacred and secular,[24] by leadership mainly by cliques of men without pastoral experience, by the marginalization of ordinary church goers, and by the unhappy union of a false theology and liturgy of magic joined to episcopal mismanagement encumbered by lawsuits and scandals. Ministry, like liturgy, is a sign of the church's health.

The approach of this book is only one of illumination. It looks simultaneously at (1) what we can see of Jesus' preaching on Spirit, service, and discipleship, and on their realization in the early churches' forms in light of (2) today's needs and directions. No age, even that of the first century, offers concretely and publicly all modes of being a Christian community, and that mystery we call the church contains within itself new resources, as the popes of Vatican II reiterated. A theology of ministry must be one of learning as well as of research: it must learn how church and ministry are functioning today in different kinds of churches; praxis as well as history are sources of understanding what best suits the Spirit.

This book is not a defense of novelty in ministry nor a liberal program for the future. It is an explanation of what in fact has been and is happening. Like the movement it describes, this theology seeks only to understand how the old is reappearing in the new, how the Spirit is drawing out the theology and forms of primal and early church for a world-church. The task of the theologian is not to establish a solitary magisterium any more than such is the ministry of the bishop. Theology is the thinking side of ministry, and the Spirit can inspire in modest ways theologians and ministers.

IV. Church and Ministers: Trajectories of History

What in the history of the church, distant and recent, is there that explains the emergence and intent of ecclesial lay ministry? What are the precedents that shed light on the present situation? Why did this facet of church life appear so rapidly and so generally?

Dynamic moments, partly from the past, are influencing the church today.[25] Forms of past ecclesiology or theology lie behind the emergence over the past three decades of parish and diocesan ministries beyond the priesthood and episcopacy. Their individual histories have differing modes of influence (reappearing, evolving, declining, dying). The following is a sketch of five trajectories, five "histories," five dynamic movements from Christian periods: each helps us understand the expansion of ministry taking place in the past twenty-five years. Five trajectories of Christian motifs and forms explain the recent expansion of ministry in the Catholic Church.[26] They are: (1) the Pauline theology of the Body of Christ with its varied activities; (2) the social distinction between clergy and laity; (3) the ministry of women; (4) passing beyond the recent past; and (5) the reemergence of circles of ministry.

The Body of Christ. A sign of living as a Christian is to find at times in one's life charisms becoming ministry. Paul welcomed all ecclesial gifts, refusing to be embarrassed by or hostile to whatever was useful to the ministry of the church. He minimized sensational gifts and accented those that were public services to the Gospel. As we will see in a later chapter, charisms lead into the life of the church and are the foundation for the ministries building up the community (1 Cor 12:7; 3:7,16; Rom 12:4), and so charism is the contact between the life of the Spirit and an individual personality. There can be many charisms ranging from momentary inspirations to lifelong decisions; at times in a Christian's life, we suspect, invitations will be given to serve the church. Paul gave harmony to the diversity of important ministries, to communal services, by the metaphor of the human body with its many activities: "...a unity in the work of service building up the body of Christ" (Eph 4:13). In the Christian community, a living organism, there is no inactive group nor spiritual elite. The ministering

community precisely as active lives from the risen Christ and
does not merely revere his memory or memorize his words. Early
Christian communities would not have understood the limiting
of charism or ministry to a few.

Beyond the Distinction of Clergy and Laity. For a long time,
the terms *clergy* and *laity*, based on the presence or absence of
the rites of ordination (or tonsure), have divided the church in
two. The origin of the distinction in the second or third century
had as its intention to enhance the ministry, to give church service to people who would work with dedication, basic commitment. The setting forth of the clergy was not first aimed at a
caste nor at producing a passive people watching a priesthood,
but at giving reverence to the sacramental presence of the Spirit
and at taking seriously the forms of liturgy and church life. But if
the clergy meant those chosen for God's service, the correspond-
ing laity were handed a religious existence that was secular, passive, removed. Yves Congar has written: "To look for a
'spirituality of lay people' in the Scriptures makes no sense.
There is no mention of laity. Certainly the word exists, but it
exists outside the Christian vocabulary."[27] In American usage,
layperson means someone who is ignorant of the area under discussion, who is out of the field of action. Most meanings of the
word are not positive, and ecclesial usage cannot escape their
overtones. As large numbers of baptized Christians undertake
ministry in religious education, health care, or leadership,
preaching in communities where no ordained ministers are available, neither biblical theology nor contemporary English meaning supports that word's "aura," which can denominate the
baptized as laity in an extrinsic, passive sense. The fullness of
baptism, the universal access to God, the avoidance of dualism,
the basic equality of men and women in the kingdom of God—
these biblical themes supersede subsequent divisions. One cannot make sense of today's parish in light of the clergy/laity
distinction interpreted in a strict dualism.

The venerable model of clergy and laity is incapable of
interpreting realistically what the church has already become in
many parts of the world. When the magisterium defends that distinction, it is defending not the words, not a dualism, and not a

division in the church between those solely active and those largely passive; it is legitimately defending the distinction between ministries. That the ministry of pastor is central and more important than that of reader is obvious, but the ministry of reader is *not* nothing, not a tolerated usurpation of clerical activity. Ministries differ in importance, and distinctions among ministries (and ministers) remain, but they are, according to the New Testament, grounded upon a common faith and baptismal commissioning.

Women in Ministry. There is a trajectory for the ministries of women, one which in a general sense reaches from the New Testament to the present day, even as it passes through centuries of neglect and minimalization. The ministry of women, however, does not appear in modern times, including the past twenty years, in the form of the apostles or deaconesses of the first centuries. It appears in the activities of women religious. The growing presence of women in ministry has followed, after 1970, upon the work of religious women, and their history began in the twelfth century. There were precursors to Francis's and Dominic's ideal of traveling evangelical groups, and those included women who desired to imitate Jesus' life and preaching. It seems that Dominic wanted to draw women into the activities of countering the Albigensians, but the church led the female counterparts to the friars back into cloistered life. There they remained for many centuries.[28] In the seventeenth century, by combining cloistered forms with some active ministry, women religious were permitted to work in education and health care, and after a century or more this led to active religious congregations (often begun as assemblies of celibate women in private associations that were focused on various types of ministerial work).

The United States, with its thousand and more schools, hospitals, and other institutions, has been the modern display ground of the congregations of active religious women. Religious women did not hesitate to establish all kinds of institutions, even in the most difficult circumstances. Most of the works of these organizations correspond to Pauline ministries. If we consider health care, religious education, the care of the poor, and retreat houses to be ministries, then one must conclude that over sixty or seventy percent of Catholic ministry in America during the twentieth century has been done by women. The time of these large, expanding, ministering congregations is coming to an end, but this trajectory leads to something beyond.

Before Vatican II, women in the Catholic Church entered ministry through religious congregations; in the first decade of the postconciliar era many sisters entered new and more directly ecclesial ministries; and by the early 1970s women without direct affiliations to religious congregations were prominent in ministry. Motifs from the Council—like the charismatic, ministerial, and priestly aspects of baptism, the welcome by parishes of Catholics who are not religious into ministries, a more subtle understanding of the presence of grace, the opening of the church's ministry beyond the Sunday masses, and the dignity of having been drawn into the kingdom of God—these have led to a broadened scope for women in ministry.

Passing beyond the Recent Past. The Baroque period, reaching from 1580 to 1720, was a time of cultural renewal and religious expansion: a great restoration of that time. With variations it reappeared and continued from 1820 to 1960; it is the most recent major era in Roman Catholic life. With Vatican II, worldwide Catholicism began to leave the Baroque era. This period is omitted or marginalized in most American overviews of religious history because its brilliance and expanse are not important for English-speaking scholars of Protestantism or the Enlightenment, whose studies of seventeenth and eighteenth century religion are limited to philosophers and pietists, omitting the important movements of Vincent de Paul and Louise de Marillac or the art of the Asam brothers. This is understandable: the Baroque, the decorous and vital offspring of the Counter-Reformation, is a kind of anti-period to Protestantism.

The Baroque spirit brought to the church new theologies, spiritualities, and arts, and these usually manifested interplays between personality and grace (e. g., as articulated by Ignatius Loyola, Philip Neri, or Teresa of Avila). A universality begun by Columbus's exploration and Galileo's astronomy offered to the Catholic mind a new worldview. God was experienced in a vastness, freedom, and goodness flowing through a world of diversity, movement, and order, while Christ appeared in a more human way, filled with a personal love, redemptive and empowering. This was a time of great missionary work and great interior conversations with the divine. The Baroque went underground during the Enlightenment and then reemerged, albeit with some new emphases, as Romanticism moved beyond the Enlightenment. The nineteenth century had its originality (it added a neomedieval restoration), but that age more often than not composed variations on the Baroque. The time from 1830 to 1960 is the period just before Vatican II, and it has its own theology of priestly, consecrated, and ministerial life and activity.

What were the characteristics of ministry from the Baroque to Vatican II? First, it was the domain of two groups—parish priests limited largely to the dispensing of sacraments, and members of religious orders, who conducted a number and variety of ministries that ranged from administering a university in Lima to running an orphanage in New York City. It was an activist ministry strengthened by a theology of actual graces effected by sacraments and by personal prayer. Other baptized Christians might help in the physical support of running a hospital or preaching the Gospel in a foreign country, but they were kept at a distance from the real, public ministry just as they were kept from the sanctuary. There were overtones that ministry was largely about the methods of spirituality and the rubrics of liturgy, that the fallen world could receive only so much redemption, and that all not under orders or vows remained in a secular sphere capable not of ministry but of a vague witness. The designation "apostolate of the laity" confirmed this, adding an incorrect ecclesiology that caritative functions alone were possible as services in the church and that the works of the laity derived from minor shares in the episcopal office.[29] The understanding of ministries flowing out of baptism and expanding around the leadership of pastor and bishop, a rejection of the strict separation of secular and sacred, grace no longer viewed within the context of a waterworks of laws and definitions, a view that there are ministries outside of liturgy, the involvement of the baptized in liturgy itself, the joining of meditation with liturgy and public action—these drew the Baroque trajectory into something new.

The Reappearance of Baptismal Ministry. Trajectories three
and four lead us to today's American church. As soon as the
Council had ended, Catholic men and women suddenly began to
study theology and to prepare for ministry in great numbers (in
1960 there existed only one or two places where a noncleric
could study theology; by 1975 it took the *National Catholic
Reporter* several issues to list them). This remarkable phenomenon had its own preparation. Various organizations were
founded in the century or so after 1830; they drew individual
Christians into active groups. These ranged from third orders
and confraternities to Catholic Action and the Vincent de Paul
and Holy Name Societies, as well as Jocists and urban houses of
Christian witness. But they were qualitatively different from
today's expansion of ministry, for they, taking for granted the
distinction of sacral and sacred worlds, did not pass beyond witness and material assistance into the essential ministries of the
church. In the 1970s, parishioners' activities underwent a pneumatic metamorphosis as men and women (and permanent deacons) became active in liturgical ministries during and outside of
mass, as well as in services of education, liturgy, peace and justice, music, and ministry to the sick and dying.

A dialectic is at work: the ministry expands because there is
more to do, and such an expansion of ministries is possible
because people are seeking ministry.

The trajectories just sketched are realizations of ministry in
the past and explanations of ministry in the present and the
future. They were stimulated by a culture and an age: they are at
work, diversely, in the Catholic Church today. Each trajectory
brings us to our present situation and suggests that this new situation is neither utterly new nor unexpected. The theology of the
Body of Christ indicates that ministry for the baptized should be
ordinary: history indicates that the ministries of women have
existed; the present age has effected a model that goes beyond
the sole performance of whatever was being done by clergy or by
religious and priests.

Change is not an instant revolution nor a chain of successes.
In old and huge organizations like the Catholic Church, change
is a complex phenomenon. The past never fully disappears; old

forms are not fully replaced; the new must be both incarnational and traditional. If these shifts in church life are considerable and fraught with further implications, nonetheless, their day-to-day realization in the life of the local church is ordinary.

V. A Ministering Church

Why did ministry expand? It seems unavoidable to conclude that it came from a deep encounter between the Spirit of the risen Jesus and the people of God. What these pages describe, a leaving and a beginning, is a difficult passage, but it is the unavoidable present time, a time that Pope Paul VI, opening the second session of Vatican II, said had come to free "the noble and destiny-filled name of 'church' " from "forms full of holes and close to collapse."[30] To reflect upon the expansion of ecclesial ministry in the past few decades is to conclude that the Spirit is determined to bestow more ministries on more people, and to disclose to the world-church how much there remains to be done.

When we look at the local church's ministry around the world, we can be dismayed. So many people to serve, so many nations, so many parishes—and a sense of vertigo over so many changes, very simple ones but fraught with implications for change in image and structure. A theology of ministry explores what is culturally new, even if theologically it is traditional and original. Gustav Thils observed the fact that the taking root of the church in various cultures occurs simultaneously with an expansion of how the church worships and serves.[31] Paul VI spoke of African "human values and cultural forms which can find their proper fulfillment, truly African": they could "formulate Catholicism in terms absolutely appropriate to African culture."[32]

Our times and the New Testament have similarities. Curiously, today's ecclesial forms and issues have little in common with the eleventh century but very much in common with the third century. Today, as in the early church, there is a large world filled with agnostics inquiring about the meaning of human life. We are increasingly aware of the pluralism of cultures and the opportunities for reaching vast numbers through the media.

Bishop Claude Dagens sets forth a number of ways in which our time is similar to the first centuries of Christianity.[33] Then, too, there was a consciousness of religion with something new, a sense of universal mission and an understanding that its good news could be interpreted in various cultures. Christianity was not just a combat against every idolatry, aimed more at the empire than at Venus or Juno, but a community with a faith that called its followers to a new experience and taught them about a deeper life. Christianity did not just set itself apart from a myriad of sects but saw them as immature and inferior. Finally, the church proclaimed a deeper, saving history *within* history and saw its own history as important, certainly more important than political developments. If these aspects recall our own time, they do so within the milieu of a church where the broad activities of the faithful, empowered by the Spirit, are being summoned to face the opportunities of each diocese. If in an unsettling way the dynamic parish of today resembles a Pauline community in A.D. 55 more than it resembles a parish in 1945,[34] it is not surprising that New Testament ideas and the basing of ecclesiology upon biblical studies has influenced the expansion of ministry. So we must begin by looking at the gift of ministry to the church, the gift of the grace of being a ministering community to the reign of God, directed by the Spirit of the risen Christ.

The American church lives and has lived for three decades in the midst of multiple sociological dynamics. There is the renewal of Vatican II in many church areas; there are the post-conciliar dynamics of which ministry is one; there are the growth in population and migrations of Catholics within the United States on a large scale, as well as large migrations of Catholics into the United States; and there is the decline in the number of priests and religious. Remarkably, the church in the United States has floated above and with these currents due to the number of teachers, theologians, and ministers in the church who have a vision of parish and diocese as a welcoming, mature, and active gathering of the people of God.

2

PRIMAL MINISTRY: SPIRIT, FREEDOM, CHARISM, AND MINISTRY

The Christian believes that God comes to men and women in a special intensity and in a history of salvation. *kingdom, Spirit,* or *grace* are words denoting a special divine presence (beyond the universe studied by physics and biology) within cultural structures and individual personalities and from this presence comes Christian community and its ministries. We begin with a look at the ministry of Jesus and of the early church: we want to see their basic contours in order to grasp some principles for a fundamental theology of ministry. The experience and forms of the early church are not so much a political rule or a single structure to be precisely reproduced, but a rich event of lasting import, an orientation, a seed of future forms, a tradition beneath traditions. The Spirit active in people joining a community is the basic impetus and gift for ministry, capable of perdurance and also of change.

I. Jesus' Preaching of the Kingdom of God

Jesus of Nazareth preached neither a separate religion nor one institution; neither did he teach esoteric information about God or himself. He preached what he called the kingdom of God. Jesus invited followers to join his ministry of evangelization, and the first Christians experienced his Spirit's call to discipleship. Jesus is minister to God: if Jesus Christ is the work and icon of God's plan for us, he is, in his own words, also its servant.

Jesus, God's Word in human person, during his ministry on

our planet was a prophet of what he called the kingdom or reign of God. This powerful but unseen reality, the kingdom of God, is the central message of Jesus of Nazareth. The metaphor "kingdom" represents the loving, active plan of God in history. Jesus did not preach primarily the formation and maintenance of an institution we call "the church." As a Jewish, itinerant, occasionally apocalyptic herald, he proclaimed the advent of God, describing this "kingdom" in metaphors and parables. He warned of its challenge to the rich and to the priestly custodians of religion, even as he pointed out its presence in honest soldiers, sorrowing prostitutes, and repentant exploiters of the poor. The Realm of God was not only a hope but a power overcoming the tragedy of history. Jesus joined it to faith in God, to love for another suffering human being, or to conversion from dishonesty and egoism. "Jesus came into Galilee, preaching the gospel of God, and saying, 'The time is fulfilled, and the kingdom of God is at hand; repent, and believe in the gospel'" (Mk 1:14 f.).

We see Jesus as the result and center not only of Israel's history but of all religious history. Jesus is not a demigod in a strange land, but the prophet and priest of God's widening power. This location of Jesus within the kingdom of God need not reduce Jesus to an ethical teacher; for he presents himself not only as the incarnation of the presence of God but as the sender of God's Spirit now and in the future.

What is the kingdom of God that Jesus announces and whose coming in history has brought not only the Christ but his pentecostal Spirit? As we ponder the metaphors for God's presence, we find that the church has stepped in front of the kingdom. The kingdom of God is not a power like the nations of this world, although the history of the church is a record of the temptation—and the church's acquiescence—to be such; nor is the church a sacral city substituting on earth for the kingdom. There have been periods, colorful if exaggerated, when political kingship claimed priesthood and ministry, and church leadership sought royal dominion. At his coronation, the son of Charlemagne was clothed not only as emperor but as deacon. Some officeholders of the church lived out their ministry not as itinerant evangelists but as battle lords. The church is human, but the kingdom is fundamentally and initially of God. The way we view the reign of God present in and after Jesus will determine the vitality and accuracy of our vision of Jesus' call to ministry. Since all ministry ultimately serves the kingdom of God and since the church itself—as ancient mosaics portray—is a deacon of the Trinity, we must begin a theology of ministry with a contemplation of God's presence in history.

The kingdom of God is the message of Jesus. From the preaching of Jesus, we learn through similes that there is a dynamic influence of God in our midst, one perceivable only through belief. Its standards and its goals, its very style of working, are not those of the world's ambition and sensuality but are love, service, and the motif of dying to self and of rising. It is, however, easier to say what the kingdom of God *is not* than what it *is*: it is not any one civilization or culture, nor any particular nation or empire; not this philosophy or worldview nor this political or economic movement. God's plan and direction is greater than any individual or collective cultural enterprise, more than history, more than the history of the world's religions, more than art, and more than economic equality. The kingdom of God is not only a condition after biological death but is the inner core of human life, a dynamic intensifying and expanding after the coming of Jesus of Nazareth.

In Ephesians, we find the images of God's reign depicting a cosmic expansion: "For he has made known to us in all wisdom and insight the mystery of his will, according to his purpose which he set forth in Christ as a plan for the fullness of time, to unite all things in him, things in heaven and things on earth. In him, according to the purpose of him who accomplishes all things according to the counsel of his will, we who first hoped in Christ have been destined and appointed to live for the praise of his glory" (Eph 1:9). Before creation, before the tragic turn of our fallen race, this planet emerges from God marked by a plan. The plan exists for me, for me to be sustained by God's love and destined for eternal life. This plan is mysterious not in the sense of hidden information or divine trick, but mysterious in its concreteness and in its movement from cosmic peace and power through sin (exemplified and climaxed in Jesus at Golgotha) and through our own suffering and sin to life triumphant. "The hour has come for the Son of man to be glorified. Truly, truly, I say to you, unless a grain of wheat falls into the earth and dies, it remains alone; but if it dies, it bears much fruit" (Jn 12:23, 28).

What is this plan and presence, the "kingdom of God," since it is not a religious empire or a set of saving ideas? We, unacquainted with kings and kingdoms, might name it an atmosphere, a world. The kingdom of God is not simply the mind of God or a future heaven. Not only *kingdom* and *reign* but words like *salvation, redemption,* and *grace* designate a subtle presence, like a cultural horizon. Although it is as intimate to us as we are to ourselves, grace is not produced by us but is God's gift. Perceived not by statistics but by the eye of faith, the atmosphere of God's plan is expansive, future-directed. Although appearing to be of religion, God's gracious plan transforms and challenges all it touches—even religion. Pro-human, it veers away from superstitious bondage to a deity, and turns toward the service of what ultimately is best in us.

The kingdom of God is the bestower of ministry.

The kingdom of God is the source, the milieu, the goal of ministry. The presence of God in our complex world enables ministry, gives ministry its life and its freedom. The church, rather than being the sovereign dispenser of ministry, offers ministry within the kingdom as something derivative, fragile, secondary, temporary. At the end of time, ministry and church will be absorbed into our life in God. A theology of ministry is basically a meditation on the kingdom, a theology of the Holy Spirit, a contemplative analysis of grace.

Jesus of Nazareth was born into a religion where priests and temple cult were of high import, and the society that witnessed Jesus' ministry was a priestly society. Jesus was not a priest and, contrary to what one might expect, did not come from a priestly family. He stood throughout his public ministry in the prophetic line of Israel. Jesus belonged to the Davidic (royal) but not to the Aaronic (priestly) line. He did not move from a sacerdotal family to service in the Temple as a cultic intermediary between God and nation. As with other prophets, Jesus faced opposition from the priests of his people; for Jesus broke through sacral caste to

welcome all as he questioned religious rules as divinely guaranteed absolutes and flared up in anger more at religious hypocrisy
than at ethical sin.

If Jesus did not bring a new cultic religion (this would have
fallen short of the revolution that the reign of God was introducing), priestly areas, however, are present in Jesus' life: the identification of the Temple with himself; his sacrificial death in blood;
the service and liturgy that he accomplished not in a shrine but in
the world; his actions, not the sacrifices of animals, but preaching, healing, and teaching (Mt 5:21). Jesus' preaching confronts
all religion in the form of the Jewish law. In different Gospels
Jesus critiques not so much the impotency as the hypocrisy and
tyranny that can flow out of religion, any religion. All this culmi-
nates in the revolutionary axiom: "The Sabbath was made for
man, not man for the Sabbath; so the Son of man is lord even of
the Sabbath" (Mk 2:27 f.). Religious forms exist to help people;
people do not exist to be the unthinking executors of rubrics.
Jesus' preaching is the authoritative critique and interpretation of
religion in order to sustain God's own reality of grace.

In Christian faith and tradition Jesus is, through his Incarnation, priest. Medieval theology explained Jesus' priesthood
through the ontological anointing by the Logos of Jesus the
man.[1] In the Word made flesh, the Christ, we have the union and
interplay but not the confusion of the human and the divine.
The divine present in the human acts within the ordinary life of
a man. The divine is not an arbitrary, theocratic will nor magic
power but is the invisible presence of God permeating and inviting. There is a certain secularity in Jesus' personal priesthood: it
is not that the presence of God is ignored but that sacrifice and
doctrine are removed from temple ritual and exist in the open
air as part of life. Jesus is both priest and victim; moreover, he is
both in terms of reality and not just symbolically, in terms of society and not in terms of an arbitrary religion. As victim Jesus is
not ritually executed by priests at a sacred place as among Aztecs
or Scythians. Jesus dies as a civil criminal and religious rebel.

In presenting Jesus as a priest, the Letter to the Hebrews
holds an innovative religious perspective.[2] That New Testament
letter is not saying that Jesus was actually a priest of the Jewish

religion, nor the first priest of a new (Christian) religion. Rather, the letter proclaims a reality and action that can be named analogously sacerdotal, but one standing over against the impotent symbolism of all priesthoods. Jesus, through what appeared to be political evil and personal brutality, changed the structure of the world and so of religion. Beyond new symbols about religion, Jesus' person and death are the reality explained by symbols. They bring the long human history of religious cult to a fulfillment which, without the events of the Incarnation, would have always escaped and deformed it.

Hebrews' central section explains the superiority of the "reality-history" of God's new covenant. Though not a priest among the religions of earth (8:4), Jesus the Christ is a priest of the reign of God and of the human race but in a new and unique way. "Since then we have a great high priest who has passed through the heavens, Jesus, the Son of God....For we have not a high priest who is unable to sympathize with our weakness..." (4:14 f.). Mature reflection upon the reality of who Jesus was, and upon what happened in him, leads the author of Hebrews to meditate upon the meaning of Calvary. Golgotha was an event in cosmic and religious history. A new priesthood had to arise, and with a new law (7:11). To describe the role of the earlier law, the writer uses several words that illustrate how it anticipated Christ: *pattern, shadow, icon* (8:5; 10:1). In this "law" and "priesthood" the Jewish religion stands for the whole of religion. As lofty as the covenant becomes through the great prophets, Israel's priestly rituals were impotent before God's being (even as in its depths the covenant bore God's grace) and in them one senses the feebleness of all cults.

Repeating rituals is a sign of the rituals' impotency. Both priest and devotee (freed from the cultic emotions of fear and gain) can glimpse that their entire sacral structure is arbitrary, one without any real connection to God's plan of mercy. This insight into the arbitrariness of most religious ritual, however, is hard to gain. Human drives and needs want finite objects and things to be divine and omnipotent. Hebrews challenges the objectifications of religion apart from human life and divine covenant. Christ's "liturgy" is universal and real and powerful. It is no longer a question of foods and animals, rites and rubrics but of reality. "But when Christ appeared as a high priest of the good things that have come...how much more shall the blood of Christ, who through the eternal Spirit offered himself without blemish to God, purify your conscience from dead works to serve the living God" (8:6; 9:11, 13, 14).

The church is on a historical pilgrimage wending its way toward that realm into which Christ has entered, ahead of us, through his Calvary priesthood. The community can and will follow him into redemption through belief in the event of Christ (3:14). "Therefore, brethren, since we have confidence to enter the sanctuary by the blood of Jesus, by the new and living way which he opened for us through the curtain, that is, through his flesh, and since we have a great priest over the house of God..." (10:19f.). The theme of Hebrews is the final priest and his free and redeemed people. Christ's priesthood is unique, for there remains nothing more, objectively, to be enacted for the human race, but what does remain is the expansion of the pilgrim people by preaching the word about Christ's real liturgy to others.

No Christian minister can be solely or essentially a priest in the sense of religion prior to or outside of Christ, and yet Jesus is not alone active in the church: he is the firstborn of countless brothers and sisters, people loved and empowered by his Spirit, and so he communicates to his followers what he has accomplished for all. If the leader of the community and of the Eucharist has resemblances to this deeply human institution as mediator, as leader, as instructor, nonetheless, Christian priesthood must be interpreted within the redemptive event of Christ and purified of traces of power, self-adulation, and magic.

II. From Religion to the Sacrament of the Spirit

From its communal, historical, and personal origins, the church stands under and amid the activity of the Spirit. This is the meaning of the biblical report of individuals receiving a share of Jesus' work during his public years (Lk 4:18ff.) and of Pentecost (Acts 2). The Spirit directs the paths of the missionaries and in the Pauline letters to the new churches we learn that the faithful have received special impetuses within their Spirit-filled life for ministry (1 Cor 12; Eph 4).

Ministry would seem to be closely allied to religion. "Organized religion" has its "ministers" and "priests." The kingdom of God, however, purifies all lesser realms and judges politics and civilizations. Jesus would not isolate into a soul or a temple the new presence of God he saw breaking in. "I saw Satan fall like lightning from heaven. Behold, I have given you authority to tread upon serpents and scorpions...and nothing shall hurt you. Nevertheless do not rejoice in this, that the spirits are subject to you; but rejoice that your names are written in heaven" (Lk 10:18). Precisely because the kingdom ushers in new times, God's revealing presence in Jesus builds upon and modifies religion. Religion in a fallen race will contain stolid error and idolatry, and so the Spirit must critique each religion and even the totality of religion. The New Testament records this meeting as Jesus encounters positively and negatively his own religion and enacts in a strange way the sacrifice of religion to God, and then goes beyond the bloody history of religion by offering life in the Spirit to all.

Christ fulfilled something. Ministry is not solely a bloody or bloodless liturgy, the Christian church is not a marble temple of a new covenant, the ministers of Christianity are not brighter and more powerful forms of Olympic or Levitical priesthood. Seeing themselves and God in the light of the coming of the Spirit, the Christians of the first century replaced much of religion with community, charism, and service. Their communities were not a new religion nor a new version of Jewish religion; they were the fulfillment of all religion.

Religion can mean an attraction to the transcendent and holy, but religion has a second, narrower meaning: the localization of the divine in objects and people encircled by mediations and castes, cults, and idols. The preaching and promise of Jesus is not a new religion nor only the next stage of one previous religion, that of Israel. To be called Son of God means to exist as definitive religious prophet. Jesus is addressing all religion, for he knows that God's kingdom now fulfills, judges, illumines, and critiques the religions of the world. "And you, who were dead in trespasses and the uncircumcision of your flesh, God made alive together with him, having forgiven us all our trespasses, having canceled the bond which stood against us with its legal demands; this he set aside, nailing it to the cross. He disarmed the principalities and powers and made a public example of them, triumphing over them in him" (Col 2:13f.). To the followers of Jesus, women and men, the cross was a scandalous event of social and religious history, and soon, when preaching the cross and Resurrection of Jesus of Nazareth, the Twelve found that often their hearers did not comprehend its consequences. The Twelve themselves did not easily grasp the new freedom within religion. People and cities long accustomed to the cultic manipulation of the divine and to the purchasing power of ritual were startled by God's wisdom: through a condemned criminal in a public sacrifice—a grotesque liturgy—God's plan entered its final era.

There are many ways of defining and dividing "religion." Neither philosophers nor cultural anthropologists agree on a single meaning. Religion can mean things: not only vessels and idols, buildings and people, but clothes, rituals, doctrines and writings—all of which pertain to knowing about and influencing the Absolute. Or religion can mean the psychological drive, the mental and emotional urges that are the ground of the concrete realizations mentioned above, for there is in every woman and man feelings of dependence (finitude), of incompleteness (mortality), of quest (meaning), and these give rise to religion, to total and personal quest, to a more or less implicit hope and faith. Religion is not just one facet of life but is capable of being the matrix of other cultural forms, of being a conscious or unconscious ground for life. Modern philosophers and psychologists have concentrated upon this second, broader meaning. Philosophers such as Rudolf Otto and Martin Heidegger and painters like Wassily Kandinsky and Paul Klee spoke of the holy disclosed in the spiritual essence of things and situations. Paul Tillich described religion as the substance of culture—the ground of being and the ultimate concern breaking forth into the concrete forms of architecture, theater, and economics. This understanding of religion is not the enemy of but the prelude to the great modern Christian theological systems.

When we say that the advent of the kingdom of God in Jesus and his Spirit clashes with religion, even spells the purification of religion, we do not mean this second understanding of religion whose forms lie within our personality. Since the Enlightenment, scholars and theologians have been announcing the arrival of a secular, religionless world. Churches and theologians for the past two centuries have been convinced that they should abandon faith in a historical revelation of God in Jesus Christ in order to be ready and relevant for a society without religion. Of course, such a time never arrived and never arrives. If charism and ministry in a sacramental mode are to be successful, realizations of revelation and faith (and revelation must become concrete to make an impact upon our sensitivity), they must not only address our inner religious drives but they must use symbols and events, actions and people to make grace concrete. When we argue that the early Christians had a revolutionary grasp of religion, we do not mean they foresaw pure secularity—*ecclesia* metamorphosed into secular city—but that they understood that external, cultic, tribal religion was superficial, and that it ended with the events of Golgotha.

We can contrast the transcendental, ecstatic, and sacramental modes of religion (all of which continue) with sacral religion (which ends). *Sacral* means all manner of things that not only symbolize or present (as the Christian sacrament does) but which may summon or manipulate the divine. In cult, the divine is often controlled; in idols, the transcendent materialized; in priesthood, the holy is controlled. Superstition, magic, and idolatry are the accompanying spirits of sacral religion. Such religion brings the perennial temptation to encapsulate the divine. Sacral religion is a phenomenon of extremes: it parades exaggerated claims and it achieves nothing. Not the dimension of human self-transcendence toward the holy, but the concreteness of sacral religion was what Jesus challenged. The reign of God brought judgment to sacral religion with its control of the religious realm in buildings, objects, rituals, and classes. In Jesus' attitude toward religion we have a foundation for the charismatic and communal life of his followers. Justin Martyr in the second century explained that Christians were priestly people because God had set them free from pagan and Jewish rituals; their prayers replaced sacrifices.[3]

The development from religion to charism has its roots in the preaching and life of Jesus, and in the interpretation of the

Christ by his followers and evangelists. In Jesus the gulfs and boundaries separating human beings are abolished. All are invited to the reign of God; all are dwellings of the Spirit; Jesus is himself the one victim and the one priest (only one realization of each is necessary) of the new and central covenant.[4] Jesus and the early church, by their use of the material and the human, turn away from a faith and life that avoid icon, sacrament, and movement. The relationship of Jesus to human religion and then to his communal Body touches upon two issues that have some importance for a theology of ministry. While an incarnational revelation and an ecclesial people are critical of sacral religion, the Incarnation bespeaks sacramentality, the union of the human and the divine, of personality and grace.[5] The new covenant is not just a space for interior meditation. The Christian is not an object of the church, nor is the Holy Spirit an indifferent abstract power source. Grace comes personally and the individual is respected. People in the church are served with the greatest respect; the baptized are not a statistic or an annoyance.

We consider the fulfillment of religion in the church not as the promotion of a new puritanism but as the effort to free sacrament and service from narrow constraints, allowing for wider incarnations in people, movements, and cultures. Religion yields to incarnation, and incarnation continues in inculturation. It is this pattern that we witness at work in the expansion of church ministry. The worldwide church after Vatican II should be free to inculturate itself in the religious milieus of the earth, always bringing the newness of the Gospel and the breadth of ministry.

III. Primal Ministry

The New Testament describes charism and ministry mainly in specific services whose names are taken from actions, for instance, from preaching, teaching, evangelizing, healing. These names and actions differ according to place, culture, and time. Because diversity of ministry is an issue in the contemporary expansion of ministry, and because over the centuries there has been a reduction to a few ministries during which ordinary Greek words became sacral Roman and European offices, we must look briefly at the structure of ministry among the first Christian churches. This requires a theology of ministry to remain with the scriptural records a while longer before moving to the transit of ministry through the centuries, and then to the exigencies of ministry today. The ecclesiologist cannot solve complex problems of exegesis but at the same time cannot appear naive or satisfied with a fundamentalist literalism. The theologian looks for basic insights from the New Testament—but its richness in the area of ministry has been obscured. Today we experience less of the being of the church than the first churches did. Developing a theology of ministry in the light of the experience of the first Christians, we turn to early church life not because it is old but because it is primal. *Primal,* or *original,* means near to the source: in this case, near a source that faith holds to be revelatory. The first communities were not only chronologically close to Jesus and Pentecost but they self-consciously display a proximity to an intense advent of the Spirit. The first churches are primal because in them the Spirit appears not fully but radically and strikingly. Our interest, then, is not in antiquity but in proximity: first churches reflect the primal event of the birth of Christian faith and community.[6] We are interested in the expression of the early church not to revivify exactly this or that form but to see in those forms what the churches view in culturally diverse ways as essential and charismatic.

Christian faith has always held that not only was Jesus' preaching and life normative but that the first generation of his disciples—called the apostolic generation—was privileged in what they saw and perceived. Their witness because of its immediacy was special. They remain primal for us today: early churches are not simply the first Christians receiving their marching orders from Jesus, Peter, or Paul. If that were so, these churches would have presented one set of lasting forms, and the church today would not reflect the church in A.D. 1200 or A.D. 1600 but only that of A.D. 50. The first witnesses and the first generations of believing disciples are primal because they are immediate; they have a lasting significance because they were creative.

The New Testament letters do not describe a pageant to be imitated but present a picture of community life. In contrast to our recent, monoform model of priesthood, the images of early Christian communities present a panoply of ideas and forms. Still, we find less ecclesiology in the New Testament than we would like. What we know of Paul's ecclesiology is conditioned by circumstances at Corinth, and we know a little of the inner way of life of the Jewish churches in Antioch or Caesarea, and only something of Rome and, later, of Ephesus.

What is striking, however, is that in this area of ministry the New Testament is richer than are later centuries of Christian reflection and practice. After the third century we have stasis and reduction, and after the sixth century, diminution. Ministry has fewer forms or is institutionalized; ministry becomes priesthood and is grafted on to canonical positions. Not every area of the Christian faith undergoes this diminution; for instance, the dialogue between grace and the human personality is more extensively developed as the centuries pass, but in ministry, reflection on faith undergoes some impoverishment after the second century. Yet, every ministerial diversity retains seeds and patterns of an earlier variety.

Theologians look to exegetes not only for information on a particular ministry—prophet or presbyter—but for a sociological picture of communities and ministry. Different regions of the Roman Empire held different views of the world and from those social, ethnic, and religious structures the first churches could not help but draw institutional forms. Ecclesiology, like Christology, displays a diversity drawn from the New Testament as influenced by different social and cultural backgrounds of the men and women who entered Christian communities and rendered the churches diverse. The religious and political structures in which they had been raised were not destroyed by baptism and the Spirit but often contributed to the manner of living in community. The New Testament's books are not systems of polity but writings of circumstance. Their situations are not fully known, their styles are diverse, and they do not intend to be comprehensive. We learn about ministry in a collection of writings of different literary genres drawn from several linguistic and religious worlds. There is a view of ministry in letters to communities in Corinth (in turmoil) and in Rome (not yet seen); there is the Acts of Apostles,

which presents the first decades of the church but not always
without the interpretation of later decades. First Peter, Hebrews,
and Revelation come from different areas and eras. Through all
of this, the difficult task of exegesis is to penetrate behind the letter of the text to authors and communities capable of influencing
the structures described as well as the written text. Development
and complexity mark distinct Christian communities—Johannine,
Corinthian, Roman, Antiochene.[7]

The writings of the New Testament bear witness to the existence of ministry, to actions and people nourishing the
churches. The word *ministry,* which has religious overtones, is a
translation of the Latin *ministerium,* which in turn is translating
the New Testament's Greek word, *diakonia.* The Greek word is
an ordinary word for service, in the household, at table, and
elsewhere. Daniel Donovan observes: "It is a surprising fact that
this basically nonreligious term should have become as central
as it did. The surprise, however, is dissipated once one recalls a
famous saying of Jesus that in one form or another can be found
six times in the gospel tradition: 'He who is greatest among you
shall be your servant' (Mt 23:11)."[8] Paul designates his high work
of being an apostle a ministry, a *diakonia* (2 Cor 4:1), and other
services are also needed for the church as they flow from the
various charisms sent by the Spirit (1 Cor 12). Service is the
essential constitutive element of office and function for
Christians. Services appear in various terms and forms, but this
does not mean that the form of ministry was of no interest to
early Christians, that church means a charismatic group, or that
a church was an ever shifting assembly of passing miraculous
charisms, or that ministry in the church today can be allowed to
be a secular bureaucratic activity whose ordinariness shies away
from the Spirit. Just the opposite is true: New Testament ministry is not simply organization and work but the activity of the
Spirit in coworkers. The typology of ministers is important.
Between charismatic anarchy and secular passivity there were,
in the first churches, groups able to develop in different ways.
Leonhard Goppelt writes: "From the very beginning we can
observe in the organization of the church, as in the service of
worship, the same characteristic tension between historical

forms and pneumatic freedom. The church conducted itself as a living organism in keeping with the consultational forms which she had taken over in an attitude of uninhibited independence from the Jewish tradition, yet she never made these forms into a constitution."[9]

We do not find in the first centuries the purely charismatic communities of the Radical Reformation or later Protestantism, a Greek college of priests, collegial or democratic assemblies with an Enlightenment spirit, or churches organized like Baroque dioceses. Leadership had several names and forms, and the relationships of presbyters, deacons, and teachers to church leaders were fluid and diverse.

The church is a community that is also the Body of Christ and the servant and organ of the Spirit. The church is ministerial. Semitic religion, Greek culture, Roman Empire offered extensive opportunities of communication and of inculturation; the age knew an intense and sometimes anxious inquiry about the meaning of human life that spurred on vigorous religious movements and the search for an experience of life in the community. In the New Testament period as today, crisis and change provoked creativity; ministries were suited to cultures and yet intent upon evangelizing them.[10] The contours of what we can learn from the New Testament of the first churches and their ministries, summing up characteristics owned by churches of Jews and Hellenes, Romans and Syrians (even when we must study them carefully and indirectly through later churches), help us appreciate a diversity of pattern and a possible chronology of development.

IV. Beyond Religion: Spirit, Freedom, Charism, and Ministry

Jesus called followers and disciples, beckoning them to a discipleship that was more than temple priesthood, more than rabbinic internship. What that "more" meant became clear only after Jesus' Resurrection and his Spirit's Pentecost. Slowly it dawned on Jesus' believers that following Jesus and his Spirit meant service, service for all and by all. *Pneuma, charisma,* and then *diakonia* are realizations of the wider, intimate horizon Scripture calls "the kingdom of God." By calling a variety of men and women and by a forceful (but not always understood) explanation of the reign of God (Mt 13:11), Jesus showed that others are to carry on his ministry. The harvest looks to workers; the future demands interpreters; his disciples are to go to all of Israel, even to all nations (Mt 28:19).

The Spirit of Jesus: **Pneuma.** At Pentecost with the coming of the Holy Spirit, the kingdom of God entered a new, more intense phase. That force and realm that Jesus had preached, the milieu and destiny of human life on earth, was presented in a further way: it was the life of the Spirit of God who was the Spirit of the risen Lord. The Spirit whose consoling presence is forecast in the Gospel according to John is the Spirit of the Jesus who lives no longer on earth but in the final, eschatological form within the reign of God. The mode in which the risen Christ lives and works is in the Holy Spirit: according to First Corinthians Jesus became "a life-giving spirit" (15:45). The Lord, *Kyrios,* is now Spirit, *Pneuma.* Ingo Hermann writes: "Paul responds to the relationship of *Kyrios* and *Pneuma* in the sense of an identity: obviously not in the sense of a logical identity but as an identity accessible to Christian faith in which the Lord shows himself as *Pneuma* and the *Pneuma*...represents the exalted one, the activity of *Lord* and *Pneuma* which for the believer is presenting one and the same event. This mutual relationship of dynamic presence (the *Kyrios* as *Pneuma*) and representation (the *Pneuma* for the *Kyrios*) emerges as the key for understanding the pneumatic mode of existence of the risen Christ (Rom 1:4; 1 Cor 15:45)."[11] It is important to rediscover the proximity of Jesus to his Spirit, for ministry is grounded not just in the imitation of the historical Jesus but in the personal response to the charismatic call of his Spirit. What Paul is struggling to express is not a full absorption of Jesus into spirit, nor an identity of two persons in God, but the Resurrection altering the way in which Jesus is present to us today. Now the Word of God Triune exists not only as the historical Jesus who, risen, is *Kyrios,* but as the Lord who is, at present, Spirit. "Through the dynamic structure of the *Pneuma,* the *Kyrios* is not merely someone coming again but is conceived as the Coming One present....The Apostle's eschatology, his ecclesiology, his understanding of Christian life cannot be understood without the identity of *Kyrios* and *Pneuma* as expressed in 2 Corinthians....Christian existence is given the task through its reception of the activity of the *Pneuma* 'in our hearts' (Rom 5:5) to gain a share in Christ, to be a member among the members of the Body being built up by the Spirit" (1 Cor 12; Rom 8:9).[12]

At first, comprehension of the accessibility and power of the Spirit eluded the Twelve. How was their movement distinct from Israel? How was the kingdom not a sect or a religion? The action of the Spirit not only shook religion but drew the disciples away from traditions and institutions that could not fully respond to the omnipresent *Pneuma*.

New Life in the Spirit. The advent of the Spirit after Pentecost was not the coming of a new sect or a new religion, even the best religion. Earth's salvation has been revealed and enhanced in a remarkable combination of universality and individuality whose poles are freedom and power. Religion continues only in the Spirit. "Now we are discharged from the law, dead to that which held us captive, so that we serve not under the old written code but in the new life of the Spirit" (Rom 7:6). As the sacral structure of so many religions is fulfilled by the death of Jesus, human religious drives are fulfilled by his Spirit. Like the physical structures of the universe existing prior to individual men and women, so in the horizon of the Spirit a sovereign, surrounding presence becomes concrete in the sacramental mode: not as magic but as the presence of grace in creation and in the human. Aidan Kavanagh writes:

> *Ecclesiologically,* the bath initiates the cleansed ones into a new People, the Body of Christ, the locale of his life-giving Spirit (1 Cor 12:13, 27). This results in their living in a community so new and different that conventional social analogues can hardly be used to describe it (Gal 3:28; 1 Cor 13:12). So radically incomparable is this transformation in Christ-become-life-giving-Spirit that only the most primal human experiences such as marriage, birth, death, and dining together offer clues to it.[13]

The Spirit brings freedom. "Where the Spirit of the Lord is, there is freedom" (2 Cor 3:17). Doesn't religion oppose freedom?

How revolutionary it was to introduce freedom into the world of religion, for temples and rituals are the opposite of freedom, both for the devotees and for the deities. Yet personal freedom accompanies God's word and life. "Now this Lord is the Spirit, and where the Spirit of the Lord is, there is freedom" (2 Cor 3:17). Christians were free from the uncertainty of prior religious lives, uncertain and fearful before idols and talismans and myths, because Jesus the Christ was for each individual existential truth and future consolation. "All who are led by the Spirit are sons of God. The spirit you received is not the spirit of slaves bringing fear into your lives again; it is the spirit of sonship, and it makes us cry out, 'Abba, Father!' It is through the Spirit himself bearing witness with our spirit that we are children of God. And if children, we are heirs as well: heirs of God and coheirs with Christ, sharing his sufferings so as to share his glory" (Rom 8:14 ff.).

Life in the Spirit is just that, a life. "Do you know that all of us who have been baptized into Christ Jesus were baptized into his death? We were buried therefore with him by baptism into death, so that as Christ was raised from the dead by the glory of the Father we too might walk in newness of life....So you also must consider yourselves dead to sin and alive to God in Christ Jesus" (Rom 6:4). The early Christians saw themselves free to live in "the household of God" (Eph 2:19) as a "new creation" (2 Cor 5:17). Free of laws, the baptized were new kinds of persons existing in the real world of the Spirit, which was neither the cosmos of past religions nor the city of ambition, anger and money. Their mode of life included service extending the kingdom into the needy, turbulent world even as it brought about the new religious law of love. "Of this gospel I was made a minister according to the gift of God's grace which was given me by the working of his power. To me, though I am the very least of all the saints, this grace was given, to preach to the Gentiles the unsearchable riches of Christ, and to make all men see what is the plan of the mystery hidden for ages in God who created all things: that through the church the manifold wisdom of God might now be made known" (Eph 3:7–10).

New life in the Spirit brings ministry.

Paul saw that the freedom of the Spirit is not a preparation for magic but a contact that flows into activity. The mission of the Spirit bears in it a drive toward activity, and this service—a being-sent to serve—flows out of the freedom and community of the Christians. The reign of God included essentially a communal place and a personal activity in all who believed in and followed Jesus.

Nothing is more basic to a theology of ministry than to see how Christian service is grounded in the Spirit. Assisted by our grasp of the revolution which Jesus' coming accomplished in religion and freedom, we must further examine how the Spirit's liberating presence transformed religion into community and ministry.

Charism. The graciousness *(charis)* of the Spirit is not only the plan of salvation-history (Eph 1:2 ff.) but the Spirit-enabled life of the baptized (Rom 8). The word *charisma* is a facet of the realm Paul calls grace, but an ecclesial facet. For Paul not only the grace of his apostleship exists but basically each person has a *charisma* in which the freely bestowed *charis* becomes concrete. Romans expresses this clearly: "...having charisms according to the grace given to you, varies" (12:6). With regards to grace there is no difference among the faithful receiving it in Christ, but the *charismata* are indeed different.[14] *Charism, gift, pneumatic* are Pauline words for the silent promptings of the Spirit in a Christian personality toward service; the most prominent among them is *charism.* Etymologically, *charism* has tones of graciousness, of generosity, of a joyful liberality. The gifts that God makes available and real in Jesus are love, mercy, and future life. Paul did not create the word *charisma,* but he gave it a new, theological nuance and richness. Speaking of powers given by the Spirit, he sometimes turned *spiritual* into a noun, *pneumatika,* but Christians have preferred *charism.* The two words explains not a bizarre enthusiasm or a miraculous display but the source of life and action in the Spirit.

Charism is found in Paul but rarely outside his writings. We do not have to conclude, however, that Paul's ecclesiology built upon charism is a narrow projection of his ideas or of the experiences of the Corinthians. Some exegetical and theological evaluations of charism for over the past century have represented forms of what we might call the spark theory. Among ordinary people in early Christian communities, the theory explains, there appeared sparks of supernatural activity, powers full of seizures and miracles. A passage from Romans, however, suggests that we see *charism* as a richer word, expressing several meanings of the Spirit's contact. "The charism of God is eternal life in Jesus Christ, our Lord" (6:23). Here we meet the primal charism, the source of all other charisms. Living in the kingdom and Spirit of Jesus risen brings pneumatic gifts, charismatic services, of many kinds, like teaching, preaching, visiting the sick. There is a charismatic ground and source from which they all flow.

Grace does not reward activity but causes actions, charisms. Paul also calls charisms "energies" (1 Cor 12:6, 11). That third member of a hermeneutical triad of the Spirit (charisms, spiritual gifts, energies) also leads to ministry. "Now concerning spiritual gifts, brethren, I do not want you to be uninformed....Now there are varieties of gifts but the same Spirit; and there are varieties of service but the same Lord; and there are varieties of working but it is the same God who inspires them all in every one. To each is given the manifestation of the Spirit for the common good" (1 Cor 12:1, 4–7). Perhaps these different Greek words represent nuances, theologies, or communities whose identities are lost to us, but the message of the Spirit's activity in variety is clear. For each word, the reality described is power from the Spirit. The community's life, freed from religion, is embraced by the horizon of the Spirit, and the Holy Spirit works charismatically in the personality of each Christian. The presence of the Spirit in baptized men and women is a life, but one which is diaconal in terms of its goal.

It is clear, according to First Corinthians and Romans, that the diversity of gifts and the view that each believer has a charism is important, and that the Body of Christ's theme is not a way of marginalizing or spiritualizing this panoply of activities. Charisms come from baptism and faith and are ordered to the expansion and good of the church. Charisms in the Pauline letters are gifts of the Spirit.

Freedom, Religion and Community. As the first Christians comprehended Jesus' critique and fulfillment of religion and as they experienced the new freedom with which the Spirit replaced cult, Christian communities must have sensed themselves to be pioneers in a process of new religion. Temple, priesthood, sacrifice, liturgy, and laws were set aside or understood in the mode of sacrament or ministry. The following chart illustrates that metamorphosis.

RELIGION	CHRISTIAN INTERPRETATION
One people, tribe, or nation	All people, particularly the lowly and socially marginated
Temple	The community
Priesthood	All the baptized with diverse charisms and ministries
High priest	Jesus the Christ, executed and risen
Sacrifice	The political and religious execution of Jesus; secondarily, the sufferings, lives, and services of the baptized
Worship	Preaching and daily life
Laws	A mature obedience with freedom and without fear to the preaching and life of Jesus enabled by the Spirit
Magic	The world is loved by God and has been redeemed; it is the place of the Spirit. Baptism, meals, Eucharist, anointing, embraces, and laying on of hands nourish the community
Superstition	Faith in the Father and communion with his will as manifest in the kingdom, globally and individually

The community desacralized and personalized the Incarnation and redemption of Jesus, while the charismatic indwelling of the Spirit permeated the life of the community. Let us look closely at four characteristics of the church's fulfillment of religion.

a. *A People.* Human religion was inevitably connected to exclusivity. The tribe or nation had its religion; normally a man or woman could no more move from religion to religion than he or she could exchange racial color or ethnic background. Tribal exclusivity fielded a claim of superiority; the gods smiled only on the tribe, and others were without importance, without even humanity (an exclusivity that has survived after the collapse of tribalism in nationalism and racism). The early Christians realized that the limiting structure of the religions around them (priest versus populace, female apart from male) was ended, and that the Gospel made faith and baptism open to, indeed destined for, all peoples, all races, all social classes, all religions.

b. *A Temple.* The word *temple* had several meanings in the self-description of the early Christians, but none of these meanings connoted a sacral building. The human body of Jesus was the place where a unique manifestation of God took place, and so it was on the cross (the Jewish temple's veil split) and then in the faith of his followers where one found the center of true worship. It was the Christian communities that comprised the Body of their risen Lord, and they saw *themselves* as their temple, replacing the holy spaces of physical temples. In a faith where a public execution had altered ritual sacrifice and where the very *Pneuma* of God had come upon each member, sacral buildings with statues and curious rituals had no meaning. Sacred space is where the divine Spirit dwells—that lay in the community of the Lord. "Didn't you realize that you were God's temple and that the Spirit of God was living among you? If anybody should destroy the temple of God, God will destroy him, because the temple of God is sacred, and you are that temple" (1 Cor 3:16 f.; Eph 2:22).

In the Spirit, God and the Lord Jesus are effectively present in the community despite fragility and weakness among the baptized. This presence, however, is not one of emotional or gnostic enjoyment. Indwelling is mission. If the immediacy of the Spirit had rendered the stone buildings of Graeco-Roman paganism or of Eastern cults superfluous, the concept of the temple as a magical place is also shattered by the evangelical mission of the community; the foundation of this "temple" is important ministries grounded in Christ: its "stones" are the members of the churches. "So then you are no longer strangers and sojourners, but you are fellow citizens with the saints and members of the household of God, built upon the foundation of the apostles and prophets, Christ Jesus himself being the cornerstone, in whom the whole structure is joined together and grows into a holy temple in the Lord; in whom you also are built into it for a dwelling place of God in the Spirit" (Eph 2:19ff.). The temple, the Body of Christ, is always being built up—there is no community without growth—and the visible actions of the community come not through its sacral precinct but through its people.

c. *Priesthood.* The English and German words *priest* are derived from a Greek word that means "elder," and so it had for the first churches no connotation of a religious cult. In the course of time the meaning of church leadership was seen to lie very much in liturgical leadership, and the priest became, for Christians too, a sacerdotal intermediary of salvation between God and man. This latter has validity, but we must understand the limitations of priesthood for followers of Jesus. The first Christians were close to the world of ritual sacrifice and temple priesthoods, even if the Mediterranean world was losing confidence in their efficacy. They were struck by the insight that Jesus was the last priest—the Suffering Servant's sacrifice needed no further complement. Jesus appears in later New Testament theology as the high priest par excellence who has come to that position not through birth or selection but through execution, partially at the hands of one religion's temple servants. Because Jesus is both God and human person, he represents both sides of the meeting between God and us. He is, not cultically but really, mediator. Jesus bridges sin and the limitations holding back human transcendence from God. The result of Calvary was redemption for all, and consequently the first Christians set up no priestly group to reproduce Jesus or Golgotha through ritual. The New Testament is very reticent toward priestly language. The Gospels do not refer to Jesus as a priest, and the New Testament writers never describe the ministers of the church as priests.

The First Letter of Peter, in a rare employment of priestly language, speaks of the Christian community as a "royal priesthood" (2:9).[15] These two metaphorical words are rooted in the Books of Exodus and Leviticus, where the people of God's covenant are promised that they will "be to me a kingdom of priests and a holy nation" (Ex 19:5 f.). This universal priesthood does not mean that each Christian is a priest for self or for others; it has a collective meaning, indicating the background of the life of the new people of God. "It is a call to the church to live as a people sanctified for God,...through its 'priestly vocation' of praising God and through its 'priestly attitude' of sacrificial service in and for the world."[16] In First Peter the priestly nature of the people is not a status but a mission. All of the priestly people are commissioned to declare "the wonderful deeds of him who called you out of darkness into his own marvelous light" (2:9). There are sacrifices (2:5) but they are of the Spirit, actions in charisms, like a moral life and preaching Christ. The Letter to the Philippians (2:17) speaks of a liturgy of faith that would be the result (Heb 12:28) of the sacrifice of Jesus the Christ (Heb 9:23; 10:12), since Christians present to God their entire life (Rom 1:9, 12:1; 1 Pt 2:5).[17] Christians do not produce a new, small, and elitist group, but a sacerdotal college imitative of and led by Jesus. When priestly language is used in the New Testament, it is used metaphorically, and the metaphor points to some reality, to a living out of grace, to evangelism. Eschewing caste by proclaiming a universal priestly people, this transforms the priestly into the ministerial.

We can find four types of priesthoods in the New Testament.[18] The *first* is that of the agents of religious cults. The priesthood of every religion before the coming of the Spirit is not continued or personified in Christ, although it does find a completion in him. Jesus' own priesthood, the *second* priesthood, is not that of high priest within Jewish or pagan religion, even to an extraordinary degree. The priesthood of Jesus both effects and sacramentalizes that which other priesthoods could not accomplish; the priesthood of Jesus turns cult into reality and brings human salvation. The *third* priesthood is the priesthood of all who in explicit faith and public baptism follow the teaching and life of Jesus. This is a priesthood of men and women conscious that they have been redeemed and given a new existence. The *fourth* priesthood could be that of leaders of communities, but there is no reference in the New Testament to the Christian ministry of leadership as a priesthood. We want to understand the depth and universality of the primal Christian revolution in ministry—a death and transfiguration of religion through freedom into grace and service. The eucharistic meal possessed a central role in the life of the Christian community. Nevertheless, Jesus, crucified and coming, was made manifest through a meal, through bread and wine—basic, ordinary, celebratory foods of humanity—and not through magic or apparitions.

Paul, writing to the Romans, did employ priestly terms in an intentional but metaphorical way. He used them to verbalize the ordinary life of the Christian: "Present your bodies as a living sacrifice, holy and acceptable to God, which is your spiritual worship. Do not be conformed to this world but be transformed by the renewal of your mind that you may prove what is the will of God, what is good and acceptable and perfect" (Rom 12:1, 3).[19] The words *sacrifice* and *worship* recalled the temples and their smoldering offerings, but this world had been transformed into a life that was both free of arbitrary rituals and committed to the active will of God in public life. Paul's second meaning of cult altered to ministry was in reference to preaching: "...the grace given me by God to be a minister of Christ Jesus to the Gentiles in the priestly service of the gospel of God, so that the offerings of the Gentiles may be acceptable, sanctified by the Holy Spirit" (Rom 15:16). Paul's ministry of evangelization was his liturgy. He took facets of priesthood out of the temples and used them as metaphors to present the real liturgy of worldwide public preaching. In Philippians, the daily life of the Christian in its distinctive morality and hopeful faith in the future was a worship of God, a sacrifice not to be consumed in the present but enhanced and fulfilled in the future (2:17).

The liturgist in the Roman and Hellenic world was someone whose acts of sacrifice, divination, and benediction represented the world of the sacral to groups of people. Paul transposed terms from Greek or Jewish liturgies as he proclaimed that his mission to all the nations was public, a proclamation and invocation of the universal and eschatological event of God acting in Jesus Christ. Paul's ministry as a metaphorical sacrifice is not a personal, charismatic undertaking but an authorized and delegated mandate that is accomplished through charism and life; he conducts in his liturgy a ministry and activity for the evangelization of the world saved by Jesus. This is not only a spiritualization of cult but a change from the uncertain, idolatrous realm of the sacral to the real: *real* in the sense of going beyond the impotent symbols of cult to the life and death of Christ; *real* in the sense of being mandated by that grace (the reality of God) which is moving to the universality of the eschaton. Worship, or what we call the liturgy, in the early communities was no arbitrary ritual. Preaching, evangelization, and Christian life were sacrifice, liturgy, and priestly office.

The Christian concept of *priest* has a complicated verbal history. If no Christian is called a priest in the Bible, the words *priest, prete, Priester, prêtre* come not from the Greek or Latin words for priest, but from *presbyter, elder.* Themes and aspects of priestly leadership had reappeared by the third century, but they do not create a traditional priest, an *hierate* or a *sacerdote,* but attach themselves to the nonpriestly elder or overseer. Nevertheless, it was inescapable that in a world much concerned with religious control of the divine, the leaders of increasingly larger and more visible Christian churches should, as centuries passed, appear not only as charismatic leaders but as sacerdotal figures of large assemblies. But this history of the resacerdotalization of the ministry of leadership belongs to a century and a half after Paul and will be studied in the next chapter.

d. *Magic and Superstition.* Part of religion is superstition and magic. Twin activities, they often are not eradicated but only suppressed in higher religions. They appeal to the human desire to know and to control. Magic is a way of controlling the deity; superstition is a way of knowing what only the god can know. Magic claims to transform the created into a sign of power of the creator, while superstition claims to draw from the finite a knowledge of the infinite or the future. The preaching of Jesus rendered these drives to manipulate the divine unnecessary. The world is loved by God, so loved that he sent his Son. As the world is redeemed and as the human person is surrounded by the

Spirit of God, the old dichotomy between finite and infinite, matter and spirit, is ended. The early Christians claimed to be "the way," "the saints," "the community," "the people." When the Creator is love, there is no need to seek the domination of creation by attempting to bribe powers, and after Jesus there are no performing intermediary magicians, because a Christian has direct access to the Father through the Son and the Spirit.

The opposite of superstition is the triad of faith, hope, and love grounded not in the arbitrary will of God but in his loving plan. Superstition wants control and knowledge to escape threats to human existence, and magic wards off the dangers of a diabolic or unknown cosmos, but Jesus and his Spirit bring a presence and plan that need not be feared, even before death. Jesus' prayer is an illustration of the termination of superstition, for it is not a prayer that our will for the future be given to us, but that we learn to commune with God's will. The Our Father reaffirms our entrance into God's kingdom, communes with God's will for us, petitions for little more than existence and benediction. Prayer for the Christian is not only *not* superstition; it is hardly even petition, since the Our Father asks God simply to place us in his plan, his will, his kingdom.

* * *

The words we might use to describe this metamorphosis within the early Christian *ecclesia* from sacral worship to communal charismatic life are deficient. It is a "desacralization" but it is not a "secularization." The sacramental, the incarnation, the interplay of the human and the divine, are more present than ever. They enable and constrain a new understanding of religion and priest, and of God and his followers. The goal of this process is not a worldly absence of religion but the incarnation of the divine in the human and historical. The temple of God is wherever the Spirit has been received. But this accessibility of the Spirit must be preached and then believed, and the ministry summons, assembles, and completes the believers in the name of Christ.

No age equals the New Testament period in terms of a radical experience of moving away from the sacerdotal, the elitist,

the arbitrarily empowered magical. The early Christians understood themselves as a chosen people open to all, but every age
must learn anew this profound shift: the church as the Body of
the risen Christ passes repeatedly through what occurred historically in Jesus Christ—the surpassing of human religion.

V. Diaconal Charisms

Paul welcomed all spiritual gifts, refusing to be embarrassed by or hostile to whatever was spiritually healthy. Nevertheless, he minimalized sensational gifts and accented those that
were public services to the Gospel. In First Corinthians he may
be contrasting flamboyant religious displays found in some sec-
taries with ordinary diaconal charisms. He led charisms out of
the life of the church and emphasized their nature by giving
examples of ministries that would build up the community. The
key to the interplay of charism and ministry is found in Paul's
repeated statement of their goals: growth of the harvest's fruits
(1 Cor 3:7); building the temple of the Spirit (1 Cor 3:16); the
growth of the body (Rom 12:4); in short, "for the common good"
(1 Cor 12:7). Harmony is brought to a diversity of important ministries and to innumerable communal services by that goal, "a
unity in the work of service *(diakonia),* building up the body of
Christ" (Eph 4:13). The kingdom is to be further realized, the
churches are to spread.

Far from charism being opposed to ministry, ministry is
mediated from the Spirit to personality by charism—diaconal
charisms.[20] A fundamental theology of grace in ministry points
to a theology of charisms leading, at times during a Christian's
life, to service, to the gifts of the Spirit in the churches.

Paul used the metaphor of organism to illustrate diversity
and unity, power and lack of rivalry. Clearly, the lists of diaconal
charisms in the letters to the Roman, Corinthian, and Ephesian
churches are not intended to be a complete list, and their names
do not for Paul exhaust or control charisms or ministries. The
lists indicate an expansivity, an openness to ministry, showing
that the manifestations of the Spirit are not to be rudely curtailed.

Paul was faced with an explosion of charisms, and he hoped

for a panoply of ministries. Early Christian communities would not have understood a limiting of charism or ministry to an elite. A sign of living as a Christian is to accept at times in one's life charisms that are ministry. For a long time, the church has had a paucity of realized charisms and only one full-time ministry. Now, more and more Christians serve Gospel and church. We have an expansion of the priesthood into several full-time ministries; we have hundreds of parishioners who wish to work not simply in church social life but in ministry as well.

If charism is the contact between the horizon of the life of the Spirit and a personality, there can be many charisms ranging from momentary inspirations to lifelong decisions fraught with risk. God's inspirations are often concerned with the depths of my personal faith or with my relationship to others. We should note: all charisms are church ministry, but all church ministry is grounded in charism. The Christian lives within a life of the Spirit, and some facets of life are ministerial; the church lives within an atmosphere of ministry, and this ministry comes from the charism of its people. An individual's life has its continents and its oceans; life follows cycles when one interest dominates over others. The ages of a man's or a woman's life are the terrains over which the Spirit sends its calls. There is an ebb and flow to baptismal ministry that follows the life of the individual Christian. Invitations to part-time and full-time ministry come according to the patterns of a recipient's life.

The charisms that come to each baptized man and woman receive their diversity through their goals: healing, consoling, service to the socially impoverished, preaching, teaching, public evangelism, leadership of liturgy and community. And so to repeat, ministry is mediated from the Spirit to personality by charism—diaconal charisms.

The word *diakonia,* ministry, in the New Testament sometimes means a particular kind of church action (Rom 12:7), and sometimes it is a general term that includes all the serving and evangelistic roles in the community (Eph 4:12). A service composed of services, it flows forth from Christian life and community and then is channeled into various Christian presentations of the word and power of God's new covenant. Second Corinthians contrasts the past religious "ministry of death" with the new "ministry of the Spirit" (3:7, 9).

This ordinary Greek word for serving and attending upon someone, *diakonos,* has not fared well in translation. The abstract Latin, *ministerium,* has been overshadowed in Western Christianity by *officium.* The Reformation wanted to rediscover the style in the word *minister,* but centuries of too close contact with state churches or middle-class ethos have obscured the active and servant nature of the word. Roman Catholics until recently saw *minister* as a Protestant term, and the English words *serve* and *service* have their own difficulties. In a society increasingly devoid of a servant class, a description of church offices and roles as services and of their holders as servants borders on piety or poetry. The contemporary rediscovery of the word *ministry* with its sharp etymological challenge of *service* looks toward a theological reappreciation of every church role as activity serving grace, and of the style of that activity as inescapably one of service—service of people, service of the Spirit in people.

In Jesus we have the source and pattern of discipleship; his work for the kingdom in which he invites others to share is marked out not by the flamboyance of an apocalyptic seer or a by the sublimity of a royal administrator. Jesus' style is diaconal, that is, the stance of the active and faithful servant. "You know that among the pagans the rulers lord it over them, and their great men exercise authority over them. It shall not be so among you; but whoever would be great among you must be your servant—even as the Son of man came not to be served but to serve, and to give his life as a ransom for many" (Mt 20:25–28). In this passage the verb form of *serve* stands in marked contrast to *lord over;* perhaps this saying of Jesus is the foundation for Pauline theology, naming church and charismatic activity in a global sense as service. Words and actions from the Last Supper as recorded by John and Luke—footwashing, suffering out of love, a commissioning to ministry, and the promise of the Spirit—complement the injunctions of the Synoptics about the style of preaching. The New Testament describes an existential and divine authority in Jesus and a real authority in the subsequent churches, but neither authority escapes the modality of service.[21] In Paul's Letter to the Romans Jesus is described in his historical life as a servant (15:8), a deacon of God's truth and of the Father's promise, and the entire fundamental theology of ministry is summed up: ministry to the active plan of God. The very real abasement of the waiter (an office for a slave in many civilizations) passes through the abasement of the founding moment of the church on Calvary to proffer a new style in Jesus and his Spirit for serving the historical mystery of God's plan.

VI. A Realm of Ministries

While scholars warn against seeing Jesus as the founder of the church in its details,[22] he did take a number of steps to initiate and continue his mission. He called disciples and sent them out to do ministries similar to his; he initiated efforts toward men and women who were not Jews, and confirmed his person and wider mission at the Last Supper. Jesus called different kinds of disciples and gave them through his teaching some general formation and commission, but he left the future forms of ministry to communities. Interestingly, the only form of ministry instituted by Jesus, the Twelve, was not continued.

The life and structure of churches came from some graced dynamic that lay deep within the Christian movement, and apostles and churches sensed themselves to be, in their forms, the gift of Jesus' Twelve and of the Spirit. Ministry grew from two motivations: the preaching of the Gospel to the world, and the service of people in light of the Gospel and the Lord until his second coming. Jean-Pierre Tillard described the development of the organizational structures of the church as a process guided by the Spirit: diversity, local, and regional; evangelistic and financial services; degrees of engagement; leader and baptismal sponsor; and those two that later times see as charismatic and institutional, ordained and lay.[23]

Three New Testament writings—Romans, First Corinthians, and Ephesians—give lists of ministries. Each expresses a community living in a different geographical and social environment over more than one decade of the first century. "Now there are varieties of gifts, but the same Spirit; and there are varieties of service, but the same Lord; and there are varieties of working, but it is the same God who inspires them all in every one. To each is given the manifestation of the Spirit for the common good. To one is given through the Spirit the utterance of wisdom and to another the utterance of knowledge according to the same Spirit, to another faith by the same Spirit, to another gifts of healing by the one Spirit, to another the working of miracles, to another prophecy, to another the ability to distinguish between spirits, to another the interpretation of tongues. All these are inspired by one and the same Spirit who apportions to each one individually as he wills" (1 Cor 12:4–11).

History and mission show that the church expands not through pamphlets and rare interior conversions but through the hard work of many. If the ministry of the Twelve is primarily the foundation of churches, of urban and regional churches, so the mission of their coworkers consists in pursuing the daily tasks of church life. We can see that this foundation of all ministries in that of the primal apostles (possibly numbering more than the Twelve) grounds a theology of tradition in Paul and also implies some continuous institutional structure centered on leadership. A remarkable moment occurred when the early Christian understood that the ministry of those around Jesus at Pentecost, the work of the Lord, would grow, would continue in diversity, and that such ministry and the basic organization of the communities would be the intimate work of the Spirit among the baptized.

When he talks about the Body of Christ, Paul is dealing with problems presented by enthusiastic congregations. Unlike today, the point is not to arouse "the laity" to activity. Rather, the multiplicity of gifts, possibilities, and demonstrations is threatening to break up the unity of the church. The task of the metaphor of the body is to give the theological reason for unity in the midst of multiplicity and to put that unity into practical effect and then to preserve it. The watchword is unity, not uniformity. Paul finds it important for the church to remain polyform. Only in this way can it pervade the world, since uniformity is petrified solidarity. The ecclesiology that is governed by the motif of the Body of Christ must radically maintain the ministry of all believers.

For just as the body is one and has many members, and all the members of the body, though many, are one body, so it is with Christ. (1 Cor 12:12)

For as in one body we have many members, and all the members do not have the same function, so we, though many, are one body in Christ, and individually members one of another. Having gifts that differ according to the grace given to us, let us use them: if prophecy, in proportion to our faith; if service, in our serving; he who teaches, in his teaching; he who exhorts, in his exhortation; he who contributes, in liberality; he who gives aid, with zeal; he who does acts of mercy, with cheerfulness. (Rom 12:4–8)

And his gifts were that some should be apostles, some prophets, some evangelists, some pastors and teachers, to equip the saints for the work of ministry, for building up the body of Christ, until we all attain to the unity of the faith and of the knowledge of the Son of God, to mature manhood, to the measure of the stature of the fullness of Christ. (Eph 4:11–14)

Two of these lists are certainly by Paul and were written not long after the midpoint of the first century; the third is perhaps by a group of Paul's disciples who were writing a few decades later. These lists appear to be illustrative, not exhaustive.[24] Exegesis and ecclesiology, after the medieval period, tried to harmonize these lists or reduce them to a single set of ministries, those of the medieval church. Actually, the lists tell us more about the theology of ministry than they do about its precise structure. It is easier to conclude that ministry was active, diverse, and flexible than to derive a job description of the ministries listed. Recently, Hermann Hauser wrote that the New Testament vocabulary for *ministry* is quite varied, that there is no imposition of titles, and that *ministry* itself (as well as *liturgy* and *economy*) can have general, metaphorical, and individual designations. The office of leadership has several titles of which "bishop" is only one.[25]

None of these lists includes *episcopos,* from which our term *bishop* comes; *diakonia* in Romans means a specific role resembling perhaps that established in the Acts of Apostles while in Ephesians the term is a generic one for all ministries, and there is, of course, no mention of a priest, which office Jesus assumed and rendered obsolete and which passed into the role of elder, *presbyter*. Nevertheless, there are ministries of leadership called shepherd, helmsman, foreman or president (Eph 4:11; 1 Thes 5:12) but these seem terms for a necessary ministry of leadership, and not titles for an all-encompassing director.

Our English words may confuse rather than assist an understanding of what a particular ministry did. The "apostles" mentioned above were not the twelve apostles but members of the community evangelizing new mission fields outside the community, charismatic and proven evangelists expanding the church.[26] The "prophets" were not seers into the future but gifted public preachers of God's revelation to the community. Sometimes *presbyters* may refer to church leaders and not to conciliar assistants to a leader often called *bishop*.[27] In the early decades the triad of teacher, apostle, and prophet was viewed as important. Was it an older or complementary form for *leader* (presbyter or bishop) and *deacon*?[28]

The period in which kingdom, charism, and ministry burst upon the scene evolved several styles and forms, some of which disappeared into history. Exegetes now struggle to arrange the temporal and cultural lines in the ministries mentioned in the New Testament. Let us pause to give some chronological order to this dynamic of ministry.

First, there was the ministry of Jesus (c. A.D. 27 to 30); second, the first communities were in Jerusalem, Antioch, and Damascus, where Jewish forms, presbyterial and prophetic, would be prominent (30–45); third, the wider foundations of Gentile churches by the Twelve and by other apostles gave an internal prominence to teacher, prophet, and apostle (45–70); fourth, bishop, presbyter, and deacon (as a specific ministry of care-assisting leadership) more and more arranged, and in some ways replaced, the earlier stages (70–110). This gives us two triads in the first century; the first is apostle-prophet-teacher; the second is bishop-presbyter-deacon. How the Christian churches understood both sets of ministries (and others like bishop and deacon) throughout the Roman Empire is unclear, and how they coexisted is uncertain.

Activities in the Community. Paul's enumeration of ministries does not have as its purpose the presentation of an ecclesiology but the affirmation that ministry in the church is diverse. Exegetes point out how First Thessalonians mentions ministers in a general way by using the terminology of work: laborers and foremen. Perhaps this describes a first level of ministry when zeal and service were paramount, when specificity and title were not as important as the expansion of the churches and charismatic harmony.

Apostle, prophet, and teacher have a prominence in First Corinthians and Romans, and then in Ephesians. As was mentioned, the ministry of the apostle was not that of the Twelve Apostles but of missionaries officially sent by their church some distance to preach the Gospel or as traveling representatives of a community (Gal 4:14). "The first place given to the 'apostles' in this triad marks clearly the missionary orientation of the church, particularly the church of the Antiochene tradition at this early period."[29] *Evangelist* means a public preacher who aimed at converting his hearers; perhaps ministering more at the local level rather than pursuing distant journeys. The prophets enjoyed an important place: were they always and only foretellers of the future? Or were they inspiring and charismatic preachers who, as frequent homilists in some communities, led the church (1 Cor 14:3)? Acts spoke of this ministry as one of leadership in Antioch and Jerusalem (4:36; 13:1), while the *Didache* suggested that their preaching led to leadership at Eucharist and in the church.[30] It is not surprising that Paul and the Twelve would conceive of leadership and evangelization as going together (while they would hardly be singling out the marginal activity of forecasting the future): "Search the gifts of the Spirit, above all, that of prophecy" (1 Cor 14:1).

While research is needed to uncover the meaning of apostles and prophets, the teachers are less opaque. Associated with the prophet-preachers, they were Christians occupied with the basic instruction of initiates in the revelation of God in Christ and later, in more profound reflection, the faith (some experts suggest they reflect a rabbinical role[31]). We know that the mystery religions, too, had not only ritual and fellowship but instruction both before and after initiation. Documents of these early centuries speak of Christians recruiting and sponsoring those to be baptized, and of teachers whose work seems to include not only basic instruction but theological reflection. For Justin in Rome, the teacher was a high ministry of someone who was baptized, while in Cyprian's church in North Africa the teachers were also presbyters. What was common to the teachers was that the Christian Gospel was truth and that they had a role to teach (and to exemplify in their lives) what revelation in Jesus, the Teacher of the Word, meant for the great and for the practical questions of life, and how he was for community and individuals the Savior. What was distinctive was that the teachers saw themselves continuing the teaching of Jesus, offering a religious truth superior to those in the philosophies and cults around them, and offering this teaching at various levels. The ministry of teaching came from the community, and Christian teachers were not fully independent scholars and thinkers; more-over, there was a variety of teaching, with some churches empha-sizing preparation for baptism while others had profound theologians attached to them. Clement of Alexandria taught cate-chumens, educated and uneducated pagans and gnostics, and bap-tized Christians.[32] The ministry of teaching then was diverse, ecclesial, biblical, and important.

These three activities—external evangelization, preaching and assembly leadership, and teaching—formed the core of many communities. New Testament lists, however, show other min-istries, and they should not be neglected nor shunted aside: min-istries of healing, of consoling, of serving those in need. Perhaps Paul implied that these are arranged around the core ministries, but all are charismatic ministries.[33]

Acts as well as the Pauline letters record proper names of people who are introduced as coworkers (*sunergos* [Phil 2:25]) in the ministry. No doubt other apostles drew Christians into their min-istry, but with Paul we have close to one hundred fifty coministers named. Some of these ministers were men; some were women. Some traveled with Paul; some were only known to him; some were evangelists on the road; and some were residents of a house where a Christian church gathered.[34] These people cannot be fitted into one type of ministerial role. Clearly, all are not presented as bishops or presbyters. When they are called *diakonoi*, not all are what later centuries will mean by *deacon* or *deaconess*. In Colossians, Tychikos is described as a faithful deacon and coservant of the Lord (4:7); in

Philippians, Epaphroditus is called a "comrade in arms" and "brother" (2:25), an "apostle" and a "coworker," and finally a "liturgist" to Paul's needs. Romans ends with a long list of personal greetings: first to Phoebe, Paul's "sister" and the "deacon" of the church in Cenchreae (16:1); next to important "coworkers in Christ Jesus," Prisca and Aquila (16:4); and then to the man Andronicus and the woman Junia (16:7), called outstanding apostles.

This variety of coworkers in the ministry and the first level of intense but formally diverse designations of them by Paul is important. Its imprecision and potential creativity will annoy us if we expect to find a single schema of two or three church offices. We should not miss the theological significance of the first believers raised to the level of coworker. The insight given into the life of the churches will, however, encourage us if we are looking for characteristics of universality and spontaneity among the first Christians.

We first find indications of women in the ministry, not beginning with the movement after the 1970s, but in names recorded in the New Testament. Full membership in the Christian community for women was itself revolutionary for the first century. The rivals of Christianity—Judaism, Neoplatonism, Mithraism—did not admit women to full initiation. As an ecclesiological principle we must ponder the excited proclamation of Paul in Galatians: "There is neither Jew nor Greek, there is neither slave nor free, there is no male and female" in Christ (3:28). Women were among the followers of Jesus from the beginning, and they were faithful to the end, and the Gospels highlighted their roles on Good Friday and Easter. Since ministry at the level of belief and theology is not derived from human social arrangement (although this influences the realization of ministry in a culture), after the coming of the Spirit to all, we would expect ministry in the Christian churches to be open to all the baptized. If women were admitted to baptism and membership in the church without qualification from Pentecost on, they were also in the communities at the active center. Consequently, ministry coming from the gifts of the Spirit communicated by baptism was open to women. There were women instrumental in the founding of churches (Acts 18:2, 18 f.; 1 Cor 16:19; Rom 16:3 f.); women with functions in public worship (1 Cor 11:5); women engaged in teaching converts (Acts 18:26).

Women prophets are attested (1 Cor 11:5; Acts 21:9). In Paul's writings a woman minister and a women apostle are named. Thus, while male ministers were more prominent and numerous in the early church and while women's activities were limited by what was culturally permissible, many roles that were associated with community service were evidently never restricted to men. "The limitations presently placed on women's role in the church and the arguments advanced in support of those restrictions must be evaluated in light of the evidence for ministerial coresponsibility and for the presence of women in ministries in the church of the New Testament period."[35] The term *laywoman,* the feminine of *layman,* does not appear in any early text, and women entered ministry as widows and deaconesses. Widows are an *ordo,* a group within the ecclesiastical orders. Their ministerial activity is not clear; some needed support, but clearly most also worked for the church. Deaconesses, in some churches ordained by a laying on of hands, did not preach and baptize but had ministries in terms of baptism, liturgy, and social service.[36]

A fundamental theology of ministry treats the theme of women in ministry past and present in the most general way. While there are knotty issues, not because tradition's view is so strong but because the issues are so new, the general response to the question of women in the ministry can only be answered in the affirmative, according to nature and grace. Women make up half the human race, or more, and the teaching of Jesus in no way is prejudicial to them. In the reign of God they cannot be secondary citizens; in the grace of the Trinity they cannot be a subclass, for then we would have old-time religion. Jesus' preaching about the kingdom in community does not offer principles where baptism and charism are limited to a natural group—one race, one sex.

Ministry of Leadership. If the words for ministries in the first communities are words of action and service, this implies a perennial critique of any church office whose reality lies mainly in vestments, honors, and titles. In the first century, ministry came not only from the Spirit and the Twelve but from the community itself. The ministry of coordination and leadership was not the whole ministry but one important ministry among others, with responsibilities and limits. Leadership in the community does not come from a play for power or arbitrary selection but from gifts of personality and grace; at the same time, to hold that authority is legitimated only by success and charismatic miracles is to deny the stability of church needed to survive history. Church structure and authority are not transitorily charismatic, but authority and ministries of leadership come from the Spirit. A church excluding its public roles from the Spirit is a schizophrenic church where community can be at war with grace.

At the opening of The Letter to the Philippians, Paul greets the community with its overseers and ministers *(episkopois kai diakonois)*. In the Acts of Apostles the title of "elder" is prominent (it is absent from the major Pauline letters) and addresses those responsible for the churches at Jerusalem, Antioch, and even Ephesus. These three terms—*bishop, priest, deacon*–are, of course, in history and etymology if not in description of office, the source for the three ministries given lasting emphasis by Christian history: bishop, priest, deacon. Do they seem to represent different cultural systems of the ministry of leadership in the community? Exegetes have thought that one title, *presbyteros,* indicated the Semitic background of elder while *episkopos* came from the Gentile churches.[37] We do not know what their relationship is to Pauline terms for leadership: foreman, helmsman, shepherd. Nevertheless, we have no evidence for a Christian church that did not contain a ministry of leadership (although we cannot give that ministry one title), just as we have no example of a church that had only a ministry of leadership. The pluralism in name and description is a further illustration of cultural and ecclesial diversity in the first century.

We can look at ministry and leadership as potentialities from which more than one precise diaconal role might be drawn forth. Two aspects of this survey of ministry may surprise us. First, varied work and a widespread invitation to ministry joined with the harmony of the community, and life was subjected to the service of the kingdom of God. Second, the roles of authority and leadership emerged from the community and existed with other ministries. But by the end of the first century, the full-time ministry of leadership had achieved a distinct importance.[38]

VII. Primal Ministry: Three Characteristics

From the churches of the first century we have only pieces of a mosaic. Pictures of ministry remain projections made from those fragments, a hypothetical arrangement. We should not use the records of the New Testament world to produce either novel theories or allegorical piety. Are there insights coming from all of the different ecclesial structures recorded in the writings of the first century? Such a theology of origins offers a guide for a historical-fundamental theology of Christian ministry that is serviceable for different cultures and eras. Those characteristics, rather than defining one or two offices, express guidelines for ministry itself.

a. Christian ministry is not sacral office. Christian ministry is something new, while cultic priesthood is as old as the human race. The Christian minister in the early church was not principally a liturgist of curiosities or a custodian of idols. Each and every minister (including the leader or overseer) was concerned with some activity that served the reality of grace. Rather than effecting distant but impotent ablutions and sacrifices, this new ministry was focused on preaching about God's event in Jesus and enacting Jesus' words of justice and compassion.

The New Testament avoided sacral words for several reasons. They reduce the efficacy of God, they cordon off an elite group from the body of believers, and they distract from incarnation and morality by leading people toward things and states. In terms of God's true dignity, sacralization can be idolatrous, while after Jesus' coming it is unnecessary. The sacralizing process insinuates an atmosphere of unreality into life; people are manipulated, not evangelized. Paul knew that the minister cannot escape being a public figure, but Christian public liturgy is verified in the conversion of hearers to the Spirit and in the sacramental activity of the minister and the community.

b. Christian ministry is action that is service to the Kingdom of God. The early Christians described their service to the kingdom of God as actions rather than honorific offices. The minister is the one who truly effects an action. Verbs such as *announce, oversee, console, teach, serve* describe ministries. The birth of

Christian ministry was a language-event: the church fashioned a language that disclosed its way of life. Prophets speak forth publicly; deacons serve; healers heal. The name of the ministry is the title of the minister and the service performed. There is no gulf between title and work, no substitution of personage for activity. In the early church, the term *ministry* actually referred to *doing* something among men and women in the public world on behalf of the reign of God. Ministry serves something beyond itself. Paul has a variety of terms—*gospel, grace, life*—for the loving presence of God toward us, made clear and tangible in the event of Christ. The church's growth is the goal of ministry, and becoming the collective Body of Christ is the norm and power and destiny of ministry (1 Cor 12:1 ff.; Eph 4:6). The church, local or universal, is itself minister—deacon to the kingdom. The dynamic of the church is one of pointing to, realizing, and announcing that which it serves.

There are no examples in Paul where life itself is considered ministry. Christian life is metaphorically called a liturgy because, though silent, it implies the Gospel or points to the presence of new life; Christian life through baptism is not itself a ministry but the origin and goal of ministry. Nor are secular jobs ministries for the first communities: being a cheerful slave is not a ministry (although the slave's evangelizing explanation of her joy to another person is). Loading ships, weaving tents, dying wool, and banking are not ministries. Ministry is not concerned with the food supply in the Roman Empire or with improved transportation on modern-day highways, although justice and the relief of the impoverished are ministries. The emphasis is upon communication of the realities of the Gospel and for Paul the ministry has an urgency, for services of these "insignificant" people are the channels of new life and salvation. The examples of ministering charisms given by Paul are unambiguous in their connection to furthering the Gospel, to nourishing and expanding the church. Paul frequently links ministry to his metaphor of building up the Body of Christ. This metaphor not only gives a sociology of harmony in the church but an eschatology drawing ministry into action. There is in the analogy of the Body of Christ a head but no spiritual elite; moreover, the metaphor is one of diverse and organic life in unity.

Ministry is placed in the community by its Lord to nourish and to build it up.[39] In the records of Jesus' ministry, however, we learn that he placed within the work of the kingdom of God the relief of men and women who bore the effects of the sinful condition of the human race: the crippled, the diseased, the enslaved, the poor. Relief of oppression and injustice, of hunger and illness, when done as hope-filled services and signs of the presence of God's Spirit, is ministry; for the kingdom is the enemy of the effects of sin like disease, poverty, malice, and death. Services to the suffering are a sign of the arrival of the Spirit and a promise of its future triumph. A ministry of healing or social care does not, however, argue that every social task done well is a ministry. There can well be implicit ministries to the deep presence of the reign of God overcoming the radical sin of human history, but our interest lies in a formal analysis of public, Christian ministry. For that, service normally is a visible and verbal expression of the existence, goal, and values of the kingdom of God as preached by Jesus and preserved in the church.

c. Christian ministry is universal and diverse. Ministry is for each baptized person; it is charismatically given in a universality and particularity, and it should not disturb a ministerial harmony in the community—these three characteristics have the greatest practical import. Paul says often that the Spirit has given ministry to all and that services are of many kinds. Each time Paul reflects upon the diversity of functions in the church he recalls the origin and end of this diversity, a diversity willed by God and the special work of the Holy Spirit (1 Cor 12:4 ff.; Rom 12:6). This diversity lives within the church (1 Cor 12:28) with the goal of constructing it.[40] The letters to the churches in the first century were addressed not to individuals but to communities. When individual ministers are mentioned, it was within the context of the greater life of the local community.

VIII. Communities of Ministers

What was ministry in the early church? Was its typical minister a replacement for one of the twelve apostles? Was the minister a charismatic miracle worker? He or she was neither. If the unique ministry of the Twelve did not continue on in history but rather served as a foundation for grounded future community and ministries, then the church was also not an assembly of independent charismatics, for that would have preserved neither Jesus' teaching nor communal continuity. We must be careful not to read modern (or medieval) church offices into the Greek words describing ecclesial roles in the first century. Exegetical studies on First Corinthians as well as Roman Catholic studies on office were often advocates of one or another extreme position. The Catholic position presumed that ministry had always been a medieval priesthood flanked by deacon and bishop, the former a liturgical remnant, the latter a nobleman. Protestant charismatic groups from the sixteenth and nineteenth centuries asserted that there was no structure in primal Christianity, for every member of the congregation could explain the Gospel and preside at the Lord's Supper, and the life of the congregation consisted not in a sustenance of institutions and traditions but in a display of supernatural powers. The early church was neither the Vatican of the Renaissance nor the California audience of Aimee Semple McPherson.

How did the community discern and encourage ministries? How did an individual Christian enter ministry? The community knew well that baptism was the entrance into ministry, that faith and baptism and charism changed the sacral into action and offered a new kind of priesthood, universal and missionary. After baptism came charisms and with them services to and for the churches. The community grew: it wanted to grow, and with growth came more responsibilities. Elements that seem normal to us in terms of ministry were surely present in the communities of Syria, Italy, and Greece: education and training built upon experience, charism, and zeal. Christianity itself became a remarkable network of communities with travel between them. J. Delorme wrote: "Paul himself in his choice of coworkers had to judge their aptitude for service to the Gospel. His companions seemed to have been proved on the job."[41] How did the full-time, central minister emerge in the community? Their appearance was momentous. An important move was the decision by a community to have ministers in full-time activity. Confirmed by the community and by some visible success in the ministry to which they believed themselves called, they took the time and expense to learn from other ministers and churches (1 Cor 9:14; Mt 10:10). There is a kind of mutual control of ministries existing between the community and the ministers, for every ministry is "in the church" (1 Thes 5:20 f.). The early communities are not so charismatically fluid that they do not need some structure and education. The interplay of gift from the Spirit with a specific activity pursued gave a role in the community.

As the first century came to a close, central professional ministry, especially that of leadership, was moving (perhaps unconsciously) some charismatic services to the edge of the ministerial circle. In expanding churches leadership naturally drew upon Christians who were full-time in a central service of the Gospel and who were capable of coordinating all ministerial activity.

Diakonos, presbyter, episkopos—these three Greek terms were in place after A.D. 100. Still subject to different sociological hermeneutics, depending upon whether one was at Antioch, Alexandria, or Rome, they survived as the permanent, basic ministries. But this revered triad is itself a puzzle. Each of the three may come from a different socio-theological source, and possibly each may have a global meaning, that is, each may stand for a group of ministers—in "service" or "supervision"—rather than for a specific task like preaching. *Deacon* is the name for the ministry itself and is sometimes so used; *elder* is a generic, Semitic office of leadership and was at first equal to and then later auxiliary to the imprecise term of *overseer* (bishop).

The fragmentary descriptions coming from the first churches have not told us all we want to know about the origins of ministry. They have not divided ministries into ones human and ones divine, nor have they offered precise offices with canonized names. We have, however, gained insight into the originality of an active community with a life and mission both universal and diverse. Different lists of ministries and layers of ministers compose the early churches. Edward Schillebeeckx, surveying the fragmentary information in the New Testament's gospels and letters, offers his picture of the late first century.

> Consequently, even after the New Testament [period], church order remains quite varied in the different commu-

nities. The fact that the *Didache* emphatically points out that overseers and helpers must be held in as much respect in the community as the prophets and teachers perhaps points toward a certain restraint on the part of these communities toward these new ministries. In the communities of a Matthaean type the old order (prophets and teachers) was clearly of longer standing than presbyters, and there was even a degree of animosity toward the (later) introduction of *episcopoi* and *diakonoi*....However, on the other hand, it is striking that all the communities of this more charismatic type disappeared completely in the course of the second century, or fell victim to Christian gnostic sects.[42]

In the place of a precise number of offices we have some characteristics of ministry that build upon our principles of community, charism, and service. These characteristics may prove of great help to a church that today finds itself called to growth and stability, to evangelical fidelity and honesty. We will take these characteristics up again in a later chapter when we reflect upon the nature of the ministry in our time.

There is perhaps more continuity in the first decades of the churches than distant scholars suspect. Social and religious forms among people and churches do not change rapidly or radically. Exchanges between communities in different countries and a firm commitment to God's revelation in Jesus would work to preserve some similarity; modern exegesis has exaggerated the differences among Christians in the first centuries, projecting back on them the proliferation of Christian sects in the twentieth century. Regardless, the apostolic church is of permanent importance for the subsequent history of the church: it is the source and pattern and principle of the church in space and time. If the early Christians were constrained by their expectation of the second coming, this eschatology also urged them to work for the reign of God, and soon the Spirit opened to them beyond cultural limitations, ever expanding opportunities for ministry among the nations.

3

THE METAMORPHOSES
OF MINISTRY

Two thousand years lie between the local missionary communities of the first century and the ministries needed for today's church. This span between the first and the twenty-first centuries is neither a void nor a linear succession of museums. History is a living drama in which characters act out lives that ultimately are encounters with God's presence. The different epochs of Mediterranean or European or American history have touched and altered Christian ministry, as the Gospel in theology and the church in ministry have not hesitated to become incarnate in various cultures.

The spontaneity of church forms and the variety of charismatic ministries in the first century suggest to us (as they did to the first generations of Christians) that the church is a living community with potentialities for the future. The church in its birth held impetuses that emerged in later centuries and in our own times. The Spirit behind church, charism, and minister is not an ideal paradigm but a dynamic fullness. The forms of church life exist on that edge where revelation meets civilization. The constellations of culture are the catalysts of ecclesial forms. From history we gain not a unique model of ministry divinely given but an understanding of the adaptability of the church. We learn why the Christian community assumed Celtic, Syriac, Hellenic forms, and why the church today searches out suitable forms, old and new. A cultural phenomenology of ministry looks at the offices, liturgies, architectures, and politics of the church in different periods. If it hopes to glimpse their underlying essence, that is because it expects those basic forms, sacraments, services to perdure and to reappear.

History is a picture painted by culture and time. As the church makes its progress through Hellenic, Coptic, Celtic, and Saxon cultures, the ministry is modified by the worlds it reaches. Ignatius the martyr, Ambrose the judge, Columcille the voyager, Catherine the mystic and reformer, Innocent the statesman, Xavier the explorer, Teilhard de Chardin the scientist—all struggled to be Christian ministers searching out new forms for the Spirit.

Christians did not write theologies of the church, much less analyses of the churches' structures, called ecclesiologies, before the end of the Middle Ages. It is true that the writings of Hippolytus and Eusebius are sources for seeing how Christians understood their churches, and we can find in the writings and sermons after the second century of bishops and theologians as well as in liturgical documents and early ordination ceremonies information on the church's offices. But a formal study of the church and its ministry is missing. Even that architectonic summation of Western Christianity, the *Summa theologiae* of Aquinas, lacks a group of questions on the church, treating church forms very briefly in segments on faith and ethical sociology. The past century, on the other hand, has spent enormous energy on questions about the church: about its nature, its teaching office, its authority, its divisions.

Ministry is a living modality of the living organic church, the Body of Christ. When it finds itself blocked from activity it seeks new channels. The external forms of ministry may be reduced or wounded, but the organic nature of ministry as a living pleroma in the church is never anesthetized. Obeying an inner spirit, new forms and styles of servanthood struggle for external realization. Beneath externals of the Visigothic, Romanesque, or Baroque eras there is not just one, perennial priesthood merely changing styles of vestments. Cultures bring their own material to the ministry; and rather than diluting it, cultural forms free ministry to live. In the colors and symbols, vestments and rituals of the liturgy, polychrome speech expresses the simple beliefs of the Christian faith. In the church's different eras, not only liturgy but social forms express the language of the ministry. This is not to say that nothing remains. In liturgy and ministry, in episcopal leadership and diaconate, a central reality assumes forms. History

shows that attacking basic ministries brings a charismatic democracy for only a short time, and then a new dictatorship with worse
sins appears. With the distinction between essence and cultural
form, we can stand a little apart from history, avoiding both relativism and schizophrenia, and see that history simultaneously limits and reveals the ministry. A historically bestowed and explored
theology is a realistic theology. We want to search out the present
and the future by pondering the past.

I. The Church in History

The blood of the church is history. Paradoxically, the longing of the human race for the divine and eternal has led theologians and churchmen to describe the church as above or beyond
history. The church, however, is not eternal. Its life is not God's
life on earth; its vision does not simply contemplate and encompass the centuries. Not only language and symbol but theology
and social structure come as gifts from history's cultures. The
metaphors of Judaism, the hierarchy of Neoplatonism, and the
lapidary orders of Rome not only preach but form the Gospel. In
the New Testament, the early churches have metaphors and theologies. In the fourth century, Ephrem the Syrian described the
church in flowery poems, while in the West, Ambrose hammered
out a logical and legal relationship between two corporations,
church and state. History is the means by which the church is con-
tinually incarnate in culture. St. Seraphon in the sixth century
wrote: "Time in the church is the reception of the Holy Spirit."[1]

We should not turn the irrevocable presence and mission
of the church promised by Jesus and his Spirit into an existence
apart from the uncertainties and tensions of history. A fear of
the historical is a sign that religion is trying to escape life for the
eternity of God. The church, rather than being eternal and perfect, is eminently historical. Just as it is difficult for human
beings to affirm that Jesus of Nazareth was true man as well as
true God, so it is difficult to affirm the church as the community of word and sacrament expressing the kingdom of God,
and, at the same time, to let the church live not only *in* but *out* of
history. Time sweeps all before it: not only all men and women

but civilizations. To a neophyte or a neurotic, history seems the great enemy to religion, for it threatens the objects and rites that hold divine certitude and power. True, history in its flood leaves nothing unchanged, but nonetheless, Christian incarnation within humanity and amid religion embraces history. Incarnation accepts history, looks for salvation in history, views history as moving forward to a fulfillment that will give meaning to all stories and all histories. In ecclesiology today we need to look in history for creativity.

History is trends, changes, wars, migrations, plans, deaths. The products and patterns of civilizations on display in the galleries of museums instruct us in the life cycles of history. History becomes incarnate in culture. Christianity is a sacramental and international faith, and so it could not be content with an empty temple, a gray room. Every period has had limitations, and history never shows to one epoch all it has to display. Cultural forces (some from within and some from without the church) make up what is called a *Zeitgeist*. Sometimes sectors of cultural life share in the processes of change but share in them asymmetrically. We do not find precise parallels in every era between economics, arts, philosophy, and religion; and parallels do not occur precisely on time in synchronicity, but often a great *kairos*, a moment of cultural history displays the same thought-forms in areas of science, art, or faith. Charism and ministry assumed certain forms not simply out of obedience to the biblical letter but also because society called or even forced the church toward patterns that seemed attractive and useful.

History is not only the situation of the church; it is the church's mentor. The more we understand periods of the church's life in its first two millennia, the less we fear history. Social forms, liturgical signs, a language and a style of preaching and praying, ministries and local communities—these are the flesh and blood of the church's life. Through them grace acts upon us, and we are empowered to believe and to act.

The church will not end, but churches do end. For over six hundred years, there was no more dominant force in Christianity than the Syrian Church. Its theologians, preachers, and poets were numerous, and monasteries and monastic schools sent missions into China or to Ethiopia. Antioch, Nisibis, Damascus—the bishops of those great centers could hardly have imagined that their power and glory would end, but today Syrian Christianity, though alive, is little known, and few know how great was its history. When we gaze upon the carved crosses of Celtic Christianity at Kells, we have the opportunity to enter for a moment into yet a different church. With its dual, episcopal-monastic organization, its pleasure in missionary travel, and its druidic interest in all types of spirits and creatures in nature, Celtic Christianity peacefully wove a rich cultural tapestry in both Latin and Gaelic. Now it barely remains. The lesson, however, from these two examples is not hopelessness before the onslaught of time, but the variety and greatness of the union of Spirit and culture in the churches.

History does not have a simple pattern: it is neither evolution nor decline, neither progress nor failure. Later times are not always better than earlier times; Gothic art is not inevitably an improvement over Greek or even Mycenaean art.[2] One age of history is not better than another, but simply different. Time brings ways of seeing life, and culture is the collection of symbols, institutions, and thought-forms that one period brings to our attention. History brings the illuminations of cultural periods, and those lighting processes of history show the kingdom of God in one set of ideas and symbols or another. Each, however, comes to an end so that another constellation, another luminous display can engage men and women with new insights into the richness of Christ. When one group of cultural illuminations goes on, another goes off. Thus it is difficult to find the essence, the nature, the original given reality of the church. There is such an essence—its giver and guardian is the Holy Spirit—but we must find the church in its own forms set up for a particular age, and nowhere and at no time do we find the essence of the church perfectly isolated. Hans Küng wrote: "Every age fashions, often out of unreflective drives and goals, its own image of the church. The theory and the forms of the church live in an interplay, and they arise out of a particular historical situation. In each age a particular view of the church is expressed by the church in practice and given conceptual form by the theologians of the age....There are fundamental elements and perspectives, there is an 'essence,' and this essence argues for the foundation by Jesus of Nazareth of some aspects of that gathering and discipleship. But the core of the church is not an element of metaphysics but inner dynamics existing in limited but diverse forms."[3] We need historical liberation in our theology because Christian ministry has been susceptive to what we might call a process of eternalization. The priesthood has changed little since the year A.D. 1000. We need to uncover the rich origins of ministry, to learn how history and culture have highlighted and limited ministry through two millennia. Still, how much richer is the church's ministry than only a few decades ago.

If history is the church's life and situation, it is also its cross. Time brings conflict, and the church feels the pain of change. The mission of the church—"to the ends of the earth"—knows the archetype of life and death; not that the church is caught up in a pagan cycle of demise and rebirth but, like its Lord, it exists in the spring of life out of death. To be faithful to the commission to preach to all nations, the church at times must die to itself, must pass through not only persecution from without but also opposition from within whenever it meets ambition, lack of hope, and sloth among its members and leaders. The church experiences the death of its labors in an epoch that is ending, the migration of its members from this or that region, the end of what had once been the right theology and liturgy. All of this is a crucifixion. Yet, the faithful church should experience this not as death but as Christian mystery from which springs forth new life. "Unless a wheat grain falls on the ground and dies, it remains only a single grain; but if it dies, it yields a rich harvest" (Jn 12:24). Life out of death is the ontology of the church, as it is for all of human life in this world. What is now taken to be an eternal facet of Christianity may be an aspect springing from the Baroque period, or what is considered to be patristic is, upon analysis, discovered to be from the late medieval period. What the Reformation vigorously rejected again returns, and what the Reformers advocated Rome now claims as its own.

In every age there are people for whom history does not exist. They are not interested in the past and imagine all of human time to be much the same. They reject the idea of the temporal succession of human culture, or they presume that their adulthood or childhood embodies the perennial form of human life. Revealed religion can accidentally further this attitude: it can exalt a golden age (Moses at Sinai, the time of Jesus, the Middle Ages, Nuremberg at the time of Luther). The trail of Judaism leading to Jesus has a complex history, and the history of the church over two millennia has considerable diversity in its forms and articulations. Fundamentalists and sects can fear time as a destroyer of tradition or as a goddess of novelty, but in fact the historical realizations of the church in Edessa in the fifth century or in Naples in the sixteenth century are ways of continuing the Incarnation. Curiously, the Catholic restorationist who identifies the Gospel with certain clothes from the 1880s, with one biblical translation, or with a vessel from the fifth century or the fifteenth century has somewhat the same mind-set as the extreme feminist who rejects the past three millennia of cultures because their attitudes toward women in public life were limited. Both fixate on one time—whether that is in the past or today— and reject variety and progress. C. S. Lewis wrote, "The unhistorical are, usually without knowing it, enslaved to a fairly recent past."[4] The deepest enemy of every fundamentalism is history.

A different approach to history is exemplified in the history of liturgies and spiritualities; it expects both perdurance and alteration. To know a little about history, to understand a little of the church's forms, whether in the catacomb chamber of the popes martyred under Decius in the third century or in the large structure of San Andrea della Valle, is to see that there are different ways in which the events and doctrines of Christianity have assumed useful and compelling forms in order to spread their message. The Christian community sees in its own history a variety of periods, and a cultural time is a kind of lighting process. In one particular age humanity understands itself in a particular way, and the church uses the forms of human culture to give this or that perspective to life and faith. In no single time, not even in the decades immediately after Pentecost, can human beings express all there is in Christian realities. The Gospel according to John concludes that it takes many human endeavors and languages to express all that was in Jesus (Jn 21:25). The church seeks out suitable forms for its worship and ministries, and history shows that the Spirit can inspire it to be present to diverse civilizations. This process not only continues the Incarnation but affirms a faith in the presence of the Spirit of the church, so characteristic of the Catholic mind.[5]

It has been commonplace to observe that Vatican II permitted the church to reenter the flow of history without condemning it or being swept away by it. "I believe that the novelty of Vatican II," Yves Congar wrote, "consisted largely in its acceptance of the historicity of the church, of scripture, etc....The vision of the Council has been resolutely that of the history of salvation completed by eschatology....It is certain, or at least quite probable, that Vatican II will condition the life of the church for a long time. That council incorporated a great density of faithfulness and wisdom coming from the entire church: it is an event of a Pentecostal type."[6] Marked changes like expansion in ministry have occurred recently around the world because the Council prompted a look at today's ministerial needs and a look at the variety of ecclesiologies in biblical and patristic times, two perspectives made impossible by the perennial neo-scholastic metaphysics dominant from 1860 to 1960. This permission for history to emerge is important for understanding the postconciliar period, precisely because history and culture drew forth so rapidly after 1965 forms and ideas, issues and problems, which were only implicit in the documents, deliberations, and actions of the Council. Edward Schillebeeckx represents the Catholic view when he warns against placing "the grace character of ministry *alongside* and *above* its socio-historical actuality." Rather, what develops historically (as a holy, healthy, and effective form of ministry, or, conversely, as unhappy forms constraining the Holy Spirit) is "precisely what the believer experiences and expresses in the language of faith as the concrete form in which ministry appears."[7] Schillebeeckx notes the pervasive influence of the interpretation and reduction of church ministry to medieval theology or to the spirituality of recent seminary life.

> The actual form of the priestly office during the previous period of history is so closely interwoven with the understanding of faith in the same period that without a historical

and hermeneutical approach all kinds of premature theological and pastoral conclusions might be deduced from it, conclusions which could completely inhibit any attempt to bring the pastoral office up to date.[8]

He explains his own extensive work into the history of ministry and church forms:

> Once we look at how the structuring and division of church office went on in history it will be clear that the church can develop still in many ways and is not bound in this matter by scriptural or dogmatic restrictions....[We need] official recognition for other forms of official ministry...and Christian faith-communities are asking for them and have a transparently clear need of them.[9]

We will not attempt below a history of ecclesiology,[10] nor will we claim exhaustive research into topics and moments in the history of ministry: for instance, the role of women in the first decades of Christianity, the evolution of episcopal office in the second century, the nature of teacher in the third century, and of deacon in the fifth. Rather we will sketch six important periods (Vatican II being a concluding bridge to the future). The ministry underwent a metamorphosis during each, and those six periods give us not only the picture but the process, as forces molded the ministry into this or that form. Each of these periods in ministry is a time when ministry was strikingly successful. Each period still exercises some influence upon theory and praxis today. No period contains the ministry perfectly, for the horizon of ministry (which is the Spirit) is capable of bringing ministry out of many cultures. Without advocating either an antiquarianism or a progressivism, we want to let the history of ministry stand forth in its broad contours.

Our six periods represent six metamorphoses in ministry: (1) a move through communal diversity and universality to a small number of ministries with prominence given to the service of leadership (episcopalization) along with a further presentation of the ministry of leadership (presbyter or bishop) as a priest (sacerdotalization); (2) the absorption by the monastery of ministry and spirituality (monasticization); (3) a dominance of

one philosophical-social structure in the cluster of offices (hier-
archization); (4) the interlude of the Reformation (pastoraliza-
tion of ministry)—a movement that is antimonastic and
antipriestly but still reductionist; (5) the Counter-Reformation's
organization of ministry along the lines of the Baroque papacy
and Baroque spirituality; (6) the romanticization of the ministry
in the nineteenth century.

Each of these ages has positive and negative facets.
Although we can and must evaluate them in terms of their suitability for our times, we must also leave each in its own *kairos,* its
own time of success. Each of these periods succeeded as an
incorporation of the Gospel. The rightness in structure of each
was at its birth stronger than the limitations we now perceive.[11]

The history of Christian ministry, however, because it is
human and historical, has limits. For the past thousand years or
more, ministry in terms of the formal ordained ministries of the
church has been passing through a process of reduction rather
than expansion, although countless men and women are always
fashioning communities and forms of ministry and so initiating
a countering expansion.

A. *From House Church to Basilica; from Ministers to Priests*

The first example of structure in Christian ministry belongs
to the churches of the first half-century after Pentecost. As we
saw in chapter 2, a picture of their communal life can be pieced
together from fragments of information contained in Paul's letters and the Acts of the Apostles. Just as Jewish and Gentile,
Romano-Gallic and Syrian communities viewed Jesus differently
in their Christologies, so we can imagine that in the first local
churches community life and structure assumed different concrete forms. Exegetes and social historians look not only at the
churches of Paul and Peter or of Acts and Romans but at
churches of different ethnic and theological groupings, as well as
at churches in different cities, such as Antioch, Jerusalem, and
Rome, about which we have some information. They also consider the kinds of people who were Christians and of whom we
have some record as active in the church. Theological libraries

have many books belonging to one of two persuasions: the first
expects to find the Catholic priest or Protestant minister of 1900
in earlier centuries without any changes; the other expects to
find free, charismatic associations of individuals unaware of
church, order, or sacrament. Both are theological projections,
and we now know that the second is the more fantastic.

The New Testament speaks of households that Paul greeted
as centers of Christian community. There is the church of Aquila
and Prisca (Rom 16:5; 1 Cor 16:19) and that of Nymphas (Col
4:15). In Acts (1:13; 20:9) we gather that Christian assemblies for
hearing the word and for the Eucharist took place in upstairs
rooms, a feature of Mediterranean households. Pierre du Bourguet observes:

> Thus, the point of departure in the evolution of early
> Christian art was not a sanctuary modeled on pre-Christian
> places of worship, nor even directly on the rites established
> by Christ or the apostles. On the contrary, it was naturally
> determined by the realities of the Christian life, lived within
> the broader context of life in general. In this respect, the
> only guidance to be derived from the words and even the
> example of Christ consists in the two complementary activi-
> ties of teaching the doctrine and celebrating the Eucharist.
> The doctrine could be taught anywhere, but more easily in a
> place reserved for the interested public."[12]

The tendency must have been to prolong such gatherings to
discuss the needs of the community. Such a celebration of the
Eucharist might involve the serving of a subsequent meal which
would require the use of fairly spacious quarters available in the
home of one of the Christians.

With the community's consciousness of being the Spirit's
temple, there had been no need for sacral buildings. The
Eucharist is not held at a mythical place, and the early Christian
apologists boasted that they had "no temple, no altar, no image
of God."[13] The church is the members with their charisms.
Christians met in ordinary rooms in private houses.[14] While
some of the first Roman communal meeting places were the
apartments and guild halls of the lower classes, even these
depended upon Christian patrons for purchase, rent, and

upkeep. Other communities, like those at the Flavian palace (San Clemente), were permitted to use rooms in the palaces of their masters. We can expect that the dynamic of the community of believers was one of diversity, and not separation. The assembly of sociologically separate classes, the universal gift of the Spirit, and the call to ministry must have been a challenging combination. The internal and institutional needs of the community were limited precisely because the ministerial expectations were external: a place for instruction, for meditative reading and preaching, for washings and anointings and commissionings, for meals and Eucharist. The house church is evidence that the typical early Christian community was personal—people knew each other and helped each other—and resembled the recent movement of base community. Contrary to surrounding gnostic and magical sects Christianity was a religion of faith and life, ordinary rather than miraculous, devoted to persons rather than caught up in the power and system of gods or angels. In writings *to* and *on* the early church, we find communities gathering in houses (Rom 16:5, 14). There were large and small gathering places, but they were at the disposal of the Christians' masters or patrons, several in a city. And when Christians moved to a new city they might join, or even found (as the example of Aquila and Prisca or the writings of Justin Martyr show), a center for instruction, sacrament, and ministerial consultation; there the social barriers between pagans and Jews, slave and free, men and women were lowered. Nourished on the sacraments of initiation and Eucharist, they understood themselves not to be clients of a goddess but a people called to be the Spirit's people. Only in the third century do we have any evidence that houses were fully set aside for worship and meeting—buildings reserved and decorated. As the number of Christians increased in Rome, tenement apartments of three stories were purchased, and the upper floors cleared for large meeting rooms.

By the end of the first century, ministry underwent a movement away from a variety of services born of a communal theology that there was a universality of charismatic ministry toward a less developed ministerial life, a fixed church order of three to six or more full-time services. This was joined to a growing emphasis upon the ministry of leadership, a leadership more and more drawn into the office and the term of *bishop.* Those who followed Jesus as ministers of Christ's people were called *shepherds* or *presiders,* then *overseers,* and then *priests.* Such a reduction to and centralization of ministry in leadership—what we might call its episcopalization—occurs differently in the early centuries and in various places. In the Syrian church of Ignatius of Antioch, the bishop had a more prominent role some years before A.D. 100. There, a monarchical ecclesiology with the three ministries we have today (bishop, presbyter, deacon) existed near or alongside the more fluid church order described in Ephesians and then in the *Didache.* There was also the world of Rome, whose writings (Romans, Hebrews, 1 Clement) show the influence of Jewish ideas on authority and priesthood. The bishop came to prominence as the local church comprehended through its expansion that it was not a cell or a sect but the world's salvation pointing to the eschaton. The Roman politics of organized centralization and the Greek love of order and vertical hierarchy furthered the prominence of the leader. Persecution and gnosticism led the church to close ranks around their community leaders. Growth from a movement to a large body brought a reduction of enthusiastic and charismatic individuals to an organization that became normative and widespread in the third century.[15] In the early second century, as the ministry of leadership become dominant, the elders, who had been collegial leaders of churches and assistants to the bishop, became individual leaders of smaller communities within the local church. Other ministers assisted the bishop or the presbyter in liturgical and extraliturgical services. There is no doubt that the three ministries of bishop, elder, and deacon found universally central roles, although local churches frequently added a further ministry of teacher, prophet, deaconess, or widow. While the prophets disappeared because of crises like Montanism,[16] the deacon's proximity to the bishop as his social minister enhanced and preserved his position.

By the end of the second century, there were Christians on all social levels of the Empire. It was also at this time that high-level theological theoreticians had begun to emerge: Justin in Rome, Tertullian in Africa, Hippolytus in Rome, Clement and

Origen in Alexandria. The full-time members of the ministry were occupied with considerable administrative burdens. Carthage, Alexandria, Antioch, and Ephesus must have had large Christian populations. Around A.D. 250 in Rome there were about fifty thousand Christians out of a population of a million, and Cornelius, the leader of the Roman church, complained about the ministerial complexity of that church, with its forty-six presbyters, seven deacons, hundreds of lesser ministers, and fifteen hundred people needing daily care.[17] These communities of diverse ethnic origins and theological interpretations found in Roman administration and centralization in the third century the pattern for the local church: leaving behind the house church and its network with others, the local church would be named, according to the Roman secular usage, "diocese," and the smaller segment called, according to the Greek for *neighborhood,* "parish."[18]

In Cyprian's episcopacy in the third century, the bishop in Carthage and elsewhere was still elected by the church and was still consulting the community. An important role in both Christian and public life, the office of bishop came to be seen as a combination of priest and high priest. We will return below to this parallel sacerdotalization of the central ministry of bishop. The bishop and his full-time clergy are rather set off from the masses.[19]

Origen in Alexandria sees a dual movement in the church, one coming from the traditional triad of clergy, and the second coming from ascetics, theologians, and gnostics. He still speaks of a universal priesthood of Christians (which he counterpoises to the distinctly pagan priestly elites) living a priestly life bestowed by baptism.[20] For Origen, there are two factors that contribute to his retention of a wider view of priesthood and ministry. The first is his scandal at the ambition and meanness of some of the Christian clergy; the second is his preference for Christian service through theology and doctrine realized in teaching and preaching and nourished by asceticism. As the Roman African Cyprian represents the bishop as leader of the Eucharist and authority figure threatened by martyrdom, so Origen, the Hellenist Egyptian, describes and encourages a flourishing ecclesial community that embraced an intellectual life nourished by the science around it as well as to the great ideas of the past.

The increasingly episcopal church is also a synodal church. The bishop does not exist ministerially alone, but as one joined in faith and activity to several groups. He is joined to the church that selected him and to his own coministers; he is joined also to the bishops of the surrounding area, and then to those of his region and of the entire world. The bishop and his presbyteral and diaconal coworkers not only led ministry, but they also absorbed it, and this new style of leadership in an organized church finds a poignant example in the selection of Calixtus from the upper class of bankers to be bishop of Rome.[21]

If the ministries of leadership were absorbing earlier charismatic services, nonetheless, readers and teachers and helpers were needed for concrete works. The deacon with a general link to the biblical institution in the Acts of the Apostles is focused upon administration, financial support, and caritative support of the needy. For a while, the centralization and numerical expansion of the church as well as the introduction of a more impressive liturgy enhanced the numbers and diversity of clergy and ministers. Singers and ascetics, assisting ministers, readers, and widows swelled the ranks. But by the fifth century, even this liturgical expansion of ministry was diminishing.

Parallel to the episcopal centralization of the church with its reduction of ministerial diversity was the sacerdotalization of ministry. Two ministries, *bishop (episcopus)* and *elder (presbyter)*, became *priest (sacerdos)*.[22] Thus the radical rejection of sacral buildings and persons by the Christians awed at Jesus' priesthood on Calvary was modified by the language and forms of religion, and justified by relating it to the history and rites of the Hebrews with their priesthood and sacrifice. Toward the end of the second century, Tertullian speaks of the bishop as *sacerdos*, but then adds: "We should be wary of thinking that what in discipline is not permitted to priests is permitted to the laity. Even we laity—are we not priests? For it is written: 'He has made of us a kingdom of priests for God the Father' (Apoc 1:6). The difference between *ordo* and *plebs* is set up by the authority of the church...but where the ecclesiastical ordo is not established, you offer and wash, you are your own priest; for where three are assembled there is the church even if the three are laity."[23] A Christian priesthood did not suddenly replace ministries of leadership, but cultural and theological developments did give sacral and sacerdotal aspects to the ministry of leadership. Hervé Legrand observes:

> The perception of the president of the Eucharist as an explicitly sacerdotal figure is not attested before the beginning of the third century (Hippolytus, Tertullian, Cyprian). On the other hand, with all the witnesses we note that it is a fact, and most often it is axiomatic (Clement, Ignatius, Justin, Tertullian, Hippolytus, Cyprian and the canonical tradition deriving from Hippolytus) that those who preside over the life of the church preside at the Eucharist.[24]

Every ministry bears facets of communal life like active service, diversity, and charism, but the ministry of leading the community easily acquired the image and reality of divine power. Two movements led to the metamorphosis of the permanent ministries of leadership into a priesthood. First, there was the natural desire in the midst of *sacerdotes* functioning in the cult of the emperor or in the cults imported from Egypt to have a priesthood. More important were the images and words of the Old Testament. In a largely Gentile church, a century or more removed from the writings of Hebrews and First Corinthians, the Old Testament was read ahistorically. An inspired page no longer struck Christians as a forecast of priesthood fulfilled in Christ but as a divine prescription for today. The Jewish hierarchy of high priest, priest, and levite was admired by Clement of Rome and then assumed a century later by Cyprian of Carthage as a valuable anticipatory type of Christian ministry. Of course, a purely sacerdotal hierarchy was what the first Christians had seen terminated in Jesus Christ.[25]

The role of the Eucharist in the centralization of bishop and priest is important. The community leader is inevitably the leader of the public Eucharist at the occasion when a large church gathers. More and more the Sunday Eucharist was the substance of the community's meeting, the work of its service. As the churches, large and episcopal, neared their final persecutions and their liberation in the early fourth century, most of the baptized met not in a home for word, sacrament, and evangelism, but they assembled passively to take part in the liturgical word and sacrament. This priestly appearance was strengthened by levitical sacerdotalism and by the image of the priesthood of Melchisedech. The emergence of a largely Eucharistic church exercised considerable influence upon the ministry. The celebrant appeared in a large hall or in a basilica as a priest of an unbloody rite. At Carthage, Cyprian spoke of the purity required of the priests whose Eucharist was the continuation of the rites of the Old Testament. The Christian assembly could be reinterpreted along Jewish lines: altar, temple, priests, and cult provided for the new sacrifice of the Christians. The figure of the bishop as teacher, example, and potential martyr, and the Eucharist commemorating Christ's sacrifice strengthened a priestly emphasis. Thus the Roman gift for distinction and order furthered not a diversity of ministries within the community but a separation into two classes, clerical and lay.

Significant in and illustrative of the shift in ministry to priesthood is the move from house to basilica. In the early third century, the expanded house church was still the meeting place of the community, but by the end of the century some Christians had buildings publicly set apart for their use. When the church found its life within the Empire undisturbed, it looked for larger buildings. It adopted, however, not a model of a temple but the plan of the Roman civic assembly hall, the imperial building, the basilica. Pierre du Bourguet writes:

> The Roman civil basilica, especially in view of its extremely flexible plan....could serve either as public building, with or without aisles, or simply as a covered or open space, with or without arcades, while at one end stood a bench for the magistrates or a throne for the emperor or his venerated image....As early as the second century the form was being adapted to the purposes of the religious sects that were free to build....Thus without excluding the possibility of a religious note, the basilica had nothing in common with the official pagan temples.[26]

The basilica offered good light and acoustics, mobility for the faithful, and a focal point for the bishop. The entrance into this large tripartite hall, whose lines drew one forward to the bishop's place, did mold the community into two groups, laity and ministers. There was still a diversity of ministries but they were distinct from the large numbers assisting at the eucharistic worship and other sacraments like baptism. The roles of the ordained, a separate group, and the growing custom of celibacy as well as a liturgy ecclesiologically inward-looking and increasingly sacral contributed to sacral forms. Constantine's conception of his own role—as the thirteenth apostle—and the imperial favor resulted in the grafting of court customs onto religious ceremony. The liturgy became elaborate, imperial, and places were set aside for the most important members attending the cult. This could only lead to a sharper distinction between priests and rulers, clergy and laity. The outward life of the church grew ever more specialized, and the ministerial climax to this ecclesial process was the constitution in the middle of the fourth century of Christian bishops as officials of the Roman Empire. Finally, due to controversies over the relationship of Jesus the man to the Word of God, the prophet from Nazareth, savior of the meek, had become the emperor of heaven.

From our perspective we can see that success also brought loss, loss in charismatic and ministerial participation and diversity. For the laity, the expansion of the church and the sacerdotalization of the clergy (which partly comprised the external forms of a public and liturgical leadership) brought to the laity inversely a spiritualization of their Christian faith and life. The symbolic, the sacramental and liturgical, the interior and ethical—these became the touchstones of being a Christian. The Christian was less and less a convert from evangelization and more and more the son and daughter born to members of the church. Ministry was a special choice by a few adults to serve the church. Charisms were lost among the daily routine of a hundred thousand Christians in an urban area. After turbulent centuries the organization of the church brought Roman order, modest diversity, and liturgical membership where earlier there had been community, pneumatic discernment, ministerial diversity, and charismatic individuality.

The growth of the church led, in fact, to the diminution of the ministry.

With the fourth century and the entry of hundreds of thousands into the Christian churches, the leaders failed to develop wider baptismal ministries within or without the community assembly. There was still a social diaconate and still some diversity in the ministry, but the universal call to ministry was replaced by a call to a virtuous life in the empire. The Christian found himself or herself partaking in what was mainly a liturgical religion with weekly Eucharist, liturgical feasts, and special moments of human life heightened by the sacraments. It would be interesting to pursue whether the elaboration of the liturgical year with its anticipation of the heavenly Jerusalem was not a subconscious replacement of the diminished ministry, where liturgy confronted symbolically the world and its power for evil.

Not only did the ministry become the activity of a small group of Christians, but ministry itself tended to appear as liturgy, and ministers sought out their places therein. It is hardly surprising that the diaconate should have suffered as a result of the process of sacralization. The field of social welfare that had been the diaconate's chief raison d'être now began to be entrusted to priests or laypeople. In 595, the Synod of Rome complained that the deacons were no longer looking after the poor but were chanting psalms instead: the liturgy had become their main sphere of activity.[27]

We cannot blame the ministers who were becoming in name and reality a clergy. They were spending themselves in leading thousands into the Body of Christ, into the people of God open to all religions and sects and races of the empire. The expanding local church from Cologne to Nisibis did not, however, recognize or solve the problem of how to sustain charism and ministry in so many after they had been baptized. Numbers brought passivity.

B. The Monastery as Minister

The conversion of the Germanic tribes to the Catholic faith gave birth to national, regional, and ethnic churches, for whom Semitic, Hellenist, or Roman cultures provided some traditional ecclesial forms but for which Germanic society offered new forms. The papacy became the advocate of the church because the pope was one of the few forces that could sustain the independence of the local church. It is not, however, the power of the papacy that interests us but the source of papal efforts to reform and strengthen the local church in the West: monasticism. Gregory the Great and Gregory VII, popes at either end of a time of turmoil, were both monks. To a church whose diocesan structure was weak and whose local clergy was feebly prepared, the great monasteries and monastic families must have appeared as the church itself.

The ministry of the local church was, of course, in the hands of priests and bishops. The bishops were in one of two positions: either they struggled against being controlled by princes, or they were themselves part of the feudal principate. The priests, little educated, served the local parishes during those eras of social upheaval through a sacramental life that joined heaven to the vicissitudes of earth. Many of the important bishops, popes, and theologians—Hincmar, Anselm, Hildebrand—were monks. Monastic renewal for the local church came not from their ambition but from their desire to revitalize the offices of bishop and priest. In that renewal, through education and morality, the monk became the tutor of the minister. From the fourth century on, certain bishops such as Martin of Tours, Paulinus of Nola, and Augustine of Hippo had favored a monastic life for their priests. By 814 councils were urging the spirit and life of the monk upon the diocesan clergy, and that movement reached a further stage in the transformation of the clergy into canons regular. Hildebrand argued at the Roman Council in 1074 for vows of poverty for the clergy, an imitation of the life of the Twelve, and for an embrace of the monastic common life.[28]

In centuries of instability, local bishops could not have competed with the resources of the monastery. The great cathedral schools were, in format and theology, monastic. Influenced by Origen and Pseudo-Dionysius, there were many proponents of the ecclesiology that monasticism was the source of the first class in the church. In the East and in Celtic Christianity, the monastic community was the normal ambiance for church and ministry. As the end of the first millennium was crossed, the monastery set the tone for the church. Monastic sites were frequently remote. Away from centers of a population ravaged by the centuries before A.D. 1000, they were secure islands for prayer, contemplation, and spiritual reading. Remoteness discouraged dangerous visitors while austerity both amplified asceticism and nourished life. The art historian Kenneth J. Conant writes:

> The larger monasteries laid the foundation of economic recovery in Europe after the Dark Ages; they presented intricate administrative problems and were accepted schools for men of business and government. In addition they were the training places for talent in the arts, and the refuge of intellectual activity. Thus the monasteries did yeoman service in creating all four of the bases on which medieval civilization was to rest: (1) economic revival, (2) the fusion of the Latin and the Teutonic peoples, (3) the afterlife of Roman law in the monastic rule, the canon law of the Church, and the Holy Roman Empire, (4) the feudal system, which set up new hierarchies of power, and enabled the monastic orders to extend their influence and their benefits generally. The great monasteries, thus developing as imposing financial, educational, and territorial corporations, were far larger, more complex, and more influential than they had ever been in antiquity. Since many of their architectural problems were new, their architecture became the living and growing architecture of the time.[29]

In the monastery two developments took place: (1) a feudalization of the ministry, and (2) a sacerdotalization of monasticism. Ministry was often seen as work within the monks' community or liturgical celebration. The great liturgies and the private mass were ministry par excellence. In some ways the monastery itself became the model of Christian ministry. In the midst of unexplored country or social chaos the monastic group was able to preserve order and learning, aid communication by furnishing hospitality to travelers and books for the studious, and enlarge the borders of Christianity by missionary evangelization. The monastery took on the ministry of deacon: it effected aid to the poor, instruction in agriculture and the arts, the cultivation of land, and the availability of other resources for social growth. The life of faith and grace could be served not only by prayer but by better techniques in the apiary and by new manu-scripts arriving for copying in the scriptorium.

The monasteries of the Carolingian and Gregorian eras like Reichenau, St. Gall, and Cluny were striking in their solid build-ings and vertical towers. They were symmetrical arrangements of hotels, libraries, dormitories, gardens, refectories, farm build-ings, and workshops. The center of all was the abbey church, where the monks, and at times the wider community of lay-people, met for the divine office and sacramental liturgy. Some ministries survived only as names and rites in the abbatial liturgy when acolytes, cantors, readers, and subdeacons joined priests and deacons around the altar. The liturgy, the *Opus Dei,* was the main ministry to grace—an iconic form in word and sacrament addressing all levels of Christian society. To serve this world other offices emerged with new names and pragmatic functions: abbot, abbess, prior, hebdomadarian, porter, cellarer, and procurator.

In good times and bad, the monastery was a fortress or haven not only for faith but for culture. A feudal world existed around the monastery, which constituted a city in itself, a sacra-mental anticipation of the city of God. In short, the direction of ministry was from the monastery rather than to it from the local church. The monastery sent out apostles to evangelize pagan lands, but that meant that the very form of the church brought by Kilian or Emmeram was from its inception largely monastic. At home, stability and maturity drew Christians to the abbey to find there, as a place of ministry, the monastic community: mentor, inspiration, magnet.

With no competitors, monastic theology and monastic spir-ituality influenced all the areas of the church. The cathedral schools of Chartres and Rheims were monastic not only in celibacy and liturgy but in their approach to theology.[30] Even devotional literature written for laity and bishops depicted a Christian life whose ethos was monastic. A new beginning in the life of grace, that is, a personal conversion in adulthood, usually meant entering not the ministry but religious life. Conversion came not in the style of a Thomas More or a Francis Xavier but in that of Bernard of Clairvaux and his companions entering a cloister. Men and women left behind the worldly struggle of knight and lady overseeing keep and lands when they entered a separate monastic island.

The widespread appropriation of monastic theology could only have an enormous effect upon the ministry. As the lifestyle of the ministry was monastic, so too was the training for ministry and for ecclesial expression in liturgy. Monasticism meant separation from the world, and the secular clergy did not always resolve well the dialectic of withdrawal and service. Monastic theology encouraged allegorical and moral hermeneutics of faith, liturgies that were an acceptance of the cycle of life and death or an anticipation of a next, better life in heaven. Sometimes reality and activity in grace, in sacrament and service, became secondary.

The results of the monasticization of ministry were several. First, the bishop came to resemble an abbot rather than a coordinator of ministries. He was the father of his people and particularly of his clergy; he was the spiritual director of his priests. Coloring this modification of the bishop's role was a second shift from ministry to a jurisdictional position. In the West, monasticism more and more defined the leader of the community as a figure of authority and order. In the East the monastic leader was such because he had been recognized as a leader in the life of the spirit and contemplation, but in the West appointment to jurisdiction replaced proven spirituality. A person canonically installed in a church office—whether abbot or bishop—was presumed uncritically to have the accompanying charisms, but he certainly had canonical church authority. Searching and testing for the right person for a specific position was slowly abandoned. Juridical appointment rendered the discernment of nature and grace at work in effective public ministry to a secondary position. Important ministers could simply be appointed with the proclamation that the Spirit summoned up in ordination would render the person a suitable abbot or bishop. We have here the beginning of a great reversal: symbols and legal positions dispensed grace rather than grace begetting life through charisms realized in office and service.

Second, the Christian life was seen not as a life of activity or ministry in the public forum but as an inner spiritual life centered on monastic detachment and contemplation. The services of the local community apart from the Eucharist and other sacraments were the hours of the monastic liturgy, such as Vespers and Matins. Since the sixth century, the popularity of urban monasticism gradually replaced the old cathedral liturgies. The prayer of the secular clergy became the monastic office, and by the eleventh century, the private recitation of the monastic hours was expected.[31] The cleric's clothes and vestments were monastic. The struggle between religious distinction in public image and excessive worldliness was resolved in favor of dress and grooming that appropriated many monastic elements.[32]

Celibacy was urged by Rome, and the monasticization of diocesan life assisted this. Cathedral and rectory had the qualities of a monastic enclosure, the cloister. Since celibacy appeared as essential to monastic life, there was an inevitable drive within a secular ministerial group to nourish celibacy, to survive in that style of life through the assistance of community life. The designated model of the cathedral canons in the eleventh century, the reformation of the Oratorians in the sixteenth, the originality of Sulpicians, Paulists, and Maryknoll in the modern era—each illustrates this tendency of celibate life to move toward religious life. Even if official church ministries were drawn into timeless liturgy, the prophetic spirit of a marginal life did not die out. Pilgrimage and crusade were each a kind of ministry in motion. More important was the large number of Christian men and women in the twelfth century, particularly in Lombardy, southern France, and along the Rhine up into the Low Countries, who took to the road to preach, imitating Christ's poverty and the mission of the Twelve. In many areas the majority were women who lived in communities in voluntary poverty, working in the care of the sick and living as a middle modality between monastery and world. Around 1144, a German priest complained to Bernard of Clairvaux that these evangelicals would do only what Scripture recorded of Christ and the Apostles. Eighty years later a leader of the *Pauperes Christi* exclaimed to his followers: "If anyone should ask to which religious order you belong, answer, 'the Order of the Gospel of Christ.'"[33] These preaching movements were a temporary liberation for public ministry, and unfortunately a few were also sources of error (ignorance more than heresy) and immorality. What had been a varied movement of free ministry was channeled into society and the church through two preachers, Francis and Dominic, who slowly formed a new, postmonastic style of religious life.

The sturdy Romanesque monasteries, which preserved and nourished the faith and culture of Europe, had an impact on ministry that lasts to this day. Some rubrics, clothes, and institutions that appear to us to be eternally ecclesial and deeply Christian are monastic and Romanesque. The monastery, source and standard for ministry, drew people to the inner life of the soul and to eschatological liturgy; it assumed or absorbed the diversity of the ministry. The monastery, which had begun as an exceptional outpost in an expanding church of martyrs and preachers, became the church itself.

C. The Ministry as Hierarchy

During the twelfth century the context of ministry as well as the igneous core of Christian society moved from the monastic to the clerical, from contemplative community to individual priesthood defined by the real presence in the Eucharist. Yves Congar writes of the theological implications:

> The theology of monasticism, for instance of a St. Bernard, remains in the stream of the fathers and the liturgy. The theology of the schools, analytic and dialectical, however, reorientates itself toward the reality of things toward their nature, status, place....In the theology of grace, for instance, we pass from a point of view which is dynamic and personal (the act of God) to a point of view more stationary and reified (our supernatural ontology).[34]

There were considerable changes in ministry during the Middle Ages. The laity no longer understood the language of liturgy and of doctrine. There was a cleavage through many political struggles and changes between the spiritual and the temporal, and so between clergy and laity. Priest and bishop were both defined more by the character given by ordination and less by the ministries they performed.

After centuries of chaos, the Renaissances of the twelfth

and thirteenth centuries brought order and creativity. Feudalism had fought simply to hold together the social fabric, but now the *ordo* of medieval society was prized for its own vitality and beauty. Parallels were drawn between the cosmos and the structure of society. The metaphysicians proclaimed that being, beauty, and truth were one, while political philosophers saw the same harmony in social life. What *ordo* and *scientia* were to philosophy and theology, *corpus* and *societas* were to church and state. As in a luminous north rose window where every segment has its own identity and yet contributes to the blue pattern of the Old Testament culminating in Mary and Child, so the medieval mind delighted in arrangement, in the "natural places" of peasant, priest, merchant, knight, prince, and pope.[35]

One philosophical source for the ecclesiology of the Middle Ages was the quasimythical Pseudo-Dionysius. The educated citizens of Paris believed that the bishop to the Parisians, the saintly Denys, was the same Dionysius converted by Paul on the Athenian Areopagus (Acts 13:33 ff.). They believed that he found his way to Roman Paris, evangelized its citizens and, before he died, wrote a series of mystical treatises, among which are *The Divine Names, The Celestial Hierarchy,* and *The Ecclesiastical Hierarchy,* works in fact composed by a Neoplatonist Syrian monk from the sixth century. As a result of his legend, Dionysius's synthesis of Christian and Platonist forms held a singular position not only in theology but in the entire cultural world of Paris. In mysticism, aesthetics, and ecclesiology, in politics and papal theory, the Areopagite's influence was unassailable. His thought-form was hierarchy. "Hierarchy was the Dionysian world itself....hierarchy makes life intelligible and possible.[36] Hellenistic cosmological theories provided a different account of the significance of ranked ministries. They were earthly manifestations of heavenly hierarchies.[37] Through the appropriation of the language of hierarchies, subtle but significant shifts occurred in the understanding of the purpose of ranked ministries. Accordingly, in the grand design of Pseudo-Dionysius's text, the purpose of the earthly ecclesiastical hierarchies was to assure progressive divinization: assimilation to, participation in, and union with God.[38] The triadic form of Neoplatonic schemata had to be trimmed to the empirical phenomenon of the church, and a double, not a triple, triadic form was posited for the ecclesiatical hierarchy. An active triad, the bishop, priests, and deacons, worked on the passive triad of monks, laity, and the catechumens, along with their penitential counterparts, in proportion to the powers each had received. In the active triad, the episcopal hierarch was said to possess a triple spiritual power to purify, to illuminate, and to unify. He conferred two shares of that power on the next in rank but only one share on the deacon. They in turn used these powers on those in the inferior receptive hierarchy.[39] Certainly, his scheme of progressive hierarchical power is not unfamiliar in Western theology, nor is his localized interpretation of ministerial mediation as residing squarely in the person of the hierarch. The episcopal ordinand, who is told through the text of the 1968 *Roman Pontifical* that it is his responsibility to act for people in matters pertaining to God, is a linear descendant of Dionysius's hierarch.

Hierarchy was the structural model of public and ecclesiastical life in the thirteenth century.[40] A number of social classes constructed the corpus of society, and within the church three orders—deacon, priest, bishop—survivors of time, gave ecclesial aesthetic diversity. There were other offices too: abbess, abbot, archbishop, archdeacon, pope, canon, friar, and provincial. Ecclesial ministry was a public dignity and a state of life inserted into the wider social hierarchy. Nothing in the hierarchical world was accidental or optional; every arrangement was *taxis hiera,* holy disposition coming from God and thus a norm or command. People and things had their place by divine choice. But the manifest ecclesiastical arrangement and the situation of each individual soul reflected the harmony of the heavenly realm. Rebellion against the given order was both futile and sinful. Pseudo-Dionysius even specified that burial sites were to be located according to this arrangement, so that at the moment of regeneration the deceased would be "in the right place." Hierarchical organization was, for him, both constitutive and expressive of intrinsic moral perfection.[41]

The theology of the church was not of major import for Aquinas, although he treats ecclesiology within the theologies of grace and faith, Spirit and sacrament. From his teacher, Albert, Aquinas learned to prize the Areopagite's works; he commented on them, and his first work was a hierarchical metaphysics of the levels of being from rocks to God, the *De ente et essentia*. Hierarchy, Aquinas observed, comes from two words, *sacred* and *principle*.[42] In a hierarchy, "a sacred principate," are ordered the apostles and all other prelates of the church. The church's hierarchy does not agree perfectly with the angelic one, but there is a similarity in pattern. The church's contribution to hierarchy is the threefold ecclesial office. Earlier authorities had shown Aquinas the vitality of the triad: three persons in the Trinity, three times three choirs among angels. Aquinas sees three sacred activities in the church: the minister purifies, the priest illumines and purifies, the bishop brings to perfection and illumines in a special way. If monks are on a rung beneath this hierarchy of active office, Aquinas argued that his Dominican friars should approach episcopal rank, for they are the pope's preachers.[43] The highest in the hierarchy is the bishop; at that ordination the Scriptures are placed over the head of this high priest to show both that he receives the fullness of light and that he illumines all.[44] With the angels as analogue and with a Neoplatonic metaphysics of light as model (and encouraged by his own personal vocation of teaching), Aquinas described the ecclesial hierarchy as a ladder of descending illumination. The lower is perfected, illumined, directed by actions moving downwards but not upwards. The higher illumines the lower because such is the pattern coming from the Trinity and the angels.

When this form and dynamic is applied to the church, office speaks and acts only downward. Diversity is vertical in direction. Service has become authority. A deacon and priest can make no contribution to the bishop. A higher office and order contains the lower eminently, and so what could a lower order contribute to a higher one, which possesses all beneath it? Movement upward in illumination or sacred action is impossible because it is redundant. We see here the pyramid of hierarchy replacing the circle of different charisms. The bishop is a divine or angelic principle within his system of orders, the church. Not only are the other ministries silent before him but he illumines and vivifies (if

not creates) them out of his being and grace.[45] Community is not
a cooperative diversity, a Body of Christ, but a fixed arrangement,
a medieval heavenly Jerusalem. The second facet in this "sacred
principate" is the sacral. One enters the hierarchy to the extent
that one has an active relation to sacred things. The center of the
sacral world, the *sacrosanctissimum,* is the Eucharist. The three
ministries are offices of the hierarchy because each has a real,
physical function vis-à-vis the eucharistic liturgy.[46]

There was, however, in Aquinas's thought an unresolved tension. To distinguish bishop from priest, he emphasizes the teaching and preaching of the latter (for both can absolve sins and
consecrate bread and wine); and yet, in his drawing of the threefold hierarchy from the sacred, he selects the Eucharist. Scholars
agree that Aquinas's depiction of the bishop is complex and even
inconsistent, for he instinctively leads the episcopacy to the word
while theologically he reduces it to a higher form of priesthood.

Ministerial reduction perdured. Not only was the ministry
formally limited to bishop and priest, but it has been reduced to
serving a single event of priesthood, the Eucharist. Yet, we can
see how right this aesthetic ecclesiology was for the Middle Ages.
The cathedral was a meeting place for the entire society gathered around a vivifying principle: priest and sacrament. The
people rejoiced in the visual transmission of their faith through
art, and through art in motion, liturgy. Out of liturgy came theater; out of social order in diversity came a peaceful process of
urbanization with a new middle class. All of this anticipated the
beauty of a city and a society yet to come; the paradigm of life
was not action but being and event, an anticipation of what
Dante, ascending through hierarchical spheres, described as *beat-
itude.* Beauty and life flow from order.

Medieval society replaced the biblical *diakonia* (with its overtones of ordinary serving) by Roman legal terms such as *status, officium,* and *ordo.* The second part of the great *Summa* treated the
human person returning to God, its source and goal in grace.
Aquinas offered a psychology of intellectual and emotional life, and
on this foundation he built his theology of Christian life. We would
expect him to have concluded this graced anthropology with activity drawn from charism and related to ministry. Evidently, in the

thirteenth century a different conclusion seemed obvious. "We will now consider," he wrote, "the variety of states and offices of human beings."[47] The Christian life ends not with ministry but with social states of life.[48]

In the thirteenth century a certain ossification of order entered, fixing ministerial activity in the flintier structure of priestly hierarchy. In the patristic age *ordo* had tones of the organic and corporate, of society arranged and collegial, but in medieval life it meant the public transmission of power in a valid ceremony of an ordination.[49] In the thirteenth century an ecclesiastical office contained two things: the work and the dignity following upon the work. Aquinas placed the action within the public institutional personality of the role; for instance, the dignity that accrues to the bishop is not simply an occasional reward but a position in medieval society. Always enamored of the Aristotelian action revealing its nature, Aquinas did not follow the popular view of the baptized as in a state of faith but saw them as active participants in the priesthood of Christ and in the cult of the church. Aquinas strove to show how an individual achieved a stable place to radiate grace. What strikes us is the accomplished shift from charismatic individuality and diversity to single stability, the uncertainty of whether life or role defines an office, and the location of ministerial grace and deed in the bishop. Congar writes: "Thomas had a vision of a pyramidal structuring of the body of the church from parish to universal church, a dynamic passing through deanery, diocese, and province based upon the ideas of the time. But he did not follow the secular academics who pieced out authority to sections of the church....Thomas reestablished a hierarchical structure, a structure oriented toward the bishops and the pope."[50] Significantly, in his analogy with the body, the church is almost always compared to a physiological organism owning an inner life with diverse functions, and not to a sociological city or state.[51]

There were new movements in ministry in the thirteenth century, but they were not the restoration of the ministries of the first century of the Christian era nor the granting of public roles beyond monastic ones to women (there were attempts in the decades before Francis and Dominic, all suppressed, to give women evangelizing ministries of preaching) but forms of a poor, apostolic life. The debate over whether new orders like the Franciscans and Dominicans (regional gatherings of mobile brothers imitating the life of Christ and his preaching) had the right to restore evangelical forms and to fashion new approaches to holiness and preaching was a controversy over the possibility of new forms of ministry in the church. What diversity there was in ministry appeared in religious orders or in local lay brotherhoods. To Aquinas, the Pauline theology of the Body of Christ suggests a diversity of activities and gifts: "Each human being has a body and a soul and through them diverse members. So it is with the Catholic Church: one body and yet different members; the soul which vivifies this body is the Holy Spirit."[52] Some arrangements of the structures of the church come not from revelation but from church law; some are of divine tradition, but many change with the times—and the latter are matters not of dogma but of polity, policy, and church law.[53]

Although his pastoral theology of bishop, priest, and deacon was considerably limited by the ecclesiastical practice of his time, Aquinas's theological principles do not exclude a diversity of orders. Still, how to account for the one sacrament of orders having different forms and ordinations, those of bishop, subdeacon, acolyte? He explained orders as a unity within diversity. The various church orders composed a "potestative whole."[54] The one sacrament of orders is a vital totality, an organism from whose life various powers could emerge. This theory leaves open the issue of whether in theory and practice ministries beyond those of leadership might be different in kind and number from age to age, culture to culture.

The facade of a French cathedral contains the thought-forms of its time and presents a diversity of elements in a vertical unity. The lines of the facade of Notre Dame de Paris express theology and ontology; its beauty comes precisely from diversity within order, conveying at the same time an impression of stability and transcendence. A vertical dynamic of lines reaches upwards, diminishing in variety but increasing in a single power, suggesting a society where historicity was not prominent, but where knowledge and belief in the transcendent were. The levels and lines of the facade present hierarchy, a progression reaching from the materialistic realism of the new Aristotelianism to the Trinity of the Greek mystics. The finite was shot through with grace; symbol and reality pointed to the next life. The laity are invited to the cathedral not to act but to see. They are separate from the clergy. Yet hierarchical forms, too, were forms for grace.[55] Because he was a genius, Aquinas's theology contains two openings toward a broader interpretation of ministry. First, he underscored with his thought on ecclesial states, sacramental orders, and the gifts of the Spirit a diversity in the Body; second, by casually noting that some treatments of church and ministry belong to the human polity of canon law ("For the study of offices so far as it pertains to other acts is a matter for jurists; and so far as it pertains to the sacred ministry it is a matter of orders"[56]), he suggested a legitimate reexpression of ministry in diverse cultural forms. For Thomas Aquinas, the church was the effect and the place of grace. His ecclesiological interests were not focused upon the foremost people in ministerial action but upon unity, harmony, stability, hierarchy, and sacramentality. In them the social and the ministerial became the beautiful.

D. The Reformation of Ministry

The Reformation was a religious protest against the localization of the activity of God in the human and the created. It was also a pastoral program to renew the life of the local church. The Reformers were inspired by the description of the early church in the New Testament, and they worked to renew the ministry according to that model. They challenged celibacy and monasticism so that they might abolish the class system within the church. As Luther rediscovered ministerial freedom and sacerdotal universality in the New Testament, he championed in the early years of the Reformation the admission of all into the ministry. Luther preached the priesthood of all the baptized and the dignity of every human occupation: being a farmer or a prince was ministry. Baptism into the priesthood of all believers was sufficient for community preachers and leaders. But when faced with charismatic and social excesses, Luther, frightened by enthusiastic anarchists, expounded a conservative reformation and insisted upon a distinct pastorate and ordination. He wrote in 1539: "Let everyone who knows himself to be a Christian be assured of this, that we are all equally priests, that is to say, we have the same power in respect to the Word and the sacraments. However no one may make use of this power except by the consent of the community or by the call of a superior."[57]

Calvin struggled to transform a city into a Christian community and to transform citizens into an assembly of worship. In the Calvinist reform, there would be no hierarchy, no sacrifice, no mediator. A complete desacerdotalization would take place. The ministry focused not on the Eucharist but on the word of the Christian community: the word and its service were priestly, and the preaching minister of the word administered the Eucharist.[58] Calvin drew out of the pages of the New Testament four ministries: pastor (shepherd), deacon, elder, and teacher. Yet his churches did not succeed in maintaining a real distinction among church ministries. The offices of elder and deacon did involve laity but without successfully eliminating the division between clergy and laity. Deacons, elders, vicars, wardens, even bishops were in the last analysis honorary or marginal services. One ministry, the pastor, absorbed the others. Entrusted with minimal ministry, the Calvinist laity more and more justified a Christian ministry in the professions of secular life. Paradoxically, the churches of the Reformation were left with fewer ministries than the medieval church, and unconsciously they seemed to have taken in the idea that there was only one ministry—not priest, but pastor.

Reformation ministry cultivated the characteristics of freedom and identity as it replaced the sacral-monastic with the secular. But support by the state could control ministry, and antisacerdotalism could end in passive support for the spirituality of the European bourgeoisie. The marriage of the clergy did not automatically liberate the minister from an oppressive monastic world for greater service to the Gospel. In fact, the Protestant clergy never lost aspects of monasticism: the manse, the close, the identification of the pastor's life with that of the church buildings, and the pressures upon the pastor's family all led to a manner of life that was evocative of both marriage and quasi-monasticism.

The Protestant desire to reform the local church along New Testament lines was incomplete, limited by the cultural situation holding sway at the beginning of modern society. Protestant ministry remains a mixture of elements from both the New Testament and medieval forms in a context that seeks to be human without being secular.

After its praise of the secular vocation, the Protestant church had difficulty with halting the identification of ministry with Western professions, difficulty with keeping a transcendence in the sacrament and service of its minister. A certain secularity and bourgeois ethos was a fallout from the Reformation. The minister failed at times to present a clear identity distinct from the family man or emerging social worker. Either the liturgical expression or the apostolic lifestyle or the depth of diaconal sacrifice might be missing from the minister—a man identified with the middle class. The furnishings of a Calvinist or Methodist church might differ only slightly from those of a law court or theater; the minister's clothes were no different from a banker's suit or an academic's gown. What was the identity of the Protestant ministry in England in the eighteenth century and in Sweden in the nineteenth? In short, who was the minister?

The Protestant theology of ministry had embarked in the sixteenth century upon a not-yet-finished search for a ministry in a free, modern society. It succeeded in some periods and countries, mainly within a homogeneous, middle-class pietism in small towns or rural settings. When such a milieu breaks up, the ministry is challenged anew from both sides, from charismatic and fundamentalist movements, and from secular or professional ethos. The minister is challenged by the sacral and by the personal.

Parallel to this secularization of the ministry ran a second current that reacted to a new bondage for the church. It tried, and tries today, to restore the New Testament vision of ministry. The "radical reformation" and its heirs formed a church that really did resemble the churches in Acts and First Corinthians. Pietism, all manner of fundamentalisms, as well as charismatic and healing churches, pursued, sometimes in a provincial or magical way, the theology that charisms come to all and lead to ministry for the community, that there are many ministries, and that a church had an outer evangelical life as well as an inner one lived on Sunday. In the small congregations praying in simple buildings in towns and cities, there survives an appreciation of the universality of ministry; there the baptized give commitment of intellect, money, and time. These fellowships of charism and ministry may focus too much on external charisms, but in such Christian communities, we often find members, at great personal expense, evangelizing in foreign countries, and we find personal and verbal service and an eager hospitality. What they lack is the bond to the wider church, past and present. These churches do not often survive cultural change, nor do they spread far. Today they become large organizations and undergo the electronic metamorphoses into televised revivals. But beneath the exaggerations and the hucksterism, beneath the narrowness and superficiality there can be found in small Protestant churches echoes of the New Testament's understanding of ministry: a world of ordinary people expecting charisms, and willing to serve their community and change the world.

E. Ministry and the Baroque

From fragile beginnings and uncertain hopes, the Catholic Counter-Reformation developed into a major movement in European history, it took shape as a new worldview, influencing both the religious and aesthetic arenas. The history of Catholicism from Trent to Vatican II is marked by five epochs: the Counter-Reformation; the Baroque, Late Baroque, and Rococo; the Romantic Renaissance of the early nineteenth century; the antimodern atmosphere between 1860 and 1960; and the preparation for Vatican II after two world wars. Catholicism largely withdrew from the Enlightenment after a Romantic restoration from 1800 to 1840. Modern views of the individual with freedom and history did not influence church life as they did some Protestant churches. It was often said during Vatican II that the Counter-Reformation was ending. That was true in terms of popular attitudes vis-à-vis Protestantism, but, strictly speaking, the

Counter-Reformation was a time of administrative and doctrinal formulation; it lasted for a few decades around the Council of Trent and held little originality. The epochal period, the time of cultural renewal and of religious expansion, was the Baroque. This has been the most recent great era in Roman Catholic life. With variations it reappeared and continued from 1820 to 1960. There are fewer than a dozen important periods in Western Christianity, and the Baroque is one of these.

The Baroque emerged reflecting the mind-set of the mid-sixteenth century and lived on to become the Rococo of the eighteenth century; its outer boundaries were the Council of Trent and the Enlightenment. The Baroque spirit brought to the church new theologies and spiritualities, new ministries and arts: these manifested new interplays between personality and grace pioneered by Ignatius Loyola, Philip Neri, Teresa of Avila, and their numerous followers. There was a universality in which Catholicism experienced God in a vastness, freedom, and goodness flowing through a world of diversity, movement, and order. Christ appeared in a more human way, filled with a personal love, redemptive and empowering. This was a time of methods and exercises, of imagination and conversation with the divine. Francis de Sales, Pierre de Bérulle, and Jeanne Françoise de Chantal offered to others their personal views on prayer and mystical contemplation. Actual grace, the great theme of the Baroque, moved from God to people, a transient force influencing adolescent vocations, validly received sacraments, or deathbed decisions. Grace was a power for life, a force to aid each individual in following God's will. Grace, however, was described in an increasingly mechanical mode, a theological style that, through the centuries and even up to the decades just before the Council, made the Catholic Church appear as a pumping station at the center of an extensive waterworks of grace. The Baroque furthered systems that reflected this mind-set: a method for meditation, the plan by Sixtus V for the city of Rome, Bernini's ensemble of St. Peter's church and piazza, and a centralized papal authority.

The Baroque world was also a theater: buildings, city squares, and baldachinos set off spaces for human performance.

Liturgies, operas, frescos, or palatial receptions were theatrical, and Baroque Christianity was filled with visions and ecstasies, with martyrs, missionaries, and stigmatics. Ornate statues told emotional stories, and crowds passively attended liturgies like folk missions, novenas to saints, or rites surrounding the Blessed Sacrament. The Baroque loved detail and arrangement, striving to express the infinite in the visual; it loved the play of light and water in the context of space and marble. In the Baroque, the hierarchical combined with the organic to give both life and motion as well as the arrangements of many pieces. Whether in a piazza's buildings and fountains or in the interior ensemble of St. Peter's Basilica, we find many diverse elements related to a single point that defines and gives meaning to all its components.[59] It is not hard to see the same Baroque style in the theology, ecclesiology, and spirituality of the seventeenth century and beyond. At the same time, grace primarily contacts the will and emotions and secondarily influences the intellect. The theater of the Christian life and the kingdom of God moved from the medieval cosmos and the arena of society to the interior of the Baroque church and the life of the soul. In the Baroque, light pours down through clear windows into the church and states that God is not distant nor utterly different from creatures. God is actively present in the church and in the Christian. In short, light is molded by the Baroque to proclaim that there is sanctifying grace. At first the Baroque church shocks us with its universe of angels, saints, and decorations. The interior of the Baroque church, moving toward the Rococo, with all its figures, is an affirmation that there is a world of grace whence come these angels and saints. Also the church anticipates the next life in the liturgy, in the religious order, in the new spirituality for lay people, in this very church building, this center for pilgrimage or meditation. Grace, in the fresco and the sculptured group, becomes concrete; there is grace in humanity.

Baroque ecclesiology continued the reforms of the Council of Trent. In a central formulation of liturgy and canon law, of catechetics and conciliar teaching we find diversity arranged around one center. A Baroque theology of the ministry is based upon two main operational principles: first, the organization of the church in detail around the papacy; second, the designation of the interior life of grace as the object of Christian ministry. The forms of a universal episcopacy and of a post-Reformation spirituality meet in their rejection of the Reformation.

The theology of the priesthood in the seventeenth century underwent an important development, one which had considerable influence on its own age but which lasted, perceived subsequently as the sole understanding of priestly ministry, up to Vatican II. It emerged out of the renewal of life in the church by priest and bishop and was formed by the spirituality of the French school (Pierre Bérulle, Charles de Condren, J.J. Olier, and congregations like that of Saint Sulpice). The spirituality (and theology was largely spirituality) was Christocentric and incarnational, but conceived within an approach like the Neoplatonism of Pseudo-Dionysius. The church "is the living image of the divine essence"[60] and its priests had first and foremost a special state grounded in union with the high priest. Heightening the divine in Jesus, sermons and books sought the extensions of the Incarnation in concrete things like the heart of Jesus, the consecrated host—and the priest. The man who was pastor or curé was a living extension of Christ the priest in his sacrificial passion. Revelation and ministry come from God to people through the high priest and his priests, through rather automatic channels of trinitarian grace. Hence, looking at the invisible God made visible in the monstrance or in the priest with his anointed hands (quite apart from receiving communion) introduced one to the central mystery of Christianity, but how that happened outside of the automatic graces of prayers repeated and rituals performed was not central. Participation in the person, suffering, and activity of Christ the priest was popularized in the nineteenth century in devotional books and in a certain iconography with such themes as "the priest is another Christ," "the priest more powerful than Mary makes him come down every day."[61] One discerns easily here a kind of Christification of ministry, which is a further, particular form of sacerdotalization. The purpose of ecclesial ministry, the power of priestly ordination, seems to be to direct worshipers to manifestations of the incarnate Word, to work as presbyteral minister in realms of the soul, to follow a regime of grace that leads one away from the world. The ministry was highly interiorized and individualized, and the deeper enterprises of the church were rather neglected in their voice and import, even as they were carefully enacted.

Intent upon church renewal, the Baroque church took organization seriously. The Roman church would be an expression of the Body of Christ, but precisely as a rational, efficient arrangement of all the enterprises of the church—missions, congregations, representatives, religious orders, bishops—around the papacy. Just as medieval theology introduced the idea of the pope as the vicar not only of Peter but of Christ, and therefore the head of the church, so the church itself appeared to be in an exemplary way the Vatican. The ministries of the universal and local church were branches of Rome.

Trent had affirmed in the face of Protestantism that Christ is not only redeemer, but the head of the church as well. Trent favored the construction of a hierarchical order, not only around the Eucharist, but also around a regimen where Rome was center and summit. In its well-intentioned and successful attempt to salvage Roman Catholicism in Europe and to bring it to new worlds, the ecclesiology of the papacy brought an end to its counterpart, the local church. The idea of a fairly independent church (or network of churches) with its own geographical and cultural identity seemed dangerous. Was not diversity the root of Protestantism? Moreover, was not Protestantism grounded upon too high an appreciation of charism and upon an experimentation with new forms of ministry? Whatever diversity that had survived the medieval period was mainly ended by Trent. *Local* meant *schismatic; diverse* meant *Protestant.* The papacy was the organizing principle of the church.[62]

And yet, diversity perdured and expanded in the new curial organization and particularly in new religious orders. Many new orders for men and women came into being in the century after 1530 (and even more after 1600 and 1830). They took as their purpose not monastic contemplation nor the general goals of the friars, such as teaching and the intellectual life, but rather pursued a specific work in the church, like the education of orphans or the direction of retreats. A new emphasis upon personal conversion and method in prayer led many to the ministry through religious life. Ministry became less the activity of baptism, charism, or local church and more a call to the vowed life that placed the baptized not in a cloister nor in a fixed state of public dignity but in a missionary post. There was a great deal to be done in and by the church; for the first time in a thousand years the church was called upon to be extra-European.

There was also a countering centralization. If a vocation was a gift of the Spirit calling adults to religious life, church office was a gift of the papacy and of its representatives. A participative theology of the community's ministries faded away, for the universal bishop of Rome and his local vicars, the bishops, were viewed not only as discerners and coordinators but sources. A bishop was interpreted theologically (and improperly) as one who possessed in a plenary and global way all ministry—that is, the one ministry, priesthood. He shared parcels of ministry, the only real ministry, with other Christians, mainly with priests. Particular, local ministries, for instance, to evangelize Indians in Brazil, to counsel the dying in a hospital, to help slaves in Jamaica or homeless girls in Boston, or to preach to the university community or in a rural parish were all aspects of the one ministry bestowed by the one minister or, in a survival of a wider theology of ministry, of the religious order.

The presumption was that, while the Holy Spirit remotely guided this distribution, ultimately public aspects of ministry came less from the personalized charisms of the Spirit or from the community but mainly from the will of church administrators. The necessary and healthy introduction of the Tridentine seminary supported that monoform delegation of ministry. Rather than being called by adult charism to a specific ministry, a young man was formed in a perennial theology and lifestyle so that at a special moment he could be given a share of priestly power. Charism, diversity, and testing by experience and by the community had disappeared. Rome's task was an impossible one: to be present in hundreds of cultures. That responsibility of cultural incarnation was avoided, however, by clothing the Gospel in a single language, law, and theology—that of Rome. The missions were no longer the world of the fourth or ninth centuries, when

Europe was evangelized through new local churches with their admirable bishops. The faith was propagated after the seventeenth century as the extension of Rome. The ministry was tied to a certain form of education, to celibacy, to Western rites. The leaders of the new churches of Africa, Asia, and South America were papal vicars, and local ministry never really surfaced.

There are successes in this approach, and also tragedies. In 1614 in Japan, there were three hundred thousand Christians, but less than one hundred Japanese priests.[63] A sudden persecution quickly and easily eliminated the ministry, and with it most of the church. The Christians who survived did so in small groups deprived for centuries of all sacramental life except baptism. That would not have happened in the third or fifth century, with Cyprian or Patrick, when bishops and ministers could rise out of the communities and adjust liturgy, leadership, and theology to local conditions.

What was the Baroque ministry? What did it serve? Like the Reformers, the Counter-Reformation and the Baroque were interested in the topic of grace. Ministry was service to grace, and grace was a power that came from God to move the free but fallen human will. Salvation was the believing obedient response to grace. This grace, however, did not find its goal only in faith but, for Catholics, extended through all of life. The individual, whether in the Alps of Bavaria or in the Andes of Peru, walked into a Baroque church and was absorbed into the Baroque theology of grace through the light that poured down onto the figures of saints in white and gold. The atmosphere of the church militant on earth reflected the church triumphant in heaven. For the average person, the life of grace was a struggle for a modicum of morality, chastity, and charity. For a more serious Christian (and the invitation was open to all) the life of grace was the inner life; the source and goal of ministry was the interior castle; daily meditation led into darkness and then light. The Baroque spontaneously seized upon two groups as exemplary saints: the missionaries, who brought grace to nations ignorant of it, and the spiritual directors, who guided Europeans into the mystery of the interior life.

This shift in the meaning of grace away from an extrasubjective, public, developmental kingdom of God to the motive force of an interior life assisted in the separation of the public from the spiritual, the secular citizen from the inner believer. Despite the glories of the Spanish, Bavarian, and Italian Baroque, much of the world came to be seen as places of dark and stubborn hostility dominated by Calvinism and then by the Enlightenment. In its model of ministry, Catholic spirituality evaluated this outer world as secular, Protestant, even pagan. The fulfillment of baptism was not ministry to God's reign but an inner call to a persevering life of prayer. The spirituality of men and women in the ministry rarely escaped a tension between prayer and work. In society, ministry faced a hostile world where God's grace seemed present only in the individual. The style of confronting history with God's kingdom was one of infiltration—infiltration *into* and anger *before* a world that had unforgivably entertained Protestantism and the Enlightenment. Hence, some evangelistic, public, and eschatological dimensions of ministry faded. Eventually a theology of entrusting the church to priests, and religion and society to lay people separated further the reign of God from the world. While Catholics struggled to sustain faith and morality in a changing world, for the elect, conversion meant entrance into the new religious congregations where external ministry was something added to the inner spiritual life. Ministry was direct but personal: the kingdom advanced from soul to soul (in France or in Brazil) much as one candle lit from another glowed in the dark. Priests and sisters, however, had a difficult time reconciling the burdens of Christian ministry with the demands of the spiritual life.

In the Western church, there were three families of men and women who lived out their baptism through the vowed life: the monks, the friars, and the Jesuits, who formed the model for the modern congregations. These were not purely chronological groupings but rather—as all lived on through later centuries—three basic styles for the vowed life. With emergence of the Society of Jesus the third period of religious life began, one different from that of the monks and friars, and it set the tone for dozens of congregations of men and women that appeared in the three hundred years after 1540. More or less these groups accepted the approach (and often the spirituality) to religious life of the

Jesuits: a method of prayer, a universal organization with control over and mobility for its members, a replacement of monastic community and spirituality with a modern, professional, ascetic individualism—all at the service of the church.

The theology and personal spirituality of the Society of Jesus influenced the church greatly for several centuries, setting the tone for much of what was new and vital. Through the creative power of the Baroque and the energy of the Jesuits, the Roman Catholic world gained new fields for its ministries. This style of Christian life was influential not only among men and women in vows but among the laity and the diocesan clergy, and among popes and bishops as well. Just as the monastic schools influenced the education of bishops and priests in the twelfth century, so the Jesuits would assume the training of many future priests, and even future popes throughout the world. We can speak of a "Jesuitization" of the ministry within the world of the Baroque as religious and diocesan priests were drawn to the new and helpful spirituality of that order and of those that followed upon its determining mode of religious life. We see this influence in the importance of retreats, in the method of prayer based upon the *Spiritual Exercises,* in the style of dress, and in the rise of private devotions and individual discipline.

A secondary influence of the Jesuits upon the ministry was the tendency of the bishop to comport himself toward his fellow Christians in the ministry as a Jesuit superior. The Jesuit rector had more control over the subjects in his community than the earlier abbot or prior. Unlike the abbot, he could touch the internal spirituality as well as the internal life of his subjects; and, finally, there was the controversial theology of obedience, which identified the superior's will with that of God. This transformation of the coordinator of ministries, the bishop, into an ascetic religious superior (without the human and subtle ethos of the religious order) is one further stage in the absorption and metamorphosis of the ministry into the office of authority. In this ecclesiastical atmosphere the Christian of charism and ministry had few rights: no questions, no insight, no appeal. Here is the final stage of the episcopalization. On the one hand, the ministry terminated in the person of a single bishop, the bishop of

Rome; on the other hand, the bishop ceased to be really a bishop—his charism and work was not realized in preaching, evangelizing, and enabling but in administering and controlling. Moreover, he became a religious superior of a post-Tridentine congregation of men who were his clergy.

As multiple religious orders grew—the Oratorians, the Capuchins, the Redemptorists, for example—a further form of lay ministry emerged, involving hundreds of thousands of Catholics, rendering service to many. That was the world of confraternities, which lasted (with diminishing strength and meaning after World War II) up to Vatican II. These brought men and women, usually in separate organizations, together for some form of study and service focused upon others; typically, confraternities might be responsible for nursing or burying the dead or for building a church of pilgrimage. As the nineteenth century proceeded, the study was usually not of the Bible and the caritative purpose usually consisted of gathering food, clothes, or money but without direct contact with the needy. By and large the confraternities (as well as the oblates and third orders) did not seize upon the post-Council expansion of ministry in order to grow and survive.

Because this cultural epoch faded into the theological impoverishment of the eighteenth century, it received no critique, was not clearly replaced, and never truly ended. Thus its influence lasted on—often without notice. Much of what Roman Catholics came to perceive as patristic or medieval in the church's liturgy and organization came, in fact, from seventeenth-century Baroque influences.

This ministry remained a ministry to grace, to the presence and power of God realized in movements and religious orders. Evangelization and spirituality presented a very real world of church and grace locked in a struggle with the Reformation and the Enlightenment.

F. The Romanticization of Ministry

As the Enlightenment arrived, that brilliant milieu of gold-edged sacramentality withdrew from a world that was becoming cold and uncertain, Protestant and modern. Thus, in the eighteenth century, the light of the Baroque heaven was replaced by the light of scientific reason. This age is probably the nadir of the history of the Catholic Church, with its few priests and its theological stagnation, a church made up of nobility and poor, awaiting the severe measures that the French Revolution would bring to it.

Contrary to its expectations, the Enlightenment did not last forever, not even for a century: Romanticism, with its accompanying Catholic renewal, rapidly replaced it. Friedrich Schlegel, early Romantic and convert to Roman Catholicism in 1804, wrote that three events made the modern world: the French Revolution, Fichte's *Doctrine of the Sciences,* and Goethe's novel *Wilhelm Meister*[64]: that is, freedom, subjectivity, and individual history. This triad led the Enlightenment to its climax, rapidly bringing something new: Romanticism. The Romantic, like the philosopher Friedrich Schelling or the painter Caspar David Friedrich, saw the world vibrating between nature and mind. Nature was a mysterious power of generation and development, and human consciousness was the creator of the world. Art and history might be tragic, but they were, precisely like the development of individual and collective spirit, also the revelation of God. Amid the turbulent world, where new powers burst out of natural sciences and new freedom emerged out of consciousness, stood the solitary, heroic person: possessed of intuition and freedom, part of the universal, absolute process, and yet alone.

The Catholic Baroque had prepared for the Catholic Romantic renewal. The Baroque period of the church did not cease in 1750 but went underground during the Enlightenment and then reemerged with the arrival of Romanticism: its forms and influences lasted well into the twentieth century, up to Vatican II. What joined the Baroque with the nineteenth century? Interest in mysticism, the presence of God in the world, ritual and religious life all encouraged the Baroque to continue, providing forms for ecclesiastical and devotional life. Clearly, the active priest and sister, multiple devotions and apostolates centered in the papacy, and the supernatural in interior emotion and awe-inspiring sacramentality were central to Catholic life in the century and a half prior to Vatican II.

What was ministry in the nineteenth century? In an age calling for universal freedom from ignorance and want, to outsiders the church appeared to be a relic whose demise was near. What was the purpose of being a Christian, of being a priest or a sister, of serving a kingdom in competition with the new kingdoms of humanity, the self, the state, the masses? The German bishops, who were still secular rulers before 1800, represented one collective vocational crisis, a shift from lord to servant; they lost their secular power and by the end of the century were fighting for the political and social rights of Catholics against Bismarck.[65]

The effects of freedom and science, democracy and human rights moved the church, with its antiquities, oppressions, and lost privileges, away from the center of society. The Catholic Church, although attracting some prestigious converts, lived at the edge of society, in a realm viewed as mystical.

In the decades after 1800, however, a surprising renewal of Roman Catholicism took place. During the period of Romantic idealism in Germany and France, with allied movements in Belgium and Ireland, new views of the church—organic, active, universal, charismatic, and ministerial—developed among Catholics. Conversing with the thought-forms of the times as personified in Schelling's romantic idealism, theologians laid a base for a rediscovery of church charism and life. Scholars in Munich and Tübingen and thinkers from all walks of life in Bonn, Münster, and Vienna created centers of a new Catholicism that were very much the products of laity and priests, men and women working together. Johann Adam Möhler's *Unity in the Church* presented an ecclesiology of startling newness: the Christian church was an organism, a living totality whose present and past flowed out of diversity in the community,[66] and F. A. Staudenmaier, professor at Tübingen, wrote a book in 1835 on the "pragmatism of charisms," elaborating a theory of the activity of the Spirit in each individual serving church and society. The church cultivated the talents of laymen like Montalambert and Görres, who confronted authoritarianism in church and state and absorbed the best of the new philosophy and literature.

During the Romantic restoration the monastic orders reappeared along with their art and liturgy. New missionary congregations, for home and abroad, appeared by the dozens, but their general style of religious life was rooted in the sixteenth century. Thus, attempts by groups of laywomen to develop new modes of service and dedicated lifestyles were inevitably directed by the church into already existing forms. The number of workers increased, but a sameness spread over the Catholic Church. Ministerial diversity and ecclesial variety could be found, but outside of parish and diocese. The impoverished position of the laity is illustrated by the reduction of the public services of the confraternities to brief devotions, by religious education identified with a catechism, and by a negative theology classifying laypeople as not monastic or clerical.[67] Pius IX and Vatican I singled out monarchical power as the aspect of the church worthy of emphasis. Neo-scholasticism replaced the leitmotif of organic community with the episcopacy as a power station of efficient and formal causalities. Charism was kept on the side (for the occasional saint or eccentric), and the independent activity of the baptized was relegated to areas of justice.

So the nineteenth century became a time of restoration. In Europe great Romanesque and Gothic churches were restored, and in England and America there was an assertion of wider ministry in controversies over parish and diocesan direction and in the founding of new American religious communities. In Europe venerable religious orders were restored. Prosper Guéranger brought back Benedictine life while Lacordaire, already a spellbinding preacher at Notre Dame and unofficial spiritual director to the youth of Paris, dramatically left the pulpit and entered a novitiate in Italy to restore the Dominican order beyond its fragile existence in Italy and Spain. Just as Solesmes' liturgy was a Romantic expression of a patristic and medieval mysticism, so Lacordaire's preaching in his white and black habit was a Romantic confrontation with secularity. Motifs of high emotion, solitary heroism, mystical faith, a transforming vision of society, and the renunciation of all that was secular were present in these figures and their communities.

But when hopes of restoration if not renewal and transformation cooled after 1848, other faces of the Roman Catholic

Church in the nineteenth century showed themselves. After 1848, however, the papacy, along with political life in Europe, grew conservative. Gregory XVI and Pius IX, popes from 1831 to 1878, directed church business from Rome. As Europeans favored strong authority so some Catholics—"ultramontanes," who sought authority beyond the mountains in Rome—joined an openness toward new philosophy and theology with a critique of civil authority and an unrealistically idealistic view of the papacy. Romanticism helped the church to continue and grow, but in a partly backward-looking style. There was a distrust of the world, society, and the state. Mysticism rather than ministry was cultivated. The literature of piety in France prepared for an isolation and individualization of the priesthood. The priest was placed in a mystical niche, exalted, described as metaphysically equal to, even higher than angelic beings. He lost his roots in the community and in the wider, diverse church. His power in the Eucharist and in penance seemed personal gifts without any source in word or community. Bishops and priests moved or were moved to the edge of society. There they experienced their powerlessness, they nourished a theology of the world as sinful, and they turned inward in their theology, away from the kingdom of God to a spirituality of the soul in prayer. The secularity and evolutionism of the nineteenth century brought with it some denial of the supernatural. The structure of church ministry crumbled as the framework of medieval society was dismantled and a new society—a secular "kingdom of God" on earth—was planned. The new politics of the secular, democratic state replaced the ministry as "teacher" of the way to heaven, as "servant" of charity in this life. An array of thinkers declared that society would render any teaching about a future kingdom of God unnecessary. They further predicted the new state would elevate the poor or disenfranchised to new heights, thus depriving the church of its chief clients. In the face of a hostile or competitive society, the church turned inward; grace became an interior condition of personal life. Christian life was mainly preservative of the state of grace.

A symbol of the marginalization of the ministry is the Curé of Ars, beatified in 1905 as a model of the diocesan clergy. The

Curé was a holy, dedicated man, but his ministry was not particularly typical of life in the local church of the time. He lived in an insignificant place geographically; his preaching and liturgy were admittedly undistinguished. He attracted and helped a large number of people, but his service was one of personal direction, of counsel and forgiveness, usually in the form of the sacrament of penance. His sanctity was his discipline; his struggle with his own personality and with the demonic was, as all sanctity ultimately is, personal. The church saw in Jean-Marie Vianney a beacon for the supernatural in a time of darkness (a motif his biographers frequently chose). Alone in the confessional, he experienced the supernatural in life, and he led others to experience, at times dramatically, that power at a time when the supernatural was ridiculed as outmoded, replaceable, illusionary. The ministry of the Curé of Ars, however, was experiential and individual; it was not a ministry to confront the world with the kingdom, but rather a ministry to the spark of real or potential grace that lies in each individual. In this ministry of exploration, of personal dialogue with grace, the Curé showed himself to be a modern person. Nonetheless, his ministry could not be viewed as parish ministry itself, but as one particular ministry, one indeed on the margin of church and society.

Noticing how the church recognized this ministry on the margin of society as exemplary for all ministry, we are not looking simply at a French phenomenon, for in Italy and Spain, in parts of Germany, in England, Ireland, Australia, and the United States, the Catholic Church was embattled. In one place it appeared to be a minority of strong believers, while in another place it represented fading clerical privilege. The church was on the defensive and could not yet understand how it might appropriate the forms of the modern world and still be faithful to Gospel and tradition. How skewed and inappropriate is Paul Claudel's praise in the first part of this century of that dark architectural curiosity, Sacré Coeur—"the final and complete achievement of the new idea: an always visible God, an always present people; the exaltation of the bread, the display of the secret heart"[68]—but how apt his words were for a church whose words were largely silent and whose symbols were little understood. The ministry of the Curé of Ars and the events of Lourdes nourished the faith of many individuals, but they did not challenge either the hostility or impersonality of the secular state. They did not lead to a Christian politics whose charisms in matters of socialization and war were soon to be desperately needed but little found. The focus of ministry was grace on earth in remarkable signs and individuals. The church of the nineteenth century almost unconsciously prepared various kinds of people for service in the modern world: the mystic, the neomedieval monk, the political activist, the solitary priest, the conservative churchman, the papal administrator. But it did not distinguish ministry from mysticism.

The nineteenth century had its originality (adding a neomedieval restoration), but that age more often than not composed variations on the Baroque. Grace, and ministry to grace, was described in an increasingly mechanical mode, a theological style that, throughout the centuries and even the decades just before the Council, made the Catholic Church appear as a pumping station at the center of an extensive waterworks of grace. A mechanics of graces, sacraments, and moral decisions had become an elaborate enterprise, as rapid but valid rituals brought grace, or rescripts and dispensations removed obstacles to grace. Piety became quite interior, capable of being cut off from ordinary life and ministry: thinking was subservient to devotion just as ministry was subservient to the *bella figura* of churchmen. Christians were passive attendants at devotions whose Baroque origins and symbolism were increasingly unclear. The optimistic splendor of the Baroque was partly overshadowed by an ethos of suffering and guilt suited to a church somewhat marginalized from society. In fact, what the Baroque had drawn together in sacramental splendor was too fixed on the heavenly and too hostile to the human.

G. *The Renewal of Vatican II*

The years from about 1880 to Vatican II, the final stage of that hybrid era, certainly had their own identity (this is the only period of the past that Catholics in this century have experienced). That era's statues and devotions may represent an ethnic tradition, a medieval theology, or Baroque devotions, but they must be explained. American Catholics in the period before Vatican II were ignorant of their history—immigrants have little time for the past. What came from the early or medieval church, and what from the nineteenth century? What came from French royalists and what from the Slovakian Rococo? Few bishops knew, much less firemen and farmers, but various past ages were brought together inaccurately under a broad rubric of antiquity. Catholics and others imagined that the preconciliar church exemplified life in Roman catacombs or Cistercian monasteries, when, in fact, its liturgy and devotions (e.g., solemn high mass, devotions and novenas, the Sacred Heart, or Lourdes) were those of the Baroque or the nineteenth century.

The expansion of fraternities in the sodalities—this was an attempt to expand the reality of the religious congregation to a wider membership—from 1700 to 1950 was extensive. They in turn led to movements of Catholic action and further into a rather anonymous, secular, individual group of the secular institute. Begun by laymen, the popes from Leo XIII to Pius XII encouraged the various forms of Catholic Action. This ensemble of movements aimed at ministry for laypeople: while it addressed the temporal order of politics and labor, it included the hope of evangelization and witness. "The lay apostolate was grounded in a supernatural ontology of the Christian—baptism, confirmation, spiritual gifts and charisms, the obligation of examining one's conscience,...an invitation to 'participate in the hierarchical apostolate.' "[69] There was considerable success in reclaiming certain sectors of society like young workers or politicians, and the ethos led to the important Christian democratic parties after World War II, but apart from narrow cadres of meetings or clear European secular hostility, the ministry of Catholic Action was unclear and frustrated. This is signified by the fact that its varied good deeds touched neither the liturgy nor the direct sacramental and preaching life of the parish; there the active laity were utterly passive. The field for this apostolate was an amorphous social field that was not quite social and not quite religious, and the ministerial activity was too often reduced to witnessing. Church and ministry were seen as a monoform hierarchy of priests (the bishop was mainly a priest; there were no functioning deacons) who could share parcels of what they alone possessed fully and sovereignly. No nuances were made between the nature of the early ministry of the twelve apostles and that of a local bishop; no questions were raised about the active role for the community in the emergence of all ministries, even in those receiving a commission from the Twelve or from other churches.[70] These forms in the twentieth century, while indications of the Spirit's intention of wider ministry beyond the ordained, were inevitably frustrating, particularly in the United States. Men and women found little to do that was directly connected to the church (washing linens, coaching boxing) or nothing at all to do. They were marked by a clear exclusion from the sacral and liturgical, and nourished by a not fully honest or realistic spirituality that viewed them as sharing in the ministry of apostles and bishops.

The preparatory importance of Catholic Action was enormous but so was its essential weakness. Vatican II's thought on the "lay apostolate" is different, for it sees it as "a participation in the saving mission of the church itself"—a stronger, more central mission—although it goes on to offer the metaphorical vision of "places and circumstances where only through them can it become the salt of the earth."[71]

By 1950 we come to the end of this ecclesial late Romanticism. New scientific, technological, political, and religious issues and ways of thinking were presiding over Europe and North America. The church in France had confessed itself to be a missionary country, and renewal in liturgy, education, and pastoral theology followed, finding its similarities in other European countries. The church discovered or retrieved biblical and patristic ideas for its new theology, liturgy, and mission. Yet, while European theologians prepared for the event of Vatican II, parallel movements preserving the Romantic, antiworldly mysticism of the nineteenth century remained influential. We see them in the novels of Georges Bernanos (*The Diary of a Country Priest* draws on the experience of France and Ars) and François Mauriac; we see them in the lives and writing of mystics, in the philosophy of Jacques Maritain, and in the early motifs of Thomas Merton.

We must note one area where the ministry did expand in a

particularly forceful way, an expansion that even today has not been fully evaluated: the new forms of religious life for women, and, consequent upon this, the new role of women religious in the modern church and society. In the twelfth, sixteenth, and seventeenth centuries, women and men had slowly prepared the church and society for communities of dedicated women who, eschewing the cloister, would minister through education and varied forms of health care to so many. The nineteenth century saw not only the formation of many congregations of religious women but also—and we appreciate them from a later perspective—witnessed the founding of communities that comprised new forms of religious life. The congregations founded after the French Revolution, and in the United States in great numbers after 1830, appear first as provinces or foundations of European communities or as sisters of the third orders of Dominic or Francis. In fact, they are something new in the history of religious life. The American sister became something more than a member of a third order; nor is she by any phenomenological standard a lay person, but a paragon of ministry. The large and numerous achievements in institutions of education and health care, and the high level of offices in education and in other areas of public life attained by these women indicate that something radically new appeared. From the point of view of quality in education, commitment, and ministry, religious women are the outstanding group in the Roman Catholic Church in America. They raise by their existence as much as by their desire for equality many questions for a theology of contemporary ministry. First, as we have just mentioned, they embody the latest revolution in the form of religious life. Second, they do well over half of the public ministry of the Roman Catholic Church and have done so for over a century. Out of these facts and paradoxes come two questions for religious life. The first questions the sense of the previous distinction between laity and clergy when ministering religious women (and men who are not presbyters) are called "laity." Second, this new realization of religious life for women—which in all appearances was ministerial—naturally raises the issue of a public recognition of women in the ministry. Theologians argued for the restored diaconate at Vatican II by pointing out that the ministry and the ministers of the diaconate existed; what was lacking was the church's liturgical confirmation in public. The same is true with the vast and varied ministry of religious women. Their ministry is particularly striking; what is lacking is the public, sacramental affirmation of it by the church, which claims to prize sacrament.

In short, the events of the nineteenth century were twofold and paradoxical. There was a new theology of the organic totality of the church, and there was the restoration of an excessively episcopal ecclesiology in neo-scholastic phraseology. There was the emphasis upon the mystical hero and the multiplicity of new religious communities; there were new institutions and services; and there was a new resurgence of papalist centrism. All, including the search for a happier, theonomous time in a restored medievalism, had contributions to make. It was as if, in the decades leading up to Vatican II, the motifs of the great periods of ecclesiology were paraded forth: the church of the apostle, the bishop, the medieval hierarchies, the Baroque and Romantic saints.

Yves Congar points out that the ministry of the priest on the eve of Vatican II is dominated by the theology of the Council of Trent and by the spirituality of the French School (Pierre Bérulle, Jean Eudes). The Council ultimately did not accept the reduction of the priesthood (the sole ministry in real existence) to the sacrifice of the altar, but it moved in that direction. In the following centuries two aspects of a religious ontology of consecration and of a ministry of communicating divine life to people are found in the French School of the seventeenth century, giving not only a deserved holiness and importance to the priesthood but unfortunately making of it a too automatic or physically privileged "object." Christ is a priest by his Incarnation, and the participation of priests in this mystery can occur through their personal sanctity and their power at the altar, but the nature and quality of the priest's concrete ministry is not emphasized. The need at that time was to have a personal spirituality of fidelity to a certain mode of life and to have zeal and some theological understanding, but the directions of priestly life were not extensive. The priest was a pastor of the interior life rather than presider over an active parish, and this period from Charles Borromeo to the Curé of Ars has joined to the activity of the priesthood an ascetical life more or less transposed from monasticism.[72] After the First World War there were new directions alongside of Trent and the Baroque. A new social situation demands a new approach. The priesthood assumed a more social and evangelistic role, and other Christians were drawn into ministry under the direction of an expansion of studies in ecclesiology, a broader spirituality involving institutions, and attention to preaching and liturgy.[73] The priest's ministry was seen within the community, within the larger reality of the apostolate. Wider communities was the challenge presented by Vatican II.

In the United States lay movements in the American church (there had been a number of them in the European church in the previous century) began to appear in the 1940s. They ranged from those with a liturgical, theological, or artistic focus to pacifist groups and sports clubs. Publishing houses and journals of a progressive nature were often in the hands of the laity (although the Paulists and the Jesuits were pioneers in richer ways of presenting the church in journals and books). Centers of social action were founded by women, and institutions in education and health care raised a consciousness among American Catholics that laity and religious women were highly capable in all ministries.[74]

Shortly after the Council, for the important series of commentaries published by Editions du Cerf, Henri Denis offered not so much a contrast as a historical movement, a trajectory, a development from Trent beyond Vatican II. We should, of course, not be surprised at developments that continue and complete. The understanding of the priesthood moved within the celebration of the Eucharist (Trent) to the mission of the church (Vatican II). The institution of the priesthood drew not only on the Last Supper (Trent) but on the institution of apostles and ministers in their totality (Vatican II). The specificity of the priesthood included not only the power of the Eucharist but action in the name of Christ, head of his Body, the church, and so the priesthood as service was not only cultic (Trent) but apostolic (Vatican II). There was finally a movement from a theocentric ministry to the activity and presence of the priest in the world, from cult to a variety of ministries.[75]

With Vatican II we reach the period of intensity in theological education, ecclesiology, and ministry itself, which this book reflects and interprets. One can no longer make sense of the church by presuming that most of its members are passive laity, even as theological and ministerial education in service of Catholicism has so expanded. Should we expect a fourth great family of religious orders (beyond monks, friars, and congregations)? We see the emergence of a large number of men and women in the service of the church (some sociologists have observed that never in the history of Christianity have there been so many in the ministry), but we do not find them founding new permanent organizations of vowed members. There will be many constellations of ministry and spirituality, but all the signs indicate they will comprise something new, outside of the clerical order and the religious orders.

II. Ministry and History

The six metamorphoses that ministry has undergone over two millennia are six acts of a pageant. Their variety describes not the entire story but rather the peaks along the cultural, ontological, and pneumatic history of Christian ministry. The triumphs and the limitations of ministry—evangelist, bishop, priest, monk, Herr Pastor, cure—all of these are the products of culture.

There are always some who claim for their time and style a perennial value. Ministers in every century have argued that their form of *diakonia* fulfilled the Spirit's reality of service to the kingdom. Frequently a period forgot part of the past and failed to imagine the future. The lesson of the history of ministry is that one should not claim an eternal superiority. The life of the Spirit in the church never ceases.

We have avoided negative judgments on these past realizations of Christian ministry. In matters of culture it is instructive to contemplate the form but best to avoid comparisons. We have been taught to view history as an evolution toward the better. In fact, history is a chain of different periods wherein one epoch illustrates one side of ministry and then another period draws out a different style. The six major periods we have surveyed succeeded in the goal of ministry. At the same time, even in their success, time and culture imposed limits upon the ministry, whether of the third or the thirteenth century.

Second, we have not been looking merely at history. Because of the importance of the primal event of the early church and of tradition, and because of the tendencies in Christian churches to try to halt time or to fear change, all of these forms of ministry have survived. They live on; they are our past; they influence our future. We have then been looking not at history but at the roots of our thinking about ministry. We have seen the sources of the church forms that we now possess.

The process, beneath the rich and complex tapestry of its records in ink and stone, is tradition. That venerable and often controversial aspect of the Christian church, tradition, can be described as the history of Christian community manifest in cultural forms and articulated in theology, liturgy, and prayer. The distinction between the primal but lasting nature of the church and its forms is at the basis of tradition: the church is committed to the past even as it searches for ministry today. The history of ministry raises two issues about tradition. Does it live within or apart from the flow of history? Is a tradition easily discerned?

Religion always longs for a golden age. Was there ever a time that did not view itself as holding a divine guarantee that no other age—all others were blank or corrupted by sin—could approach? There is never a golden age: every period has its limitations. For American Catholic reflections on ministry, it is unrealistic to imagine a golden age of many vocations: for many parts of the United States such a time did not exist or existed for less than a decade. Moreover, that age did not have to minister to the vast churches of today, and many of those large numbers of priests and sisters never remained within the active ministry. In Latin America and Africa, there never was a period when a celibate clergy reached an indigenous and extensive level. Other areas have always been dependent upon Europe and North America for ministers. No time is perfect, no age is the standard, no culture was sublimely integral or especially theonomous. There never was a golden age. Churches look back to a golden age. The Church of Byzantium looked back to the time of the great theologians and councils of the church; the churches of the Reformation imagined that the sixteenth century was a time of singular evangelical freedom. How much effort did Roman Catholicism spend in the past hundred years trying not only in theology but in art and educational theory to reproduce the thirteenth century? If there was an *age d'or* for the church, then faith in the Christian community would not focus upon the life of the Spirit but rather upon the view of a scholar or an aesthete. A single golden period would accomplish the impossible; it would contain the entirety of the kingdom of God, and it would have harnessed all the powers of the Holy Spirit. The idea of a single normative, historical time for the church is dangerous and close to idolatry because it locates the Spirit of God within very finite limitations. Moreover, it strikes at the mission of the church (and how often evangelism has been crippled because the fullness of the Gospel was hidden in the propagated civilization of its preachers) as it communicates that the church is not capable of nourishing the mustard tree of Christ living in all times or spreading to the ends of the earth.

Patristic and modern theologies interpret tradition not as texts and written principles but first as the living consciousness of the Christian community reflecting upon itself and its past. Tradition includes not only wisdom from past epochs but failures as well. Upon closer inspection we see that the history of ministry is often a "negative tradition." The church has long periods of not having this or that ministry; earlier ministerial forms or faithful interpretations of ministry were not always retained. A devolution implies a negative tradition, that is, the historical record is often not one of hammering out ministerial forms but of letting ministries and structures of community life fade away. Centuries passed during which there was no discussion of ministry outside of that concerning the spirituality of the celibate male priest. Negative tradition does not transmit fully Gospel and Spirit in tradition. Because tradition is so important a safeguard of revelation, we should be slow to call a particular tradition a fact or view it as a practical area. We should be aware that there is in certain areas a lack of discussion and theology—in those areas the Spirit seeks to enlighten the church, even to the extent that we must speak of "negative traditions," that is, questions that have been resolved over a period of time but without any discussion of them. A negative tradition is not an engagement of the organic life of the church whose soul is the Spirit but simply the nonconsideration or minimal consideration of an area.[76]

There was an extraordinary variety in the first decades among the Christian churches when Easter and Pentecost were new. Every subsequent generation looks to that experience—not as to a confining law but as to a revelatory experience rich with more and more possibilities for ministry. Modern theology interprets tradition not as written norms but as the living consciousness of the Christian community reflecting upon itself (its world and its ministries) and its past. Similarly, change is neither an instant revolution nor a chain of successes. In old and huge organizations like the Catholic Church, change is a complex phenomenon. The past never fully disappears; old forms are not fully replaced; the new must be both incarnational and traditional. If these shifts in church life are considerable and fraught with further implications, nonetheless, their day-to-day realization in the life of the local church is ordinary. The Spirit never fails to offer the church charisms adequate to the opportunities, and thus through pastoral responsibility rather than grandiose administrative centers, "We are shepherds of the future."[77]

A MINISTERING CHURCH

What is ministry? It is not fashionable in contemporary culture to define something: to describe precisely a social reality, to see its nature and to accept its limits. If we do not have some clarity about ministry, we will not be able to understand what is perduring, what is changing, and what is new. We need to distinguish (but not separate) the gifts of Jesus' Spirit to his followers from their vital cultural form. The expansion of the number of serious ministries and the quest by willing baptized men and women for part-time and full-time ministries is not in America a return to trusteeism nor in Africa or Latin America a presumption of leadership, but an awareness of a richer Christian life than attendance at Sunday mass. The number of men and women desirous of entering professional ministry is climbing. Deciding on the basis of recent devotional phrases that only priests are really active in church service or locating ministry in every good human enterprise weakens ministry.

What is ministry?

If we follow too empirical an approach, ministry will be whatever a church group decides. When ministry lies everywhere at hand, after a short-term exuberance it lies neglected. Soon it loses its attraction and fades away. On the other hand, when a definition is too ready and a meaning, given by language or ontology is imposed as divine and eternal but comes from Carolingian or Renaissance societies, then there can be nothing new in ministry, for the realm of the prophetic and diaconal tinted with the blood of missionaries and martyrs has been turned into an ecclesiastical and legal set of identification cards, external appointments without a clear reference to reality, either divine or ecclesial.

There are different ways of defining ministry. One approach is to set forth a metaphysical definition (largely Aristotelian)

139

according to which all problems can be logically solved. This approach, however, overlooks the fact that ministry, like revelation, is God's Word and event in human history. Theological expressions of revelation can never attain the ultimacy of revelation; they are always reflections in human conceptuality and language upon revelation. The New Testament bestows ministry, commands ministry, describes the characteristics of ministry, but it does not define ministry nor proffer lists or job descriptions.

A second approach is to search for the nature of ministry in the tradition of the Church and the churches. The Christian churches, as these chapters show, have received ministry from charisms given in the midst of various cultural moments. We should take seriously these different ecclesial-cultural forms and perspectives, for they contribute phenomenologically to a definition of ministry. For instance, in the perspective of the Syrian Church, poetry replaced logic, and liturgy and spirituality were more prominent than organization; the ecclesiology of Ephrem's hymns contrasts with the rigor of Bellarmine's tracts. History's diversity is, however, a guide and not a definition.

A third way, suggested by our society's preference for rapid changes, finds the best guide to ministry in what is actually being done. What works is the real; the newest is the best. Certainly the thought-forms of society and the needs of the world are the forum of ministry, but they do not determine fully its nature or its forms. Revelation, church, Gospel, and tradition have a role. Times change, and when a church commits itself too precipitously or too fully to one ministerial style or rejects the Spirit present in other or past ministerial traditions, or when it identifies ministry with this work and style here and now, that church will have to fight for its life when the next cultural epoch arrives.

Our Western minds long for unanimity, and so we may be disappointed in our search for one rigorous definition in ecclesiology, just as a Christian is disappointed in a search for one view of Christ or one eucharistic liturgy. We do not find just one ministry or a single definition of ministry in the New Testament. We can see, however, that plurality and potentiality help the Gospel appeal to a succession of civilizations. Without pluralism the church would already have exhausted itself long before reaching Persia or Ireland.

The variety of the New Testament is not a sign of relativism but an affirmation of its ability to present the definitive religious event of the human race in all its richness. For that reason, not only before the mystery of Christ, but before the style and forms of Christian life in community, we stand as learners, researchers, contemplatives, ready to draw forth things old and new.

When the approaches of fundamentalisms of the Bible or of canon law and neo-scholasticism are set aside, complaints are heard that Christianity, even Roman Catholicism, has lost the ability to give certain answers. Some questions, however, are too close or too removed from the Word of God to support only one certain answer. Ecclesiology is not at the center of God's revelation in the way that God's grace or the person of Jesus is. In the daily life of the local church we should be slow to find easily God's sole format. Because history and society intrude into the Christian community's life, one way of answering a complex theological question is to sketch the parameters of an answer. To disclose what ministry might be, let us draw forth some characteristics from the New Testament. They establish parameters (positive and negative) for describing the nature of ministry.

I. Characteristics of Ministry

We return for a moment to the world of apostolic churches, not to present antiques from the sacristy or to claim a canonical delineation given by Jesus, but to draw out a phenomenology of ministry from its essential aspects already sketched in a previous chapter from biblical sources.

Six characteristics stand out in forming all ministry and each ministry. Theologically they compose a kind of nature of ministry. Let us look at each briefly. Ministry is: (1) doing something; (2) for the advent and presence of the kingdom of God; (3) in public; (4) on behalf of a Christian community; (5) as a gift received in faith, baptism, and ordination; and (6) as an activity with its own limits and identity existing within a diversity of ministerial actions.

(1) Doing Something. The Christians in the first churches, avoiding any appropriation of sacral language, depicted church

life by using words that reflected the ordinary and the active. With only a few exceptions, verbs used to describe the ministries connoted actions undertaken to sustain and spread the Gospel. Over the centuries those Greek action words became sacred offices. We are rediscovering the original language-event of ministry, its linguistic preference for doing. A Christian is not baptized into a tribe or race or into a passive group of neophytes or into a gnostic study club but into an active community: into church but also into service in the church. Some English words (inevitably with their sources in Roman legal and political life)— *office, role, state, order*–when used to express ministry, have drawbacks in their meanings and implications, because the element of action is suppressed, and too, activity as service can be obscured by the structures of laity, religious life, and clericalism.

(2) For the Kingdom of God. Not every noble movement or good deed is ecclesial ministry. *When everything is ministry, nothing is ministry.* We are looking for characteristics of Christian ministry (we admit that ministry to grace can exist in other religions, since grace can be present in them, a grace which Christians believe finds its full revelation in Christ), and that ministry has the clear purpose of serving the kingdom of God as brought and preached by Jesus. Ministry makes the kingdom explicit, turning its ambiguous presence into sacrament, word, or action. Word and deed are offspring and servants of the kingdom of God. The first Christians were intent upon preaching the newness of this kingdom broken into history, and the public nature of their faith converted or antagonized their world. While Christian ministry must display patience in leading to (and not forcing) faith, and while ministry ultimately serves the inner conversation of a person with grace and not church politics, a ministry normally is a recognizable service of the kingdom. Call it "grace," "salvation," "faith," "Holy Spirit," "justice," or "reign of God"—they are all the objects of direct and immediate ministry.

(3) A Public Action. The New Testament speaks of Christians announcing their faith in God's presence "openly." Public preaching is ministry and liturgy (Rom 15:16). There is no doubt that the first Christians saw the witness of their lives as a

service to the Gospel (Rom 12:1; 16:19). When we say that ministry is public, we mean that the ministry normally takes on a visible and public form in words and deeds; this does not mean it is caught up in politics or the media, or that it is always ostentatious or articulate, but that it passes beyond the interior and silent and communicates its message or action to other people clearly. Its inner dynamics moves away from vague gesture to explicit statement. Through the centuries the communication of the Gospel has not been done mainly through uncertain signs, such as justice in commercial dealings or in a casual neighborliness (although these may be part of Christian life). When we recall the incarnation of grace, according to which the prophetic Jesus confronts the world's sin and death, we understand the uncompromisingly public nature of ministry.

We should not accept an interpretation of baptism which asserts that the main activity of the baptized is only a passive participation in liturgy. The theologies of the laity in this century failed in their attempt to give the laity a place in the community precisely because they joined a liturgical role that was passive or routine to a vaguely defined role of witnessing in the world. Liturgy is the nourishment of life and therein the root of the sacraments, but liturgical life is not the single goal of baptism. Liturgy nourishes a life holding some ministerial involvement. It is difficult to restrict, a priori, all public evangelical and liturgical activity to a small group in one ministry and at the same time be realistic about how baptized Christians are active in their evangelical faith. The public characteristic of ministry challenges any rechanneling of Christian service into liturgy alone or into inner piety.

Some Christians, because of age or illness or some other factor, are limited in the public aspect of their ministry. Their limited service in prayer and in the symbolism of their life can be a great grace for the entire Body of Christ. But this is not the norm of ministry. Prayer and suffering may be the life's blood of ministers but they are not the ministry itself. Prayer communicates between an individual or a group and God, but it too must be translated into concrete service.

With the entry of large numbers into urban churches, the leader of the Christian community in the third and fourth

centuries faced (and, from our perspective, never solved) the
problem of how all the baptized could be in the ministry. Today,
at a time of expansion in ministries, we should not present
Christians in prayer as the norm of ministry, nor should we cloak
Christian communities' passivity with a sacral language of offering and suffering in order to locate everyone easily in the ministry. So the public nature of the ministry questions members of
the clergy whose work is not clearly ministerial just as it challenges the existence in the churches of a passive laity.

The church through the centuries has struggled to overcome this reduction of the ministry. Religious orders served this
purpose as did associations of laity (the very popular brotherhoods, sodalities, and third orders). After the Reformation and
the French Revolution, the ministerial side of the church's life
looked inward. Often contemplative monasticism was seen as the
ministry par excellence. Canonized saints were by and large cloistered contemplatives or foreign missionaries; some were eccentric or reclusive. The laity had been rendered largely secular and
immobile, and church authority in Europe and in North America did not trust what it might not be able to control. In Christian
countries (which were in fact becoming de-Christianized) ministry at the parish and diocesan levels was only feebly addressing
the modern world. If the religious orders kept alive the diversity
of ministry, movements such as *Action Française,* Jocists, secular
institutes, and various forms of the "apostolate of the laity" struggled to offer ministry. But those movements from the first half of
this century occurred largely outside the church and its liturgy,
in the secular sphere. Moreover, they were to be seen as a share
in the bishops' or pope's ministry: ministry was an "apostolate,"
something to be grounded in the twelve apostles' successors, the
bishops. The roles of Spirit and community were overlooked.
The theology of baptism as a primal commissioning was awaiting
rediscovery. One could praise the baptized in devotional language, but neither the code of canon law of 1917 nor a modern
form of Christian life such as the secular institute succeeded in
calling the baptized to real ministry. Moreover, the apostolate
held out to the laity was generally limited to tasks such as collecting old clothes or coaching sports. When ordained ministers did

try to find ministries for the laity, the alloted tasks were often restrictive and trivial. Where the baptized took up public service, as with *Action Française* or the Catholic Worker movement, the work was significant but it was *outside* the church—in social or political issues, services, and structures.

The legal usage of *laity* froze all Christians who were not ordained priests in a passive state, as Karl Rahner pointed out in 1955.[1] It did not touch the teaching and sacramental life of the church, and so it could be kept at a distance by the hierarchy. Nevertheless, in touch with the inner mind of the church and with the Holy Spirit, the twentieth century has seen a generous, genial surge of activity by Christian men and women; zealous and imaginative, they worked well, often independent of official leadership, and they have been precursors of the present expansion of the ministry.

The church must encourage real universality of ministry and not reduce it to symbols and metaphors or casual kindness. If the first Christians had exercised only good cheer, the Gospel would still be in the suburbs of Jerusalem. A sign can be an image, a gesture, and so serve grace, but normally ministry is more than signs. True ministry connects eleemosynary and caring deeds with the values of the Gospel; it develops social programs out of the inner dynamic and Word of the kingdom of God. It is an external expansion of an invisible internal faith. Through the Council, Catholic Action on the edge of the church enters the church to take part in liturgy and then moves into other areas of parish service.

Christian life is not the same as ministry. It is certainly the backdrop to ministry, but it is wider than church ministry. If aspects of evangelical life such as justice, courage, and temperance flow from commitment to faith in the Gospel and are requirements for being a true Christian, they do not inevitably comprise ministry. Ministry brings something more specific: namely, public voice and action directly for the kingdom. Justice and mercy are incumbent upon all Christians. The bank teller who witnesses to his faith by being joyful and honest lives as a Christian and may even exercise a ministry of sign, but a sign is slow in its efficacy and unclear and needs interpretation. Upon the virtuous bank teller too, during stages of his or her life, is incumbent some public ministry for the church and kingdom.

Even as we insist that ministry be both action and public action, we recognize there is room for the ministry of sign. The Christian gesture, an exemplary life, and involvement for good can be symbols that speak to people. Signs are usually ambiguous; they need interpretation. Lack of interpretation is the reason why ministry as sign is an analogous form of service and why sign is not the place to begin a definition of ministry. The sign is a secondary expression of faith, and the interpretation of the sign—the explanation of a Christian's honesty and joy, witness, or limited lifestyle—is necessary for the sign to be ministry. Signs are a silent ministry. Interpretation turns signs into public addresses.

(4) On Behalf of a Christian Community. Ministry begins with the Christian community, flows out of the community, and nourishes and expands the community. Many ministries are needed to sustain a community because there are many things to be done in word, sacrament, service, and evangelism. A community evangelizes new members as well as educates Christians young and old. There are ministries internal to the church, and also ministries from the church into the world; all men and women may respond to the presence of the Gospel and the Spirit. This brings us back to the conviction that ministry serves the kingdom just as the church does; both are the results as well as the catalysts and sacraments of the kingdom; both are creations of the kingdom and have their justification not in themselves but in the kingdom. Whether on a university campus or in an urban hospital, the minister ultimately ministers to grace, while the church is the wider living source of ministry and servant of grace.

Both biblical faith and ministerial experience show that the dialectic of sin and grace in today's society is not easily mapped. One thing is clear: life in the church and obedience toward the church and its creeds are not lines corralling grace. The rediscovery of the breadth of the kingdom of God around the church brings a theological conclusion: ministry is not only the administration of churches but the enabling of the church itself to serve and to speak the grace of the kingdom. The minister does not have the responsibility of judging the presence of grace, nor the tiring burden of insisting that salvation is simply church membership. Ministry is not a badge, not an office,[2] not a cliché, but a spectrum of various concrete and helpful services to grace. Ministry's place lies within the buildings of the church, but its milieu is the human personality permeated by God's plan. For the ministers, the prayer "Thy kingdom come," is one of commitment, but also of consolation, for that kingdom enables ministry.

Jesus' ministry in the New Testament is not only a ministry of preaching the kingdom but one of confronting the antitheses of the kingdom. These evils—sin, illness, madness, injustice, and death—are the visible effects in our human condition of fallenness or original sin. Ministry against them is prominent in the New Testament, and yet, is helping the sick and the poor a direct ministry of church to revelation and religion? Christians have traditionally answered affirmatively. Following Jesus, all human efforts to relieve these signs and effects of sin are fields of ministry. Apparently, for the Savior's particular perspective on world illness, injustice and want are not chance occurrences. He views them as endemic tragedies flowing not only from natural or social causes but from sin; they are opposed to the Father's plan and so the advent of the kingdom cannot leave them unchallenged. The act of nursing the sick not only imitates Jesus but serves the triumph of love and life over sin. In areas of personal and social service we should not be too strict in delineating what is and what is not ministry for the Christian community. Jesus places service to the kingdom not only in words of faith and hope but in deeds of justice and mercy confronting sin and death. It is not that ministry to the human person is added on to religion but, for the Christian faith, it lies at the heart of what religion proclaims. By the Incarnation the human person is profoundly affirmed. The Word in Jesus is a sign of God's love for each person; each man and each woman is a sacrament, and serving those billions of sacraments is the liturgy of ministry (Mt 25:41).

As sacramental initiation bestows new life and confirms faith, baptism also initiates a person into charism and diaconal action, into a community that is essentially ministerial. The initiation flowers in ministry and not in a moribund state called "laity." A Christian church does not have the option to live liturgically but not evangelistically. "On behalf of" demands action born in the local church. Each church should be as intent upon witness in the world as upon its own inner life. Like the kingdom, the church lives on the boundary between its own institutional sustenance and the winning of new nations to the Word of God. The church leaves the ninety-nine for the one lost sheep—but in our time this single lost creature is entire movements, cultures, and nations. The church at every level—from diocesan offices to a rural parish—should be zealous for public action.

(5) Gift of the Spirit. Ministry has not one but many sources. Its sublime, encompassing, and intimate source is the personal inviting presence of the Spirit of the risen Christ. Josef Hainz sums this up: "The Spirit must be seen as the *pneuma* of God and of Christ. It is the medium of mediation, the sphere and force-field in which Christians, and too the churches, exist as the 'Body of Christ.'"[3] A developmental understanding of *person* grounds a developmental theology of charisms. Not as an automaton of the supernatural but as a modern adult, the minister steps into the hope and ambiguity of ministry. The second chapter on the horizon of the Spirit and its charisms flowing into ministry has explored this at length.

(6) Diverse Services. No characteristic of ministry is more challenging than that there is a plurality of ministries. Jesus himself is followed by different groups—the Twelve, the disciples, the women—and his ministry has a variety in preaching, healing, forgiving, confronting injustice. Jesus is interested in men and women responding to the call to follow him and not in a monarchical arrangement of ecclesiastical strata (Mt 20:25).

For Paul there are many ministries within a harmony of community life. The Letter to the Romans offers a theology of the Spirit as life and power. The *charismata* of the Christians are different in different people, but all result from union with God in Christ. Some living examples are teachers, preachers, ministers of mercy and aid. "For as in one body we have many members, and all the members do not have the same function, so we, though many, are one body in Christ, and individually members one of another. Having gifts that differ according to the grace given to us, let us use them: if prophecy, in proportion to our faith; if service, in our serving; he who teaches, in his teaching; he who exhorts, in his exhortation; he who contributes, in liberality; he who gives aid, with zeal; he who does acts of mercy, with cheerfulness" (Rom 12:4–8). None of these charisms necessarily consist of elements that are essentially miraculous or ecstatic, but all are necessary aspects of church life. Paul illustrates communal diversity-in-harmony by the theological analogy to the human body. In First Corinthians, the Apostle first mentions spiritual gifts, and then charisms, ministries, and powers; an exemplifying list includes preaching, healing, prophecy, instruction. The metaphor of the body is offered to unify a second list of gifts: apostles, teachers, leaders, workers of power. Christian freedom, ministry, and diversity are referred back to the Spirit.

> Now there are varieties of gifts, but the same Spirit, and there are varieties of service, but the same Lord; and there are varieties of working, but it is the same God who inspires them all in every one. To each is given the manifestation of the Spirit for the common good. To one is given through the Spirit the utterance of wisdom, and to another the utterance of knowledge according to the same Spirit, to another faith by the same Spirit, to another gifts of healing by the one Spirit, to another the working of miracles, to another prophecy, to another the ability to distinguish between spirits, to another various kinds of tongues, to another the interpretation of tongues. All these are inspired by one and the same Spirit, who apportions to each one individually as he wills. (1 Cor 12:4–11)

The mission of the Gospel, the power of the Spirit, and the richness and the misery of human life are such that ministry emerges in different forms. The connection of ministry to personal charism grounds variety. Ultimately, diversity in ministry is necessary and normal, ranging from a reader or distributor of the Eucharist to parish and diocesan services involving lengthy preparation, expertise, responsibility, and commitment. This question is at the center of a fundamental theology of ministry today, and so we will turn again in the next chapter to the issue of diversity.

II. A Definition of Ministry

These six biblical characteristics sketched above constitute the fundamental identity of ministry. Pointing to a reality richer than now exists, they lead us to consider calmly the possibilities which our own times require. These characteristics cannot be easily set aside, although no single ministry or church may perfectly realize them.

Christian ministry *is the public activity of a baptized follower of Jesus Christ flowing from the Spirit's charism and an individual personality on behalf of a Christian community to proclaim, serve, and realize the kingdom of God.*

Is our definition of ministry too narrow? Limitations are intended, and that nature of ministry challenges several theses:

a. Every act an ordained minister does solely by virtue of ordination and not necessarily by the action itself achieves effectively a ministerial goal.

b. Acts of the baptized that resemble ministry are either secular actions or actions motivated by Christian virtue in the secular sphere because the layperson by definition is excluded from formal ministry.

c. The Christian perspective posits the baptized influencing the secular order by personal and public ethical stances and the ordained acting in a liturgical and teaching sphere.

d. The ordinary professions pursued by honest baptized Christians are their only ministry for the Gospel.

e. Baptism is only metaphorically a commission to real, formal, charism-grounded ministry; baptism constitutes a person in the Christian laity, which is by definition outside of serious church activity.

f. In the layperson, neither zealous intention, baptism, nor professional preparation can turn an activity into official church ministry; in a presbyter, bishop, or deacon, however, a good intention can easily cause grace even through incompetent teaching, preaching, and liturgical leadership.

g. There have been and can be only three serious ministries

that deserve ordination and the designation of church office: deacon, presbyter, and bishop.

All of these propositions are, upon reflection, incomplete if not false. We must permit the theological definition of ministry to appear diversely in preaching, teaching, social care, and leadership. Various ministries (of quite diverse intensity and ecclesial importance to the baptized and the world) participate through their personalized charisms in ministry. Other full-time ministries—traditional or new—are not rivals to deacon, pastor, or bishop. The ministry presented in this book has been called "functionalism." It does focus on pneumatic activity and charismatic service. This active view of ministry, largely one of common sense, finds advocates in St. Paul and in the Aristotelianism of Thomas Aquinas. A functional ministry and ecclesiology does not say everything and presumes the importance, even the primary importance, of spiritual life and church order. These, however, although comprising the background to ministry, are not the ministry itself, nor can they replace ministry or correct poor ministry. Ultimately one must be freed from a church life that is only a cult and contagion of sacrality.

III. Language and Ministry

Language is drawn from human experience, but then it can also return full-circle to determine reality. Language can control ministry and can diminish and demean it as well.[4] Originally in the New Testament times language empowered ministry. There was an originality, something revolutionary in early Christian religious language, connoting that cultic function was service and honorific office was ministry. Ministry, as the letters of the young churches in the New Testament show, began with verbs: preaching, evangelizing, being sent, and serving. One cannot help but notice how in the course of history Christian theology, in its dialogue with Greek philosophy and Roman political structures, exchanged some of its dynamism for more static ways of being (of course, it also gained doctrinal and organizational assistance). Verbs became nouns, actions became social states: for example, priesthood, clergy, hierarchy, office. This linguistic shift came to depict improperly a reservoir of beings (people marked by grace) rather than a concert of agents (graced people in service).

Order and *ordination* are words from Roman political structure and law.[5] In the patristic period there was a flexibility in the usage of *ordo* in the Roman Empire. After Tertullian, and more solidly after the peace of Milan, in the West a terminology of *ordo* drawn from the political and social life of the Empire was applied to the church. It referred to the bishops, and soon to the church's hierarchy over against the faithful *(plebs)*. Augustine presented the church as existing in groups of *ordines,* which are offices and grades, and arranged them in a descending hierarchy that ends with married couples and people active in the world.[6] Not all early Christian writers employ this term, certainly being aware that its prime analogue and meaning was fixed in Roman society. Sometimes a church order is called an office. Finally, in the Latin-speaking world *ministerium (diakonia)* is present but more and more yields to clergy, order, and office. *Ordo* was a significant interest of medieval culture. There is order in creation, and there is a further order of grace.[7] *Ordo* attracted artists and lawyers, theologians and architects. What was more exciting or profound than order drawing a diversity of motifs and media into a harmonious whole? From the twelfth century on, there had been a search for patterns wherein a myriad of elements could achieve an effect greater than their parts. A divine plan (predestination) and a presence (trinitarian mission) unfold that *ordo* in a new mode of existence, grace. The Word and Spirit of God come to people and live with them to summon forth and enable a special life and destiny, and move forward under the leadership of Christ, the head of the new human race. An ordination is a ceremonial action by which one enters an order.

Can ministry be constituted and defined purely by words? Does not the word *laity* in and of itself reduce and exclude? Why are there bishops who cannot preach or do not preach? Of course, we would not want to dabble with the uncertainty of Donatism, which held that only a verifiable presence of grace (always impossible to discern by humans) created true ministry. With that and similar sects, since grace could not be verified, one was never sure of a baptism or an ordination. Retired elderly deacons remain deacons, bishops for whom their ministry of leadership is too demanding cannot be ignored (permanency needs ecclesial order and tradition), but, at the same time, ministerial incoherence and ineptitude should be an infrequent exception. Normally ministry serves grace, and ministry as a public action on behalf of the Gospel in a church should be empirically viewed and tested as to whether it exists and has any potential efficacy. Ministry is not a document or a state, but an action. Language found in canonical, rubrical, or nominalist theologies (where church office exists without a necessary connection to efficacious service) defeats the energy of the church. Certainly, drawing upon a past metaphysics or ideology to structure a language that diminishes diaconal charisms in people is insupportable.

Ministry's language has ended up in a confused state. The word *ministry* has become a prize. Everyone wants to have a ministry, just as every organization and self-help huckster wants to found a spirituality. The other extreme is for some in purely administrative offices of the church to reserve ministry for vestments and titles. Biblical ministry asserts the empirical to be the master of the linguistic, while Christian realism defines Christian ministry narrowly and yet insists that the defined reality be applicable to more than one or three ministries. Concepts and words should not hold absolute mastery over ministry—and words from biblical churches should not be relegated to piety. Today diversification in ministries questions old regulations.

How will we speak of readers, of coordinators of liturgy and music, of theologians and directors of religious education, deacons and pastors gathered together in a local church? While doing is more important than naming, and we should be happy over the great interest in ministry, nonetheless, it is important eventually to have some clear language about the structure of the church. Clear-cut terms are no longer available for every Catholic reality, but it is important to educate people regarding the diverse reality of ministry; to explain with somewhat accurate words the roles, responsibilities, and sources of various ministries. The use of inadequate or pious language signals people that the subject at hand, far from being sacred, is curious and insignificant. People understand that revelation cannot be fully enclosed in a word or idea, but they should be led to see the real parameters and the true nature and varied aspects of church life.

Merely verbal solutions have been suggested: sets of words that might distinguish one group of ministers from another. First, there is *lay ministry* and *clerical ministry.* Second there is the pair, *nonordained ministry* and *ordained ministry* (the precise identity of baptism is left unclear). A third approach is only typographical: *Ministry* and *ministry.*

The problem is that none of these sets does justice either to the church's revelation or to its life. A prior law or an administrative decision could create a virtual ecclesial vacuum for any of these ministries. The designation of what ministry is at all or what constitutes important, lasting ministry could come from one historical period or one law and would perdure apart from the empirical needs of the community.

All these pairs seem to be rooted not in an ecclesiology of ministries but in a past sociology of one important office over against a passive lay state. Permanence, a supernatural source of ministry, and a stability in powers and roles are all important. But ordination and offices should not imply that they exist for themselves or for that which is not divine but ecclesial. On the other hand, behind new terminologies may stand a sincere will to expand the ministry.

One should be aware of a nominalist theology behind the scenes in all that touches the church. Nominalism—the approach by which laws and definitions determine external reality—is the temptation of every bureaucracy. A realism drawn from Thomas Aquinas's theology, so influential in the Catholic Church,[8] opposes the nominalist preference for terms. What is nominalism? It is a reversal of realities into ideas and words. Although Tridentine theology opposed the nominalist aspects of Protestantism, several times in this book we have criticized a rather nominalist perspective present in the practice and theology of the church from 1860 to 1960. Nominalism (and fideism, its religious companion) is attractive because it offers what appears to be immediate clarity and importance. Within nominalism, authority and will—things are not allowed to emerge as they are—impose meaning. Intellectual arrangement decides what is good and real

in realms both human and divine. Nominalism constitutes reality
by words or mental forms; these are rooted not in created realities
but in the increasingly arbitrary will of God. Nominalism presumes that philosophy or law is more significant than reality.
Here ordination and ministerial title are bestowed not by charism
or service but by juridical decree.

A nominalist ecclesiological mind-set selects certain rites,
devotions, and phrases and decides they are eternal. Eventually
this stance becomes a schizophrenia, playing with reality and
seeking to control much that cannot be controlled. Every nominalism—and each implies a legalism—is imbued with its own psychology and ontology. The nominalist worldview reduces
ordination to a liturgical exercise of episcopal power. The role of
the bishop seems cut off from the realities of Spirit, and community as his will or that of superiors in the hierarchy determines
every aspect, divine as well as human, that touches ordination
and subsequent ministry. Yves Congar points out the theological
implications of the legal or nominalist stance:

> There is ultimately no insistence upon an actual interven-
> tion of God's grace, nor on the need for man to pray for this
> intervention and to prepare for it by discipline. There is no
> explicit relation of authority to sacred acts such as charity
> and prayer. In short, legalism is characteristic of an ecclesi-
> ology unrelated to spiritual anthropology, and for which the
> word *ecclesia* indicates not so much the body of the faithful
> as the system, the apparatus, the impersonal depository of
> the system of rights whose representatives are the clergy, or,
> as it is extensively called, the hierarchy—ultimately, the pope
> and the Roman Curia.[9]

A serious example of a nominalism is an arbitrary designation
by church authority—apart from the activity of the ministry and the
trajectories of tradition—of some ministries and ordinations as
given by Jesus' institution and existing apart from history in time-
lessness. We have already rejected immature divisions of ministry
that have no foundation in reality but only in terminology. There
are distinctions to be made between Christian ministries, but such
distinctions flow out of the empirical service of each ministry and
out of the visible life of the church. Since ministry is not a sacral

state but an action, anything touching its definition must take into consideration what this ministry does. So distinctions like *Ministry* and *ministry, lay ministers* and *clerical ministers, hierarchical* and *pastoral offices,* and *ordained* and *nonordained ministries* find their foundation in legal decisions secondary to baptism and clearly defined ministries, rather than in the essential distinctions born of church service. *Lay minister* involves a popular linguistic usage; *clerical minister* ineptly combines action and class.[10] New terms, too, can be a nominalism, because the words are disconnected from the actions they should represent. In our time, nominalism has its old form, the rules of church administration, and its new form, theological fashion.

The puzzling over language is a theological quest. We have mentioned the difficulties of nominalism and of setting out church roles according to those church laws that remain medieval or Baroque. A general difficulty is the pervasive presence of the problematic word *laity.* A lay person, according to contemporary English usage, is a man and woman who is not involved in the area under discussion, or who is ignorant of what the educated and initiated in a certain field possess. The exclusion of the majority of Christians (precisely as "laity") from ecclesial power, the traditional counter-poising of them over against a limited clergy, the present and past meaning of the word—all this makes *lay ministry* a contradictory term. Aristotle suggested that words be used as they are commonly understood. The pejorative meaning of *laity* appears even in the patronage by which minor realms of "ministry" are given to lay people. *Laity* always appears to carry an intrinsic obstacle to ministry, its "lay-ness." In fact, baptism is the essential opening to ministry. In France for the past century and a half, the term *lay* has meant aggressively secular, even antichurch.

Words can be obstacles, opaque or self-justifying. A word's meaning is what must be unlocked. For ultimately, as theology repeats from Aquinas, faith and its graced obedience are movements that terminate not in words, but in realities.[11] Language is not simply a tool but an expression of life and reality. Language does not descend from God but is the creation of human beings, through which God speaks. God speaks to us silently and his Word is caught up in our words. Human languages inevitably provide the words, ideas, and grammar for God's revelation. God's Word uses our words and undergoes various linguistic and social translations in history. Modern hermeneutics makes us aware of language as an event, a liberation, or as a tool to enable propaganda and control. A fundamental theology of ministry should be critical of language, should criticize unsubstantiated or schizophrenic frameworks, and finally should stand apart from every dictatorship of concepts.

IV. Circles of Ministries

An underlying permeating (transcendental) presence of grace and its realization in charism and theology, in historical changes in liturgy and devotions, the existential individuality of God's self-sharing—themes of this book—support a basic pattern of considering ministry: namely as circles of ministries around the leader of the community (who could be Christ or his Spirit, or the pastor or bishop). The communal leader stands not over against or in competition with other ministries, but as a leader who enables. The other ministries themselves are not all the same, but they are all truly ministry: the ordained and those working full-time in a church along with all kinds of part-time ministers, volunteers, and assistants in the parish. It is best not to try to find their identities fully in the linguistic division into *lay* and *ordained*. We live in a time when simple linear divisions into two groups are not adequate.

The model of concentric circles helps here: it stands in contrast to the line dividing this group from that, a division unable to recognize degrees of ministry. This new model recognizes concentric ministries as such and makes allowances for degrees (some very different from the others) of ministers. Here all ministries are based upon the underlying animating force of the Spirit in the community and unfold from charism and personality vitalized by baptism and drawn to ministry. Circles of ministry indicate a similarity in ministry but also point to differences and distinctions among degrees of ministry ranging from leadership to occasional services. The distinctions and differences are

initiated by baptism, commissioning, and ordination but are ultimately based upon the goal of the ministry.

Karl Rahner's theology helps to fashion a fundamental theology of expanding ministry. Rahner's theology is a theology of
grace: of the self-sharing of the divine persons active in the individual, or collective, person. This theology, particularly in its
later decades after the Council, focuses upon the history of the
ideas and forms of the Christian community, and its goal is to
permit diverse participation in a unique and central Christ.
Christianity is "not a castle of truth with innumerable rooms
which must be occupied in order to be 'in the truth' but is the
opening from which all individual truths (even errors) lead into
the Truth which is the inconceivability of God."[12] What is true of
expressions of revealed truth can be applied to forms of church
life. Around the time of Vatican II, theologians came to see a fullness in the ministry. Rahner finds and preserves the primal gift
of ministry within the historically manifest forms. The church,
distinguishing between a single potentiality ("one pastoral ministry") and its "degrees," is interested not in quantitative control
but in fullness and quality.[13]

In 1955, in a very different ecclesiastical world, Rahner
wrote a prescient essay on the lay apostolate, that loose assembly
of devotional ideas and social enterprises dating from the first
half of the twentieth century that categorized some ways for
those not priests and religious to serve the church in "action" or
"apostolate." He argued that the term *lay* needed to be presented
in such a way that it did not mean "profane." Further, a layperson
cannot be someone outside the circle of the sacral but should
have, through baptism, a role in the church; the church could no
longer be an institution of clergy and passive laity, a social format
that had lasted for a millennium and a half and that could not
easily be altered.[14] Even as he pointed to promise and charism,
Rahner did not foresee such a rapid shift from passivity to ecclesial ministry for laypeople. In 1958 he showed that the church
could not be divided between institutional offices and charismatics, that every ministerial office was to be linked to the Spirit,
and that church leadership should recognize its potentiality for
frustrating the charismatic and should pass beyond the separa-

tions (not distinctions, for there is always a distinction between the divine and the human) that the medieval and Baroque times had brought into the church's ideological structure.[15] When the local church is enhanced, the charismatic and diaconal appear; when all is produced in a universal sameness, they lie dormant. "The future presses in upon the church, a future in which the premium set upon the characteristics present in the local church...will perhaps be higher even than it is in the present....Life in the church in the new form which it will acquire in the future will first, and by anticipation be experienced *here* in the local church."[16] *Charismatic* refers not only to charisms in the church but to the charismatic reality of the church as well; it is not a violent, anti-institutional, sensational phenomenon but the role of the Spirit viewed dynamically in history. The charismatic element is simply God's Spirit guiding salvation-history in ways that cannot be foreseen or fully planned or solely drawn from the past.[17] "The charismatic in the church" means the varied and universal presence of the Spirit at a depth that prompts personal and ecclesial realizations; this is "the first, the most proper and ecclesial among the formal essential characteristics of the church." The church is an open system, a kind of community whose concrete condition as already given and as coming to be cannot fully be determined from a single point within itself but from a point outside of itself, from God, so that each condition of the system can rightly be said to be effected charismatically and not institutionally. Fifteen years after Vatican II he described the church of the future as "declericalized." The church's mission and origin imply that its ministries are quite different from secular officeholders. "Office has a functional character in the church as a society, even though this society with its functions (proclamation of the word, sacrament, leadership of the church's life as society) constitutes a sign of the reality of the church—the free Spirit, faith, hope and love."[18] Whatever is of the institution or the hierarchy (which term is ambiguous) is not the foundation of the church but flowing from what Jesus and his Spirit have bestowed. "Office is never simply identical with the Spirit and can never replace the Spirit; office is really credible and effective in the sight of people only when the presence of the Spirit is evident and not merely when formal mission and authority are involved, however legitimate these may be."[19]

Before the Council Rahner was offering ideas that would further the expansion of the ministry before this expansion had really begun. He sensed that Catholic Action was not enough and that both parish and Catholic men and women held a potentiality awaiting liberation. He maintained that the second millennium of Christianity, for historical and pastoral reasons, had at key moments ranging from the Investiture Controversy to the Reformation, kept the ordinary Christian in a state of inactivity. Conversely, he viewed the middle of the twentieth century as having produced movements and theologies about "the church becoming a living force in the spirit and heart of the faithful, about the fact that the Christians are the church and should not merely be regarded as subject to her directives and the object of her solicitude and protection."[20] One can today discern "the Spirit pressing the church to give practical effect to this new awareness." The ecclesial source of the new vitality is baptism: "...by sacramental consecration every Christian in the church has been authorized and empowered for the task of actively cooperating in the work of the church both interiorly and exteriorly."[21] Rahner in a new way for that decade described baptismal grace as giving the right, the task, and the interior power to help the church realize itself today. Baptismal grace is incarnational and ecclesial and personal, all in terms of working within the church and not just as an occasional voice or random witness in the secular sphere. Nonetheless, at this time Rahner could not foresee the expansion of new ministries beyond pastor and deacon, and so his general theology speaks of Christians having "a share in the active function of the church both in internal and external affairs," even as he cannot get beyond that activity taking place in the public and secular sphere.[22]

The relationship between the church and its individual structures, between the New Testament and today's church, "is an important and difficult question,...for within the time of the New Testament itself there is a history and a becoming of the constitution of the church."[23] It is not a sacral officialdom from which all prophets, innovators, and charismatics have fled (and they can be diocesan or school ministers with new ideas, and not just long dead reformers of religious life). The church, far from hoping for a time without forms, is itself the place of the concrete presentation and realization of invisible grace. The church is very much an historical institution: it is like a landscape that changes its contours in different areas. The church listens to revelation and the call of the age in the same moment, receiving in a new way that which from the beginning was entrusted to it.[24] Such a church existing in history for human beings cannot be a closed but an open system; revelation and even theology are never exhausted by this or that form. A theology of grace and of baptism that is personal and existential transcends a static ecclesiology of elite priesthood and passive laity. "The hierarchy of orders is not identical with a 'hierarchy' of free charisms in the church which also belong to the essence of the church; nor is nearness to God a privilege of the clerical state which is also not simply the sole bearer of the realization of being the church."[25] Ministry is wrapped in faith: it serves the content of faith; it is possible only through faith; it is responsible to faith. This faith is the faith of its entire church and is capable of insight and of newness. "Each member of the church is an active cobearer of the self-construction of the church, and precisely as this self-construction of the church means concretely the mediation of salvation to the individual. But this fact does not mean that the function through which the individual Christian is cobearer of the self-construction of the church is the same for all individuals."[26] This theology remarkably anticipated the ideas of the Council, but it does not reflect or foresee the close interplay of ministry and the baptized, which becomes, after 1970, the expansion of the parish ministry.

In the 1970s the German church instituted ministries of pastoral assistants, and Rahner reflected on the expansion of parish ministries. After noting that such a step—the introduction of full-time ministries into a parish team, and the leadership of the non-ordained in directing parishes for which priests were not available—had considerable theological impact and produced consequences some of which were not thought out, he offered anew his theology on the objectivity of graced realities. The priest, for Rahner, is "based in a community and commissioned by the church to be the full and official preacher of the word of God so that the sacramentally highest level of intensity of this word is entrusted to him."[27] The center of incarnational life is seen by Rahner to be closely joined to preaching the word and the eucharistic action. If the priest-pastor is at the center of the life of the church, that ministry does not exhaust all ministry. In the church before Vatican II, there was really only one ministry; now there are others. Even if the church does not endow a service with a title or an ordination ceremony, it might still exist. Rahner called attention to the fact that by Vatican II all aspects of the diaconate were being done by men without ordination. Reality had preceded ordination, and he believed office and ordination should confirm that reality. Rahner often referred to the reality of ministry, noting that the baptized were doing ministry habitually and professionally without having received any sacramental commissioning, which commissioning existed in the church precisely to assist them in ministry.[28] The emergence of pastors of parishes for which there were no priests raised theological issues, for in practice the distinction between the two was the absence of a few sacramental powers. But the various roles of leadership, of service to the word and Spirit, of functions not tied to a particular sacramental power must be permitted to stand out, to be leadership and sacramentality. The response to this is not to constantly list lay and nonordained aspects of these ministers but to fashion a ministerial identity in the "conferment of an office of a permanent character...regarded as sacramental."[29] Rahner spoke of "the ministerial basis" of the church, which it needs to fulfill its functions, and how the social and evangelistic services draw out ministries; he viewed positively the expanding number of ministers, the diversity of ministries, and expected for some an appropriate liturgy of commissioning. This was not to make the church more, but less, clerical and hierarchical, giving a wider group responsibility for the church and displaying its true sacramental nature.

That sacramentality of the entire church was not original with Rahner, but he placed it at the center of the church's ecclesiological issues, along with the questions relating to the mission of the church in the wider world. The church is not simply "Christ living on."[30] It is the living realization of the grace of Christ, "the *fundamental sacrament* of a grace, precisely because it is offered to all, presses forward to express its sacramental historical nature," a sign and realization of salvation for the world, the leaven of a supernatural humanism. Sacramental ecclesiology liberated Christians from the constraints of legalism and clericalism; the liturgy of sacraments and sacramentals offer people a worldwide liturgy of grace.[31] A Rahnerian theology of degrees of implicit and explicit grace has a variation in church life. Just as Christ is the definitive center of a world of religions with some revelation and grace, Rahner maintains there are degrees of grace, all drawn from the event of Christ but not all explicitly recognized as such, working within vastly different times and peoples. In church life the center is retained but not at the expense of the condemnation or diminishment of those who exist in other degrees. Looking back on his years of work in church structure, Yves Congar also found a linear model inadequate. He proposed a return to a deeper tradition in which Christ's Spirit underlay a community with various circles of ministries within it.[32]

> The church of God is not built up solely by the actions of the official presbyteral ministry but by a multitude of diverse modes of service, more or less stable or occasional, more or less spontaneous or recognized, and when the occasion arises consecrated, while falling short of sacramental ordination.... It would then be necessary to substitute for the linear scheme a scheme where the community appears as the enveloping reality *within which* the ministries, eventually the instituted sacramental ministries, are placed as *modes of service* of what the community is called to be and do.[33]

Theologians like Congar and Rahner, and also Edward Schillebeeckx and Otto Semmelroth, offer a similar theology of the sacramentality of the entire church linked to the primal charism of a ministerial fullness.[34]

V. Reversals in Ministry

A new theology of ministry will introduce a reversal. The reversal, however, is a renewal, for it gives more of the church's life born at Pentecost. The shift in emphasis is not something radical or novel but an understanding of ministry old and new. The reversal is one of direction and inclusion, not of upheaval: it is a move from symbol to reality, from solitary priest to community, from liturgy to service. The liturgical aspect is affirmed but as one side of ministry, the all-important symbolic-sacramental (sacramental in the broad sense of all the mediations of grace in people and things and movement) side and source of ministry. Ministry is more than liturgy, preaching is more than preaching during the Eucharist, and love is more than the kiss of peace. Service to the kingdom of God flows from liturgical enactment into real, public, social actions. Liturgy is intended to confirm and nourish these actions, these ministries in the world. Ministry partakes of this deep but sometimes forgotten principle: first ministries, then liturgy. For centuries, Christians rarely entered their parish church outside of Sunday morning. Catholics can easily view the priest solely as liturgist and presume that other ministers are active only in secular service.

When we compare two ecumenical councils, Trent and Vatican II, we see a move from defining church and ministry in terms of Eucharist to a wider perspective including both liturgy and pluriform mission.[35] The roles of presbyter and bishop, correctly defined, are not the same as those of educator and deacon, not because their roles as community leaders set them apart from extraliturgical ministry (indeed they are the center, the enablers of all ministries and not just liturgical ones), but because the role of a community's leader is not the same as a community's social advocate. With an expanded ministry, with new ministries realizing the old services of prophet, teacher, evangelist, and deacon in the public sector—they may have liturgical roles—the community's vocation and breadth is evident.

The movement by which Christians withdrew from public ministry to liturgical attendance is being reversed. Christians do not enter the world as ministers because they have been consecrated as liturgists. Just the opposite is true; offices and roles in the liturgy are justified by public service. Liturgy reflects real ministry.[36] A deacon has a liturgical role because of an external social ministry. Although deacons' identity and origin seems pluriform, the dominant forms that characterized their ministerial role in the ages of the martyrs and of the Constantinian establishment centered around extensive programs for the urban poor or the Christian needy. For them, too, whatever liturgical role they had was derived from this. This reversal by which diaconal action in the world grounds liturgical symbol is a central facet of a realistic theology of ministry.

The most sharply delineated example of this is the role of community leader. The leader presides among the ministries of a church's public services. Hence, this coordinator is thereby the normal minister to preside at that special expression of the community's life, the paschal liturgy of Sunday. Hervé Legrand observes that most Christians believe that their eucharistic assembly is possible because it is enacted by a priest whose personally possessed and unique power effects this event. In fact, the bishop and then the presbyter preside at the eucharist because their ministry is one of leadership and spiritual discernment in nourishing and building up the community. "Thus presidency of the eucharistic assembly is seen as including the liturgical, prophetic, and ministerial dimensions in the pastoral charge of building up the church, a charge conferred in ordination."[37] Legrand finds in a variety of patristic and liturgical documents from the first five centuries of the church that reversal by which not sacral priesthood but leadership in charism, liturgy, and public life is the foundation of bishop and later of presbyter as eucharistic leader.

Beautiful and profound theologies have been written about the sacramental representation of grace in the motions of the liturgy, but there is also a real, corporeal incarnation of grace in other ministries. Liturgy serves the spirit of the Christian by word and symbol, by silence and sacrament, by sounds and colors. There is a way in which liturgy remains secondary (for even sacrament is not full reality), the symbolic and verbal nourishment of the Christian having some further goal beyond the church building and Sunday morning. Thomas Aquinas concluded that there was a diversity of ministers in the Body of Christ, because there existed a diversity of actions "necessary for the church."[38] If the ecclesial source and effect of liturgy is ministry, nonetheless, a parish has to do not only with a priest attracting attendance at Sunday mass but with assembling a people whose being as the Body of Christ requires sacraments and expects ministries.

The reversal we have sketched by which diaconal action for the world grounds and flows from liturgical ritual and sacrament is a central facet of a realistic theology of ministry. Charism precedes ordination, whose sacrament that liturgy is. Just as the varied graces of the community fashion the constellation of a public commissioning for a ministry, brief or permanent, baptismal or ordained, so the goal of ministry, service to the kingdom in the world, permeates every service and every liturgy.

5

MINISTERS IN THE CHURCH

Ministry is the internal and existential work of a local church or a diocese. Ministry is an aspect of baptism, a facet of each Christian's life. Ministry is grace in structure, charism in ecclesial service. Christian ministry is *the public activity of a baptized follower of Jesus Christ flowing from the Spirit's charism and an individual personality on behalf of a Christian community to proclaim, serve, and realize the kingdom of God.* But who, then, are ministers in the church? It belongs to authority to structure a particular ministry and to coordinate other ministries but not to absorb ministry itself. Leadership does not compete with other ministers by excluding them from graced roles. In this chapter we will look at the diversity of ministers, for it is not church office that is a new and prominent presence, but the variety of ministries.

I. One Body, Many Activities

Christianity is not a monism or a single cell, not a dictatorship or a monarchy; and it is not a uniform society. In its origins were distinctions: between Jesus Christ, the Head, and the Body; between the Spirit and the baptized; and between different kinds of ministers called, inspired, commissioned, and sent. This diversity was obscured over the span of the past millennium and more in which a single ministry, priesthood, and a passive universality, laity, composed the church. One of the results of Vatican II, as we have seen, is the restoration of a diversity in ministry, a restoration made necessary by the expansion of the church and the diversity of needs and cultures.

How should we describe diversity in ministry? We have seen in previous chapters that the experience of the early churches concerned the ordering of charismatic diversity, communal service,

167

and leadership. Michael Himes insightfully, but without any desire to compromise the identity and authority of the ordained, speaks of a

> universal episcopate and a universal diaconate in the church [just as there is a priesthood of all believers], an episcopate and diaconate of all the faithful. All are called to the episcopal function of maintaining the unity of the community. All are called to the presbyteral function of responsibility to and for the word. All are called to the diaconal function of direct service to those within and outside the community. The vocation to these universal ministries is given in baptism, which is the principal sacrament of ministry.[1]

The early Christians came together with the insight that the Spirit's presence brought to Jesus' disciples an invitation to ministry, but that ministry would have various forms.

II. Diversity in Ministry

The issue of diversity in Christian ministry is at the heart of the church today. To bring together an expanded full-time ministry with bishop and pastor, and to solve confusions about the make-up of the Christian community, we need an accurate and incisive theory of diversity-in-ministry. The priesthood of all believers in the First Letter of Peter, Thomas Aquinas's understanding of a potentiality within the sacrament of orders, Trent's insistence upon not one but three offices, and Paul VI's restoration of ministries are moments in the church's consciousness of a will toward diversity-in-ministry.

Not a few important theologians and ecclesial moments support in their own way this diversity-in-ministry. We have, of course, the Pauline "Body of Christ" motif. The analogy of the body rejects the idea that some charisms and ministries are essentially superior to others in the eyes of the Spirit. In the concept of diversity-in-ministry we find that each particular ministry's identity and its relationship to other ministries bring power, humility, and holiness. This metaphor has both influenced greatly the life and structure of the church and, at times, been largely suppressed or replaced by others' view of the church as perfect society or bride of Christ. The church is the Body of the crucified and risen Christ, who shares his life in sacraments, faith, and the call to ministry. St. Paul was thinking of one local church and viewing a basic elevation and equality among its members as the foundation of all the charisms and activities of the community.[2] Thomas Aquinas supported a theology of ministerial potentiality, despite the commandeering role in his society played by order, office, and hierarchy. Aquinas presented orders theologically as a potentiality, "a potestative whole." "The distinction of orders is not that of an integral whole into parts nor of a universal into individuals but of a *totum postestativum....* "[3] Aquinas, moreover, will not admit that only the major orders are sacraments; rather, all of the levels or orders are realizations of a single *ordo,* which is a sacrament and somehow one sacrament.

An argument against a wider diversity of ministries is that three orders—bishop, priest, and deacon—are of divine institution. That divine establishment could mean either an express constitution by Jesus on earth or a decision by God communicated later to the church. Some theologians over the past millennium have presumed that Jesus communicated to the apostles in detail certain ministries, and they were only three; thus those ministries instituted by *"divina ordinatione."*[4] But prophet and teacher had as great a centrality in the first century as did presbyter (today's "priest" might well then have been called "prophet," that is, preacher-leader), as historical studies show.

What of the three ministries found in the Council of Trent? We interpret the teachings at an ecumenical council through its historical context and theological language. The hermeneutical key to the Council of Trent is the Reformation as it had progressed up to 1560. Trent did not present a complete doctrine of orders nor a full theology of priesthood or episcopacy. Its statements were replies to the denials of the Reformers. Luther, Calvin, the Anabaptists, and the Zwinglians had given the impression that the ministry was purely human, legal creation of the church; they identified ministry with actual preaching and seemed to neglect the ministry of eucharistic leader. Furthermore, they accepted only one ministry, that of the preacher-pastor actually functioning in office. Ordination, character, episcopal power, and cultic priesthood were minimalized by the Reformers. There is no doubt that Trent insisted upon a real distinction between important ministries and baptized Christians, and that it searched for the ground of that distinction in the eucharistic sacrifice cult or hierarchical power (which are particular sources). With regard to the question of the diversity of ministries, however, Trent was arguing precisely for a diversity: *"Plures et diversi essent ministrorum ordines"* [The orders of ministers are plural and diverse].[5] Its list of three received with veneration is presented as a rejection of the Protestant idea that there is only one church office, the pastorate—a view upheld by the Reformation to attack the magisterial and jurisdictional power of the bishops. Trent affirmed the sacramentality and the permanence in character of ministry, objected to a reduction of office to laity, but insisted that "the hierarchy (of orders) includes by divine institution bishops, presbyters and ministers." Trent argued for the distinct identity of important ministers; the laity were not to move *"promiscue"*[6] in and out of orders. It is unlikely that the conciliar fathers intended the following meaning, but the letter of the text admits of an extension of ministers under the third, vaguely categorized group, *"ministrorum."* The burden of Trent is to affirm real, stable ministries; more than one order of ministry; and ministries other than preaching. The line of argumentation is away from monoformity in orders.

We have seen how Karl Rahner explained the perduring reality of ministry and office. (The two are combined in the German *Amt* amid forms which change, disappear, and reappear). For Edward Schillebeeckx, too, Jesus and his Spirit did not bestow one or two offices on the church but a fullness of ministry. He argues that the church not only has the right but the duty to determine its structure in each period. A single structural arrangement may be an isolated incident of the essence of the church for one age, but it should not be used as an obscuring hermeneutic for the past or as a procrustean bed for the true. The *jus divinum* of ministry is not the judge but the gift of history; it looks backward through tradition but also forward to mission. "'Divine Origin' includes a historical growth of various forms and divisions."[7] The sociological process within the church that brought forth ecclesial office is not rooted in plans from Jesus or Peter. Yet important ministries do go back to the apostolic church, and ministry is present in the early church not only in charism but in an inner drive toward order and effectiveness. Consequently, the pneumatic process of naming and describing, of creating and arranging ministries has a sociological and historical dynamic. Jesus established a reality of ministry with certain characteristics of service, detachment, authority, and universality. The Spirit in history enlarges or focuses this *pleroma.* Why did some apostolic ministries fade away if a primal constitution established them? Why did others remain but, while preserving their names, change their roles? The history of ministry is not a progress from good to better: there is newness and antiquity, gain and loss. Ministries that were once of crucial importance might appear again, while preaching might be separated again from the community leaders and healing evangelists might emerge. If ministries can be lost, ministries can also be regained. A single order of church office, whether medieval or Baroque, cannot be set forth as the sole pattern, the essential definition. History shows that different arrangements and names for ministry in the church have occurred; there are more than three ministries but different arrangements in church order which, nevertheless, guarantee all that is necessary for service, evangelization, order, and tradition. Simply because a church form does not now exist need not mean it is lost or has no right to exist anew. The parameters of the apostolic period and the limits of the time of primal revelation in Christ are unclear. When we compare the historically conditioned forms for a specific office (or ministerial title) we see both an ecclesial essence *(jus divinum)* and a history. Is it the historical action of Jesus or the subsequent constitution of the Spirit that brings divine institution? Is there an ongoing revelation of the Spirit and a penetration into the unique message of Christ that encourage both discovery and rediscovery of different forms of ministry? Can a later church alter, improve, diminish the forms of the past given by the Spirit? The original constitution of Jesus and his Spirit bestow adaptability and diversity to insure the survival of ministry in the ages.[8]

Vatican II did not accept the medieval and Baroque reduction of ministry to priesthood alone but took steps to reestablish diversity within traditional church offices. First, the Council established a true ministerial role of *deacon,* open to men from various manners of Christian life. Although the restored diaconate has not escaped difficulties (the deacon can become clericalized, can lack adequate theological and pastoral education, can miss having an extraliturgical dimension), this restoration has its value. In the permanent diaconate we have a ministry and an ordination that do not lead to priesthood; we have Christians being ordained who are not pledged to celibacy, men who are not members of a quasi-monastic state. Second, conciliar theology designated the priest as a ministerial representative of the leader of the local church, the bishop. The original meaning of *presbyter* was reintroduced, and this gave an identity to this ministry other than that of sacral priest or routine-bound assistant to the pastor. Finally, Vatican II described the role of *bishop* as a proper ministry rather than a dignity added to, or a version of, the priesthood. We now have three separate ministries with three ordinations; no ministry leads to another nor does one by essence encompass the others. The bishop is the minister to whom presbyter and deacon relate as coworkers. The roles of pastor and bishop and the sacramental ethos of the liturgy have not been and are not diminished by the expansion of the ministry. There is a clearer idea of the role of pastor today, and circles of liturgical ministers represent the norm and offer the church ways of proclamation. The central offices are enhanced, not reduced.

Hovering around all our considerations, however, is the most famous ministerial distinction of all: that which exists between clergy and laity.

III. The Clergy-Laity Distinction: History and Reality

For fifteen hundred years a structure of the Christian churches, the form (often the sole form) of diversity has been not

Christ and his Body, not the Spirit with its gifts, but clergy and laity. This line of socialized diversification assumed modes of being and created not services but classes. Both historical theology and the expansion of the ministry have challenged the claim that the distinction between clergy and laity is basic, exclusive, perennial, or decreed by Jesus. The dualism intends to protect revelation and church, but in its historico-social forms it also exists as a product of culture. One searches the New Testament in vain for a theology of the laity. Neither laymen nor priests can be found in it, at least in the sense in which the Middle Ages or Vatican II understood those words. Being a Christian in faith and baptism grounds all ministry and exceeds all position; Christians share a joint inheritance as I Peter proclaims them to be "a chosen race, a royal priesthood, a holy nation, God's own people." The *Apostolic Constitutions,* issued at the end of the fourth century state: Moreover, let not a bishop be exalted against his deacons and presbyters, nor the presbyters against the people: for the subsistence of the congregation depends on each other. For the bishops and the presbyters are the priests with relation to the people, and the laity are the laity with relation to the clergy. And to be a Christian lies in our own power.[9] We know at once that there is something not fully accurate in this division when we recall that when a man enters the clergy he does not cease to be, theologically and at the deepest level of his religious life, a Christian, a member of the people of God. Baptism is not removed by ordination but indeed is its necessary presource. Perhaps this division of states, too severe in its separation, is not adequate for a ministering church.

Clergy. The etymology of *clergy* lies in the Greek *kleros:* a "lot" or a "portion." In the Acts of the Apostles (1:15 f.) Matthias is elected by the casting of lots and receives the share of the apostolic ministry that Judas had abandoned. By the time of the *Apostolic Tradition* of Hippolytus (c. A.D. 220) the word was used to define a general ecclesiastical state to which bishop, presbyters, and deacons (Did the Eastern churches include deaconesses?) belonged. There is another New Testament meaning for the clerical reality. In Acts, Colossians, and Ephesians, the word is used to define the share that all Christians, all members of a church have in the Word and reality of Christ; "the inheritance of the saints in light" (Col 1:12) comes to all its "heirs" (Gal 3:29). Lot means the share in eschatological salvation that God gives to each individual believer in the communion of all believers. This share is understood not simply as a fortunate lot, a windfall, but as a good reality prepared for the brothers and sisters redeemed by Jesus. A sharing in the Lord comes precisely not just to the clergy, who exist in their ministries rather than in a collective group, but to the whole people of God. As we have seen, that breadth of the Spirit is the originality of Christianity (Rom 8:1 ff.).

In a letter of Clement, a church leader in Rome, written around A.D. 95 we find links of Christian ministry to the Aaronic priesthood. Clement described how the great apostles planned that Christians would succeed them in ministry. Those bishops and deacons functioned (as did Moses and Aaron) as leaders of the people, as directors of the order among many charisms and activities. Clement did not describe the Christian ministers as priests, nor did he use sacerdotal language in referring to Christians. Jesus is the significant high priest. With Ignatius of Antioch early in the second century we have the triad of bishop, presbyter, and deacon highlighted and given particular importance among ministries, some of which like *apostle* or *prophet* are fading away, while others like *teacher* will remain.[10]

It was the third century that spoke of a laity apart from the active clergy (before that time one finds few references to this dyad). Alexandre Faivre notes how little we know of the church before A.D. 200 and how the church in the following decades emerges with vitality and organization. "It was only from the 3rd century that the word 'layman' came to designate an ordinary Christian belonging to the great body of faithful people. Throughout the second century, writers preferred to describe Christians in general as 'the holy portion,' the 'elect,' or the 'chosen,' and 'the brethren.'"[11] Clement of Alexandria was the first to use the term *layman* to designate explicitly a category of Christians, but this usage of *layman* referred to a monogamous man accepting a high moral code; it was not a term connoting every baptized Christian (it is interesting that one designation of all Christians in the second century, "holy portion," is in fact the word *clergy*). The usage of *layman* corresponds to the expansion of the church and its necessary institutionalization. "It was in this climate that a frontier came into being and then shifted within the Christian social group: the cleric/layman frontier. This frontier and the justifications for it were not accepted by everyone."[12] Issues over liturgical roles and those of forgiving sins also accompanied this. The impression we have from Tertullian, Hippolytus, and Origen is that there emerged a line between two Christian social groups, clergy and laity, and yet who was in which group was not so clear. "Within each of these two groups, various functions lived side by side. Attempts were made...to define and justify the outline of this frontier separating the clergy from the laity and to define the duties and the roles."[13] At that time the focus of the community began to shift from evangelization to solemn liturgy and orthodox teaching, although the external mission of the church was considerable. The separation of clergy from the people may have been nourished by the tendency of the churches to want to resemble the Jewish people of the inspired Pentateuch, or by the desire to resemble the religious life of their pagan neighbors' cults. Particularly important was the ahistorical reappropriation of the Old Testament. Some Gentile churches looked upon Jewish Scripture not so much as a prophecy of Christ but as a collection of inspired beliefs and ethics. Hippolytus's liturgy of ordination and Cyprian's argument for the purity of the *sacerdotes* cited Old Testament texts. Origen used *clerics* as a term for those in special orders, and he contrasts them with the people; he presents the clergy as the maintainers of the church's organization, but with his preference for preaching and theology, he occasionally implies that the most important ministry is accomplished by those who teach and preach at an advanced level.[14]

During the period from the reign of Constantine to that of Justinian and then on to the Byzantine Empire in the East and feudalism in the West the clergy were constituted as a separate social class endowed with religious and civil privileges. The episcopacy, which was earlier an acceptance of a potentially dangerous and self-denying service of the community, became a privileged state. In the medieval church clerical tonsure was a minor quasi-ordination that guaranteed membership in a state with religious and ascetic obligations and separate legal protection. Feudal and preindustrial societies prized stability because they had to struggle to maintain existence and society itself. Medieval and Baroque theologies of the church looked at ministry, that is, "church office," much as they looked at marriage: the church defended its legal rights, its public image, its contribution to a stable society. The being of ministry analyzed by law and the sacramental ontology of structured grace were paramount. Later secular societies prizing freedom, individuality, and action could only find the clergy-laity structure sociologically inept.

Laity. Class distinctions come in pairs. While the clergy became an elevated, sacral state, the laity became a passive group. The first Christians saw themselves as the people of God, a people open to all, male and female, slave and free, Jew and Greek (Gal 3:28 f.). God's people, a universal people, had access to the Spirit through Jesus. At the heart of Israel's faith and revelation was its theological sociology of being the people of God. People (*laos* in Greek) is contrasted with the *goyim,* the nations. Israel is a people because God's love and care touch them. Aware of both the intensity and universality of the advent of God in Christ, the first Christians saw themselves as the people of God. This title is not withdrawn from Israel, but the reality of being-the-people-of-God in a more intense fashion is open to all, male and female, slave and free, Jew and Greek (Gal 3:28 f.). In the midst of cults and sects, Judaism, Germanic, or Syrian religions, the Christians saw themselves as an elect people blessed by God: unique, powerful, in a sense untouchable. God is bringing out of the nations a people (Acts 18:10); those who were once alien from Israel and at war with God, looked upon as "no people," are his people (Eph 2:19). The idea of the new, pilgrimaging people of God, broader and stronger, is often found in the New Testament writings that challenged sacral religion.

The Latin *laicus* and the English *laity* have generally been thought to be simply an adjectival form of the Greek word for *people.* Was not in Christianity a *layperson* (a term not applied to a woman) simply a member of the people who participated in the new covenant? Critical studies, however, have argued that this was not the case. In secular literature and in translations of the Old Testament after the Septuagint, the meaning of the word is like our contemporary meaning: ordinary, outside, not holy, even profane. The word is almost never used in Christian literature before A.D. 200. Obviously bishop and presbyters, deacons and readers, teachers and widows emerged from the Christian people, but within two centuries *laity* became a term for the mass of Christians who are not among the ordained deacons, presbyters, and bishops. Faivre concludes:

> The term "lay" became more widely and more generally used throughout the course of the third century....At this period the laity was not contrasted with the clergy. The term was a name that was intended to remind Christians that they were called to the same dignity and—at least at the level of morality—to the same duties as the presbyters and the deacons....It was not long, however, before the laity was fully placed in contrast to the clergy and all who were not members of the clergy and belonged to the church became laity.[15]

The Reformers rightly spoke of the priesthood of all Christians, but did not succeed in developing a praxis of universal ministry. Luther's conservative reform, frightened by Calvin and the enthusiasts, hesitated and then returned to the single pastoral office bolstering it up. Some Protestant churches may still be frozen in a monoform ministry rooted in medieval office. Others show a bizarre switch in universalizing not ministry but the laity: they speak of all Christians being lay people in an attempt to get free of the sacramental. Such a flattening secularization process can now be seen as the suicide of a church. Christians are not all destined to be laity but to be new creation, a new people whose psychology includes charism and ministry.

Class distinctions come in pairs. While the clergy became an elevated, sacral state, the laity became a passive group. What were originally titles of glory, "heirs" and "people" become prisons of status. Certainly without diminishing diaconal roles of pastors and bishops today (except when these lay claim to creation and control of grace, structure, and ministry) it can be suggested that it would be more proper to refer to the Christian community as originally and essentially "clerical" in the sense

that it is spiritual and ministerial, and that the vast majority of
the baptized cannot be "lay" if that means passive and secular or
religious in a solely internal mode.[16] Dualism usually means that
one pair has an inferior position. Catholic Christianity certainly
had a history in which that occurs, for the layperson had less and
less activity in the church until finally in postmedieval times the
laity, most Christians, had no mention in theology and little mention in canon law. It was social history and not revelation that
guided this sad decline. The church leaders became priests, and
priests were sacral and holy, and other Christians were profane;
the church became not an organic community of ministries but a
hierarchy on whose lowest rungs were found the laity. What a sad
reversal of the revolution of the coming of the Spirit of Jesus to
his disciples, in which the baptized were not quite spiritual and
holy and in which those whom the Spirit called to ministry were
ontologically and religiously inert. But in some countries a member of the people of God, a "layperson," became an individual
committed to the Enlightenment, one who stood opposed to
church and faith. In France "lay" in the course of the nineteenth
century and into this century connoted the advocacy of reason
alone, of secularity against religion, of faith as a private affair
without any public role, something left to clerics and devotions
(we see this curiously influential even in past theologies that too
sharply divided the secular and sacred spheres).[17] So today the
word can be employed only with an accompanying theological
and linguistic qualification. At the same time in ecclesiology and
in the code of canon law of 1917 the laity "always occupied *the
lowest place* and was defined *in function of contrast* to all the different kinds of classification that took hold in the church."[18]

   To be a layperson is to have a modality of being or, better, of
nonbeing: not-being ordained a priest or bishop or deacon (married deacons are often contradictorily referred to as "lay deacons"). A phenomenologically pejorative or at least passive
meaning of *laity* excludes a baptized person from acting publicly
on behalf of the community and reserves activity to the
ordained. There are, however, actions in the church that are not
performed by either presbyter and bishop or by reader and
teacher but by men and women of the entire people. In no way

are these actions "lay" but are eminently sacramental actions empowered by the Spirit's presence in the baptized. Some of these actions have been long repressed but now exist again; similarly, when the spouses administer the sacrament of marriage to each other, the understanding of *layperson* from recent centuries is inadequate in terms of theology.

Members of religious orders (who are not priests) are, canonically, laity. The canonical status of brothers and sisters vis-à-vis their roles in ministry presents a particularly poignant example of the collapse of the clergy-laity division. In the United States perhaps 70 percent of the ministry is being performed and has been performed by religious women who have not been officially in the ministry. Because real ministry through jurisdiction is tied to ordination, women's roles have been subordinated. They are canonically laity but formally ministers. The piety of the official church, when it views them, addresses them out of the context of vowed laity. Religious women present the most dramatic phenomenological "noncompute" in the world of clerical and lay states; for in their "nonministry" lies great services, and their nonsacral spirituality has created countless institutions, services, and disciples. Not a few religious orders of men, dating from the medieval or Baroque period, have built into their constitutional structure a clericalism, that is, they are primarily communities of priests whom a minority of nonordained members assist. Now these orders are finding this sociological distinction injurious to their very existence. Religious life challenges the separateness of clergy and laity. In its own renewal mandated by Vatican II it has rediscovered a diversity in ministry within the community life and services of the larger orders and congregations, male and female.

How is the ordained secretary in a church office within the ministerial group ("clergy") while the educated, full-time Christian employed in the team ministry of an urban hospital remains in the lay state? We could cite dozens of such paradoxes. To reduce the ordained ministry to a once given character or office that no longer has any ecclesial activities is not helpful (although one would not want to deny the permanency of ordination). A solution can only come from a coherent theology of the ministry that replaces the clergy-laity structure with a pattern of concentric circles of ministries and ministering groups, with important distinctions preserved. Yves Congar described how a shift took place in his own thinking.

> Ultimately there can be only one sound and sufficient theology of laity, and that is total ecclesiology. That theology I did not write. [I have come to see] that the pastoral reality described by the New Testament imposes a view much richer....Proceeding along this line of double recognition is extremely important for an accurate view of things, for a satisfying theology of the laity. Eventually one sees that the decisive pair is not "priesthood-laity" as I used in my book on the laity but much more that of ministries or service and community.[19]

As baptized Christians assume ministry to the sick, various teaching roles, and preaching or leading in communities where no ordained ministers are available, some churchmen struggle to establish a rationale explaining how they are *not* in the ministry. They do this because they fear that any entry into the ministry means entry into a state of priesthood, and such access is closed to those who are not male, celibate clerics. Defenses of the distinction between clergy and laity have their source in a legitimate anxiety that the denial of this patristic and medieval theological sociology will lead to a church without diversity and without ecclesial competence. One could argue that just the opposite is true: the clergy-laity distinction suppresses diversity and standards of competency in the ministry. Church administrators fear that a pietist universalism will appear where anyone can perform any service in the church. In fact, distinction through education for every ministry will increase in depth and rigor as the general Christian population grows in education. The identity of and differences among bishop, presbyter, and deacon, and also between teacher and counselor in a parish is far greater now than it was twenty years ago. Clear ministerial identity brings not monoformity but distinction and demand for competence. There is more distinction in a church through a diversity of responsible activities than through two levels of class. It is hard not to conclude that the impetus of the texts of Vatican II and the spontaneous pastoral response around the world suggests not rejecting the inner meaning of distinctions in the church but the importance of an ecclesiology of unity and diversity. Giovanni Magnani speaks of "the novelty of Vatican II as regards the laity," its "positive vision," and the "remaining tension," while Edward Schillebeeckx wrote:

> Although the Second Vatican Council strove to dissociate itself from this historical background which resulted in a clericalized view of the church, this nonetheless continued to have an effect in many of the statements of the council. A laborious search was made for the layman's place in the church, as though this was the real subject for discussion. But, from the point of view of biblical theology, the problem is exactly the other way around—what is the place of the church's office in the people of God?[20]

Remi Parent notes that "one cannot even count anymore the books and articles dedicated to the tremors that shake...the pair clergy/laity."[21] He analyzes different ways in which the traditional distinction operates within the church. One can see it in terms of the basic organization and ethos of the Catholic Church itself, in terms in of the structures that give power to some and exclude others, and in terms of the daily ministerial life of a church.

Will a theology of the laity last? Yves Congar has written: "To look for 'spirituality of lay people' in the Scriptures makes no sense. There is no mention of laity. Certainly the word exists but it exists outside the Christian vocabulary."[22] Alexandre Faivre asks whether the theology of the laity has not always been since its origin is ambivalent, and asks whether today the theology of the laity is at a dead end. Its emergence at the beginning of the third century pointed to a change in ecclesiology. It enabled some Christians to feel that they were still members of the people of God, despite the place that the clergy was increasingly occupying in the life of the Christian community.[23]

For these various reasons, the social framework given by the clergy-laity distinction cannot survive and one must place several ordained ministries at the center of circles of ministries, themselves of varying importance and activity.

IV. Kinds of Ministries

The new ministries emerging in the church (which are often rooted in old and primal ministries) own different degrees of intensity. What has been called "lay ministry" cannot simply be applied solely to volunteer parochial helpers. Social action, education, liturgy, and health care are central. A realistic theology of ministry in today's churches includes Christians who are in the ministry in quite limited and temporary ways—readers, occasional bearers of Word and sacrament to sick and dying—as well as Christians in weekly ministry, those in the full-time ministry, and those ordained. Part-time ministries are also part of the global expansion of ministry and there is a wide spectrum of these. Each ministry should include some preparation and some public commissioning. Some ministries and ordinations are less intense or of shorter duration, but these make a contribution. Ultimately, every Christian at times would be involved in such services. The pastor and the bishop are responsible for developing the theology of ministry and the identities of the ministers.

Furthering diversity in the ministry calls for a few alterations in the pattern of ministry:

a. The ministerial image and service of the baptized should be enhanced, and the levels of involvement in the life of the community should be recognized.

b. The leaders of the local churches, bishop and presbyter, find their identities in leadership, but this leadership is not purely administrative or liturgical. The pastor's leadership is not simply directing but being a Christian as a source of community life in a ministry. The pastor directs Christians through enabling them in their own ministries—that leadership is expressed in preaching and made manifest in leading the eucharistic liturgy. An integral aspect, then, of being a presbyter and bishop is to facilitate and coordinate ministries: for the local church this involves attracting, educating, and directing an ensemble of ministries and not just hiring or controlling people.

c. Certain ministries, considered important by local or regional churches, may warrant recognition as professional types of ministry, that is, they begin after lengthy training. Their permanence and preparation might call forth a serious installation or ordination in the church.

d. If this expansion of the ministry appears too abrupt, diverse ministries could be established as forms of the diaconate, a diaconate for women as well as men. Such a step has the advantage of giving the permanent diaconate clear ministerial activities. This would also mean that male and female deacons receive subsequent training: for instance, deacon for education, deacon for peace and justice. This revives what may be one view of the early churches where *diakonia* was not at first a specific liturgical or eleemosynary ministry but represents (as it does linguistically) ministry itself.

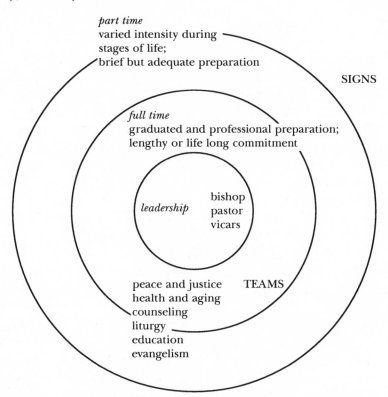

One of the many benefits of collegiality and communion emerging from Vatican II has been its ability to address national and regional differences and stimulate the diverse ways of being the church. A country's ecclesial needs along with its prior traditions in spirituality and liturgy may necessitate modifications to a particular ministry. Just as ministry can assume culturally this or that pattern, the spirituality and devotions of a particular Christian church influences the forms of its ministry. While Scripture and tradition show how certain ministries are always present, the pattern of ministry and the addition of ministries, with public commissionings, can vary from place to place, time to time. Monoformity in the number and description of ministries is not an evangelistic advantage, nor is it an apt way for the churches around the world to manifest their unity. While ministries should not be too easily moved in and out of church structure, the nature and number of the ministries can expand and diminish as culture and church need them.

What distinguishes ministry, baptismal and ordained? We will not return again to the issue of language and pairs of terms. One basic distinction in the ministerial life of the church is quite mundane. It is the distinction of full-time or partly full-time ministers from those who are part-time and then from a third group who are in a transitory mode of service, like readers and distributors of communion. The members of the parish team whose central ministry is their vocation and livelihood and who have been prepared for this work by education and experience form a central core and have, based on tradition and a particular commissioning, a certain importance. "Full-time" includes today the ordained triad and others who have equal preparation and are considered important in the essential life of the church.

We would expect, in light of the theology of the New Testament letters, that baptism will lead many Christians to various ministerial activities during their lives, activities in liturgy, preaching, teaching, or service. We can expect, too, that some Christians enter upon professional ministries, three of which Western tradition holds as particularly important (although Catholicism has witnessed and tolerated their reduction to one). The prosaic term, *professional ministry,* raises certain issues. The word *professional* may contain pejorative overtones from the world of secular or elitist professions. Originally, a profession was a commitment, an act of faith in a work which was often a service, such as, medicine or social service. The United States views Orthodox and Catholic priests as well as Protestant ministers as members of a profession along with teachers, lawyers, and doctors. Professional ministry refers to a group of people in church service (the ordained and others) who have a general theological education proper to a particular ministry. Through education and pastoral internship, through a church's sponsorship and through mature dedication they enter upon an important, specific ministry. They intend a lengthy commitment to this public ministry. This ministry is their profession (but not a job or a status). So professional ministry refers to: (1) services in the church that require a serious call and extensive preparation, (2) services that are full-time and include a strong possibility of lengthy, lifetime commitment, (3) ministries that draw on such preparation and commitment because tradition and contemporary pastoral practice consider those ministries to be central, important, and foundational for the church in its full life. Such ministries imply permanence (whose pictorial theology is the tradition of character), responsibility to the entire church, and qualities of leadership. Normally they would be permanent, although the mobility of Western society threatens the permanency not only of professional ministers in religious education, health care, and peace and justice, but also that of deacons and presbyters. The employment of the words *professional* and *full-time,* building upon baptismal ordination as well as by further ordination in some cases, may not be the right words but they are grounded in reality; the distinction between professionally prepared, permanent, important, and publicly established ministries, and other baptismal ministries is grounded upon the reality of different degrees of ministry—ministries enabled by education, commitment, importance, and church recognition.

Diversity[24] is to be grounded in the reality of the ministry and the church's life. There is considerable difference in preparation and responsibility between the public entry into an episcopal ministry of leadership for the entire diocese and that of a reader at Sunday mass. Nevertheless, the identity of both, bishop and reader, is ministerial: the reader is not a tolerated lay adjunct to the Eucharist. The reading of the inspired Scriptures by a baptized person is a high service to grace. We cannot equate a eucharistic acolyte with a full-time minister in a hospital, nor is the acolyte involved in Christian service as intensely as the presbyter, but the health-care minister may well be. A formal Christian ministry, witnessed to in the early church and needed by this region, should not be ignored or given the vague designation of lay employees. Christians who are active seven days a week in the improvement of political policy and community life are important ministers. New ministries can fulfill the essence of ministry even if there is a difference in service, quantitatively and qualitatively. A solution to the issue of new professional ministries must begin with a theological realism that discerns ministry where the characteristics of ministry are active.

V. Ministry and Life

Being, being-a-Christian, has a place in a theology of ministry. Being is the ground of all that is done, and so the Christian life is deeper and broader than its services. Although ministry is more than the day-to-day life of a Christian, the daily life of every Christian can be ministerial. The lives of Christian men and women have served as voices of revelation, sources of hope and care, and lives of radical commitment have attracted others to the faith. Christian life is often a sign serving the kingdom powerfully. Being and doing, sign and activity are clarified through the following typology (see next page).

Let us turn to three areas where venerable theology and church practice have mixed being and doing in the ministry and where we are challenged to distinguish a mode of Christian life from the church's public ministry: (a) the monastic, contemplative life seen as ministry; (b) secular, professional life as Christian vocation or ministerial sign; (c) ecclesiastical life without real ministry.

a. The ways of being a Christian that we call contemplative, monastic, and eremitical are, as such, not active ministry. These forms represent Christianity in one of its aspects. Daily life is a backdrop for ministry, always prior to and nourishing ministry, but it is not a direct, public action. These forms may be, however,

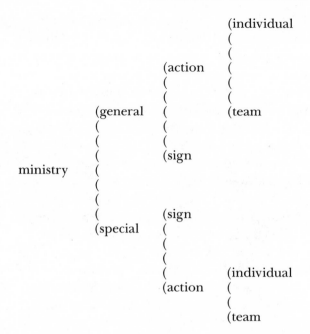

This can be viewed from a second perspective.

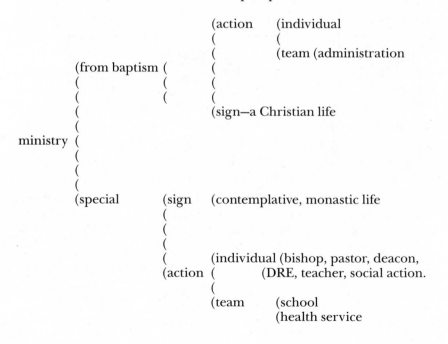

ministerial as signs. This does not mean they are not important; for those called to it, the monastic and contemplative life is a rich way of being a Christian. Contemplatives *are* ministers, however, when they minister to each other in community, or to occasional visitors, or when they write or teach (ministries not central to their chosen life). But the monastic and contemplative life is precisely that—a life. The world can ignore or misunderstand the unspoken words of the contemplative life, of a silent Christian life; society may never even perceive or accept that in silence and symbol something saving is being expressed. In its ambiguous witness in being and life the contemplative life is a sign. In some times and places the signified Gospel of contemplative men and women may be the best mode of preaching, but normally the Gospel is communicated through more direct actions, and it is in direct, full-time professional ministries that we must search for the essential character of ministry. If silence is ministry, if prayer is preaching, if solitude is apostolate and social service, ecclesiology becomes a self-defining spirituality touching only obliquely church or world. We must let the good things of Christian life stand on their own, and also let the analogous complexity of ministry challenge our analysis. Only then can ministry struggle for a wider life. This is only to say that monastic life has its own identity and value but in terms of ministry it usually finds a further realization in direct ministry.

In areas like education and health care, we must note that Christians participate in the ministry not only directly (or by sign), but also indirectly: as members of a group, team, or community whose goal is clearly ministerial. "Team" invests secular professions and activities with a ministerial goal. The universal church is made up not only of dioceses and parishes but a variety of Catholic institutions, particularly educational and health care ministries. What is not explicitly ministry—maintenance, bookkeeping and such (there are no Christian pipes or ledgers) can be an integral part of the team ministry of a group or institution. For the primary ministry of a hospital is not radiation therapy but health in the widest sense, just as the ministry of a Catholic university is an education that preaches the values and message of the kingdom. To this primary goal the entire team contributes.

b. Our insistence that ministry is something the Christian

does explicitly for the kingdom and church (not the justice and love that results from Christian life) leads us to question considering as normal ministry in secret and symbolic modes of Christian life. Life can be witness and can influence secular life without explicit religious proclamation, but is this the typical, the biblically described ministry?

Secular institutes and other groups once presumed that in the modern world explicit ministry must diminish and that covert and symbolic action would be normal ministry. This may have been true of earlier decades in the nineteenth and twentieth centuries. Roman Catholicism, after the Reformation and Enlightenment, felt that the modern world was hostile toward it. Without direct control over society, church leaders encouraged the laity, formed by doctrine, sacraments, and spiritual discipline, to transform the secular order—but slowly, implicitly, and from within. The theological rationale for this low-keyed ministry was not all that congenial to the Catholic mind. First, it suggested that faith was a matter of individuals and religion solely for souls; second, it implied that grace was absent from the world; third, it entrusted to the laity what was in fact an infiltration of the worlds of science and politics; finally, it divided grace from nature, handing over soul and sacrament to priests but world and history to laity.

Ministry makes explicit the reality of the kingdom of God. Christianity does not have a monopoly on justice or joyfulness, but what is proper to Christianity is precisely an explicitness, an exposition of God's plan. Normally, a church expresses the Gospel publicly and explicitly, not by infiltration. It is confusing when Christian ministry becomes no more than a gesture, a hint of a change in the world's future. The Incarnation of God is the ultimate expression of explicitness, as are Jesus' teaching and commissioning. There are times and societies where only the ministry of sign is permissible, for instance, in a Muslim country or a refugee camp, in a factory or an Asian village. There, a patient ministry of being speaks more loudly than sermons. The ministry of silence and symbol, however, is never the norm of ministry. That would deny the incarnation of God's Word and would reduce Christianity to a static sect.

Activities such as teaching French, being a bookkeeper, and farming are not Christian ministry. They are the vocations and professions of Christians and as such are good and holy. We cannot continue the past theory of ministry in which every legitimate and moral human enterprise is ministry. How does teaching chemistry well announce Christ directly in a manner suited to the age of the Spirit? A lawyer's work should be judged not as ministry, but as the work of a Christian; not every legal transaction is ministry, even if legal aid to the oppressed intentionally done as a confrontation of sin by the power of the kingdom of God can be a ministry. Preaching and teaching are direct ways of spreading the Gospel; farming and mining are not. Producing food, directing the flow of money, and making and selling furniture may be important, but neither ledgers nor fields evangelize directly or publicly. Only those already converted by word and sacrament can perceive what message there might be in a bucolic spirituality. This does not mean to imply that the way men and women work is unblessed. Life pervades our work and so do baptism and grace. We are, however, complex beings; we are called to be, to work, to live, and to minister. Considering all of life to be ministry reduces grace to secularity or hands over ministry to a professional class. Defining ministry narrowly does not produce an elite group of ministers but lets ministry challenge the potential ministry of every baptized person. When everything is ministry, ministry fades away.[25]

c. Our narrow definition of ministry as more than a monastic or clerical state questions also the way in which the church is administered. Ecclesial administration developed after the Middle Ages and the Renaissance into something approaching a sacral court. Some of its actions may be ministry but many are not. Churches at the international and local level often employ as administrators those whom the church has liturgically commissioned to be preaching leaders of local churches (bishops) or eucharistic communities (pastors, presbyters). Many of these men now perform what are in fact secretarial and administrative functions. Behind this staffing of the church by the celibate and the ordained is a laudable desire for honesty and discretion and a questionable desire for secrecy and control.

The curias of the church, Roman and diocesan, have been, from the beginning, administrative circles of men whose dedication and self-effacement recall a religious order. Episcopal and papal households were patterned after religious orders. Tradition tied many administrative offices to priestly ordination as an entrance to the curia, and to episcopacy as a fulfillment. This led to priests who had no real ministry in a local community and to titular bishops who more often than not did not fulfill the ministerial definition of a bishop but existed as such only by virtue of their ordination. There exist archbishops who rarely preach, presbyters and deacons who are secretaries and archivists. Goals of ecclesial administration without ministerial identity altered the meaning of priest and bishop, while the mix of monastic clericalism and bureaucracy was exemplified by ministers who were in fact defined in ways extrinsic to ministry: bishops as juridical leaders of nonexistent communities, solitary Christians with the power to confirm and ordain. Nominalist views of the ministry joined with a clerical mode of living to give a public office to an ecclesial administrator. This can lead to a confusion between what we will call a *mode of life*–celibate, male, quasi-monastic, clerical–and what we term a *ministry*–bishop or presbyter. What the church needs for its administration is perhaps a religious order (although nonmonastic Christians, too, can be trustworthy and efficient). They would serve, without ambition and without any hope of honor and wealth through the misappropriation of ministry, as the curia of the church's leaders. In a healthy religious order, service to the community and its leadership as well as to the world is done not only with dedication and humility but with some anonymity. We can see how the employment of the semi-monastic clerical state was a quest for this kind of administrator who would retain a dignity and quietude while restraining the noises of modernity that threaten to turn every church into another business. But today, because of the mix of the monastic and ministerial, some ordained ministries have become honors for administrative posts.

VI. Ministers for the Church

The legitimacy of ministerial diversity is established by research into Scripture and history. The ways such diversification lives in churches, however, comes from experience and theology. How is diversity appearing today in church structure? Which ministries stand forth to complement deacon, bishop, and presbyter? What are the possibilities and needs for a community or a country? There are different ways by which churches will find other ministries: (1) Some would do it by reintroducing ministries found in past tradition. Ministries from the New Testament or from the patristic periods in churches, East and West, are brought back into church life, especially into the liturgy. (2) Others look at the needs around them and the interest of Christians for a particular ministry; churches are, consciously or unconsciously, involved in a discernment and location of people and offices in the official ministry. The ministry, however, is not aided when the goal and function of a ministry is left unclear or when a variety of jobs are gathered together into one office without a specific, extraliturgical purpose, or when a particular ministry is demeaned or ignored as something lay and secular. There are ministries based not upon Scriptural or liturgical legitimization (although both can be present) nor upon a pool of interested people but upon the needs and priorities of a local church (parish, diocese, region, country). Ministry as a function of building up the church begins not with an extrinsic charism nor with a liturgical restoration but with the community's consciousness of its needs; communal goals lead to an ecclesiology, a plan of ministry. Needs and opportunities may indicate God's will while offered talents may indicate charism.

In the early 1970s Pope Paul VI and some Vatican departments addressed the issue of the traditional minor orders and, indirectly, the issue of emerging ministries.[26] Archaic orders such as porter and exorcist were suppressed, while reader and liturgical assistant (acolyte) were retained. Reader, acolyte, and communion distributor were given their own identities apart from the orders of deacon and bishop and were entrusted to Christians as a share in the ministry of Christ endowed by baptism. This beneficial renewal joined two traditional services to some real action in the church and thereby recognized somewhat the ministerial dimension of baptism. There were, however, two drawbacks to this positive move, both involving the realm of the priestly. First, in some of these ministries, if priests were present, they were to be preferred to the laity. We see here the idea of the absence of baptismal consecration and the motif of sacral priest over against profane layperson; moreover, the tradition of the church is that ministries should remain within their proper confines—distributing communion is not the proper ministry of a presbyter. Second, women were first excluded from the restored service of reader and minister, but then an act of ecclesiological nominalism established that women could function in these ministries in an "extraordinary" way.

David Power pointed out that the effect of this Roman encounter with expanding ministry is minimal if we remain with the documents themselves, but that the documents did recognize a new worldwide situation in ministry.

> Whatever the indecisions and ambiguities, the church is working out the implications of the Vatican Council's teaching on the laity and is trying to do this in conjunction with the facts of church life rather than in a purely abstract manner. Thus, the ecclesiological principle which states the call of the laity to share in the mission and ministry of the church on the basis of their share in Christ's own ministry, is everywhere accepted....The extent, however, to which these concerns postulate a new ecclesial structure is not often found in statements. It is more the lived experience that calls this to our attention.[27]

Could there be a further diversification of ministry, a diversification into ordained ministries parallel to bishop, priest, and deacon, a diversification recalling the early churches? Paul VI suggested to national churches that they might add their own ministries to the lower levels of reader and acolyte. "Besides the rites common to the Latin Church, there is nothing to prevent episcopal conferences from requesting others of the Apostolic See, if they judge the establishment of such offices in their region to be necessary or very useful."[28] This suggested expansion of part-time ministries (a suggestion the Vatican subsequently has not approved) indicates a path that should have been extended to full-time ministries twenty years ago. Power, treating ministries other than bishop, presbyter, and deacon, suggested a number of levels of ministry arranged not according to their present or potential importance but according to present Roman Catholic recognition.[29] First come the ministries of acolyte and lector preserved formally in the church's law and liturgy; next are the extraordinary ministers of the Eucharist, whose identity is unclear; then there are ministries of liturgical presidency, that is, ministries that perform an important work for the community but are recognized only obliquely: preaching or assisting the pastor (similar to what was established by the German Church); occasional services, for instance, to the sick and elderly, so often needed in a parish; finally, daily Christian involvement through sign and Word in the course of secular society. Power's sketch is valuable, for it illustrates the present lack of recognition of the ministries of the baptized. There is also the interesting downplaying of ministries involved in liturgy alone and a telling location of the traditional lay witness to and transformation of the world at the end of the ministry's spectrum.

The German bishops set up three ministries: the pastoral assistant works in areas such as teaching and personal counseling; the community assistant helps the pastor in his work, both in the parish and liturgy, except where the pastorate requires priestly ordination; and the administrative assistant relieves both pastor and ministers of the burdens of administration. Here rather than establish clear ministries in the parish, the single minister has been given assistants. The overall impact of the German plan is a pool of random ministerial services. Another step by the German bishops is more interesting. They approved for preaching Christians not ordained to the presbyterate.[30] This has introduced a range of men and women into the liturgical preaching of the community's worship and has established baptism as a ground for important ministry. Moreover, while permitting occasional preaching by valued Christians, it has set up theological education and training as the criteria for becoming an ordinary preacher in a German parish. If we could change "lay preacher" into "preaching minister," we would have an example of the diversification of significant ministry.

France tends to expand ministry through teams, looking to goals and areas that need service, but not particularly focusing on identity and education of particular ministers. This approach, a contrast to Germany and the United States, offers both insights and contrasts. Bernard Sesboüe writes:

> Is there a need to reexpress ministry? Certainly, for two reasons. The first is that the ecclesial usage of "ministry" for laypeople is dubious and needs a new interpretation. It is necessary to reaffirm clearly the ecclesiological import of the existence in the church of two ministerial realities, the one pastoral and ordained, the other baptismal. The second reason is that in the development of the participation of laity in pastoral responsibility we run the risk of an underestimation of these ministries which are the proper field of laypeople and which are in their order irreplaceable.[31]

By the latter Sesboüe means the evangelization of society, which he rightly notes should not be diminished by the entry into proper parish ministries by some laity. At the same time, there is still an overtone of a separation of ministries, which is not always true. For instance, the minister of peace and justice in a parish is involved in aiding society on behalf of a worshiping and ministering parish.

The United States, in a second stage of the expansion of ministry, has been marked by two directions beyond the general increase of ministers. There is the emergence of parishes with large staffs and the increase of parishes directed by a man or a woman who is not a presbyter.

To conclude, should one be afraid when we imagine a church with a variety of ministers, some of whom are not priests? Should there be order but also diversity? Cannot leadership be sustained amid a universality of charisms? The de facto structure of the parish or diocese needs a coherent theological arrangement and ecclesial recognition. At Vatican II, theologians argued for the restoration of the diaconate by pointing out that the church in fact already had the diaconate active in certain areas; what it did not have was the grace and form given to both community and individual that come from the public recognition and commissioning of this ministry. Today this is even more true, and of more ministries.

Nothing is clearer from history than the fact that excessive sacerdotalization leads to an unjustified laicization. When one ministry draws all to itself, it leaves most of the members of the church in a purely secular world and in a church where passivity stifles baptism. Does this mean the clericalization of the laity or the confusion of sacral and secular roles? Thirty years of the introduction of the nonordained into prominent ministries gives almost no examples of this.

There must be more planning for what the American church will be in the next century. The growth of the number of Catholics is an unfaced problem. Some dioceses look ahead in planning for the decline of priests, but the new model is only tolerated, left unexplored or unformalized. The growth of the Catholic population insures that the question of ministers cannot be ignored. Through baptism and confirmation 150,000 adults enter the American church each year; they are potential recipients of education and of a call to ministry. The Hispanic population of Chicago increased from 850,000 to 1,100,00 in the 1990s, and sociologists project that the population of American Catholics will rise from sixty million to seventy-four million. While there is great interest among young Catholics in temporary ministry, one must face the relentless ending of the church of the nineteenth century. For instance, one can expect that the withdrawal of thirty thousand religious women from active ministry in the next fifteen years can be met only by the expansion of ministry.

Ministry other than presbyter (and deacon?) is not taken seriously in terms of incorporation into the diocese (this is less true of the parish) in terms of adequate salary, benefits, appreciation, and spiritual life. Too many still leave in place a weak ecclesiology of "parish workers"; they are replacements for the absent clergy, employees with a job. But "ministry" is never a "job." All those serving the presence of the Spirit are bound by a higher calling, a spiritual life. The renewal of the ministry from the 1960s to the 1990s is the rediscovery of the revolution of the early church: first, the kingdom of God is open to all; and second, its ministrations are incumbent upon all.

The needed expansion of ministry and the new model presume financial support. They require greater contributions from Catholics who support other institutions (such as high schools and universities) well but who have not been educated in the realism of the financial costs of the new model of parish and diocese.

In some circles of leadership there is the gloomy hope that perhaps ministry, other than that which the priest does, will fade away. In this daydream full-time ministries of the baptized seem expendable, doomed to exist outside of the life of the diocese. Poor retention of young priests after ordination is a further problem. It points to dubious quality. In fact, four out of ten ordained are needed just to replace young priests who leave, and so the other six can barely replace priests lost by death or retirement. While the diocesan priesthood will decline by 40 percent between 1996 and 2005, the Catholic population will be increased by 65 percent. The idea of a golden age and its return is not only historically unlikely but is pastorally inadequate. One cannot imagine these declining numbers being reversed by a new surge of priestly vocations. The new ministry is not that solely of the presbyter. The diversity of ministries today precludes a return to the medieval and Baroque theology of one minister, a theology that is less rich than those of the first centuries and that is not the theology of Vatican II. Still, the priest or pastor remains central, for the leader of the community must be a presbyter and not vice-versa. The Church needs local church leaders—pastors and bishops—but the idea of a sudden shift to anything approaching the needed number of competent priests is fantasy. This miraculous nostalgia presents a poor theology. The presbyter/pastor is not the only minister, although he was from the eighth century to Vatican II. The pastor has not been threatened by the diversification of his world of ministries but in a way has been set free and given a clearer identity. This is a difficult position and the pastor is the unsung hero of the postconciliar period.

Each group in the church, from readers to cardinals, has its own distinctive calling and graced life. The church is not composed of people most of whom are failed aspirants to the one sacerdotal ministry. There are many gifts and services in the Body of Christ, and they are not in competition. The role of pastoral administrator illustrates the difficulty of pursuing pastorally the new model of ministry while refusing to accept its theological implications. At the same time, this role has effected a positive influence because it has helped people become used to new images and realities of ministry at the local level. The ethos of a ministry that is only "lay," of the temporary church employee, is dangerous because it undermines the Catholic presupposition that ministry and spirituality are joined together. Can the lay minister follow just any lifestyle? There must be demanding Christian lifestyles for all in the ministry, ways of living the Gospel that are neither solely monastic nor purely secular. We must admit that we do not know what the church would look like at the international level, although we know something of what it looks like at the parish level.

6

SOURCES OF MINISTRY

Ministry comes from the Spirit of God and from the individual's personality.

The Incarnation of God's Word in Jesus affirms that God does not disdain the created, the material, the human, while the preaching of Jesus proclaimed the personal offer of God's reign. Ministry in its divine source and direction comes through various sources, mediations, and confirmations. Ministry comes from God, the Creator of our personality, from our faith in the reign of Jesus, from baptism into the new life of grace, and from our personal gifts. The ministry serving the church and the community is sacramental, and there is a sacramentality of ministry.

The nature of ministry is public action by Christians for their church as service to the kingdom of God. The psychological ground or "matter" of ministry is the baptismal and social life of a Christian in the community, where throughout a lifetime being and doing intersect. The goal of ministry is to serve God incarnate in Jesus and present in history, often through the church. The source of ministry is the agent (or agents) who bestow in private and in public those special ministries that flow out of baptism; we are considering here mainly full-time ministries (with their considerable investment of preparation and time) although part-time ministries, in bearing word and sacrament and social service to others, come from the same sources.

Does ministry arise from a private vocation akin to a conversion experience? Or is ministry solely constituted by an episcopal ritual? Searching for the efficient cause of ministry should not detract from the dignity and responsibility of ordained ministers in the church. We want simply to disentangle the phenomena and structures connected to office and ordination; some of them have been claimed as words of divine rule while others have been ignored by church discipline.

When we look at neo-scholastic textbooks up to Vatican II and their picture of the church, we find a neatly drawn Aristotelian ecclesiology. In that theology, the form, the cause, and the goal of the church are all the same: the hierarchy of bishops and church administrators. People, even presbyters and deacons, are only the material cause, the passive stuff to which a supernatural ministry comes. When we recall how passive the material element is in Aristotelian philosophy, we appreciate how marginalized in the ecclesiology of the late nineteenth and early twentieth centuries are baptism, charism, and Christian person. The role of the Spirit is central and the role of ecclesiastical coordination is important, but Christians respond to the various forces prompting ecclesial service, and the theology of these pages follows the church of the first centuries with various levels of people in diverse ministries in the church.

There is no one source of ministry, and so we will explore the Holy Spirit, the individual personality, charism, ministry, and sacrament and community.

I. The Spirit's Gifts

Is not God the source of ministry? Yes, but the difficulty with such a statement is not its affirmation but its analysis. Without going into the question of what is traditionally Jewish and what is novel in the first commissionings of Christians, we see that a constellation of forces was believed to be present as ministry began. God is active in all of them, and all of them refer diversely to his Spirit, and to his servant Jesus. God chose as the definitive mode of his presence to us the man Jesus, the Summoner to and the Pattern of discipleship.

Is Jesus the source of ministry? Certainly, but such an affirmation says too much and too little. Jesus' call and his Spirit's charism are different modalities of an invitation to ministry. A move from Jesus' invitation to discipleship and then to the activities of the small communities after Pentecost is a move from universality to diversity; from, we might say, prophecy to ministry.

Jesus came to his cross after he had associated individuals and groups not only with his person but with his ministry. The Twelve and the larger circles of disciples were summoned specifically to share in preaching. The post-Resurrection appearances do not begin the ministerial call to men and women but confirm it. The women, groups of brothers, Galileans, the Twelve, and seventy-two disciples—these are examples of variety and universality in calling. These people are not left as students with, and then without, a guru or rabbi, but are urged to share in Jesus' ministry, in its style, even in its divine word and power. Jesus' calling of his first disciples is a forecast of the explosion of charismatic ministry in the churches. Sustained by an eschatological presence of the risen Christ, believers have the impression that Jesus is coming toward them out of the absolute future, which is God. Jesus' second coming is a fire or a magnet that gives further meaning and power to his members' discipleship.

The historical Jesus, after his withdrawal from earth, remains present under the modality of *Pneuma,* "Spirit." The Spirit, which is the source of a commissioning to ministry, is not an abstract deity but the Spirit of God and of Jesus. By baptism that Spirit is present as source of a new life where every Christian is a new creation, a full member of the people, a part of a living temple. Baptism does not merely lay out unformed material for the Spirit's whim, simply mix the clay for the ceramist's wheel to form into a vessel. The human and divine forces that lead a Christian into special ministry through baptismal or public ordination draw on the structure given to a personality by birth and by the spiritual life begun by baptism.

Frequently Christian groups have thought of charism as a spectacular personal gift or a miraculous phenomenon. Does not a charismatic speak in foreign or self-composed languages, cure the terminally ill, read interior thoughts, foretell the future? (On the other hand, in Catholicism any public activity was within an ecclesiastical office.) Although Paul had heard of effects of the Spirit that seemed to have been extraordinary, he always led charism back to ministry for the community, back to spreading the good news of and in Jesus, back to ordinary, daily life and love. Inward maturity, holiness, and outward growth are the goals of the church, not flamboyant miracles. The merely sensational is not the charismatic. Paul rejects the idea that the Spirit acts in bizarre or arbitrary ways. Signs and wonders also occur in the pagan religions and cults (1 Cor 12:2), but in the Holy Spirit there is not just power but also order, utility, consolation, and success. Charism, then, in the Pauline ecclesiology is not the alternative or rival to daily ministry but the source of ministry.

Much of modern exegesis and theology along with the ecclesiologies of some churches have been characterized in the field of charism/ministry by a drive to separate the two; they always pit pneumatic power against community. Overly intent on finding at the origin of Christianity an opposition between liberty and order, between personality and grace, Protestant scholars throughout this century overlooked the context of charism—Body of Christ—and charism's fulfillment, ministry. In Protestant ecclesiologies—behind them lies the negative dialectic between law and Gospel—there is a hostility between individual and social nature (both sinful), and grace. Structure is mistaken for authoritarianism. This takes attention away from the real counterpart of charism: not the threat of authority but the fulfillment of ministry. Adolf von Harnack rejected connections between charisms and the lasting, central, traditional ecclesiastical offices, while H. F. von Campenhausen described the charismatic empowering of the Pauline churches but then concluded that there could be in these communities no "legal system" or "formal authority"; that free fellowship developing through the interplay of spiritual gifts and ministries fully excluded office and authority.[1] Those theologians' language portrayed the Spirit as soaring freedom snatching the baptized from lurking Jewish or Gentile structures, which could contain only the arrogance of human authority. Protestant theologies of a free church tradition accepted only a ministry based originally and continuously on manifest charisms, while some of the traditional churches of the Reformation had accepted the dangerous exceptionality of charism but also had fled any true sacramentality and authority in church ministry by establishing ecclesiastical offices as merely organizational necessities.

The Roman Catholic mind tends in the opposite direction. It

has a different view, a perspective of sacramentality as the intersection of nature and grace, a belief in the continuance of the Incarnation. It sees harmony between grace and creation, spirit and structure. Catholicism, however, later gave its own coloring to the relationship between charism and ministry in Paul. Strangely enough, a harmony between the charismatic and the ecclesial was set aside by medieval and Baroque theologies, and this lasted up into the mid-twentieth century. An emphasis upon hierarchical ministry constituted by legal code was so strong that the charismatic had to flee to the edge of church life, to the monastery or to a spiritual life from which women and laypersons were permitted occasionally to utter a prophetic word. The history of ecclesiology and spirituality shows how easy it is to draw a sharp line between the charismatic/ministerial and the priestly. As early as the third century, the great church was frightened by the Montanist ecstatics, who no doubt retained true facets of charism in ministry. Control through priestly rather than charismatic office came to the bishops, but the charismatic dimension reappeared in Egyptian monasticism and in groups of educated women in fifth-century Rome and Jerusalem. It entered anew through the founders of religious orders and through mystics who were theologians and teachers. The frequent explanation of charisms as extraordinary and transient graces comes not from Pauline theology but from later centuries, each with its own reason for separating spiritual act from legal church office and for offering some marginal activity in the church for women and laity. Charism is defined over against the ordinariness, the stable sacramental power of office; freedom and spirit are in the charism; obedience and church are in the priesthood. The church may need the charismatic for inspiration, but the charismatic ultimately must yield to the authority of the church. Teresa of Avila is the charismatic; Domingo Bañez, her confessor, is the Dominican priest. Francis of Assisi is the charismatic; Innocent III is the ecclesial center. Thomas Aquinas expressed what he saw as a tendency toward social separation by distinguishing among charism (*gratia gratis data*), grace (*gratia gratum faciens*), and public ministry (*officium*). Those "freely given graces" are transitory and clearly distinct from the official ministries of the church.

The medieval distinction between transient charism and permanent office neither accurately depicts the early church's theology of charismatic services nor helps us to understand the expansion of ministry today. Roman Catholic ecclesiology (and spirituality) has now moved away from the past marginalization of charism just as it has moved away from the identification of ministry with one office. Hans Küng explained how charisms are universal and primal, but not miraculous:

> We have seen that charisms are everyday rather than funda-mentally exceptional phenomena, that they are various rather than uniform in kind, and that they are found throughout the church rather than being restricted to a par-ticular group of people....Hence one can speak of a charis-matic structure of the church which includes but goes far beyond the hierarchical structure of the church...it (charism) signifies the call of God, addressed to an individ-ual, to a particular ministry in the community, which brings with it the ability to fulfill that ministry.[2]

Theology should not identify public ministry only with insti-tutional position, nor should charism be reduced to personal spirituality. Today the purpose of aligning ministry with charism is to avoid continuing a dichotomy between the baptismal life and episcopal ordination (both of which have their extreme, irra-tional forms), a division that can lead to an arid separation of being a pastor or bishop from life in baptism and community. Such dichotomies encourage a dictatorship over ministry by a structure uncontrolled by humanity or divinity. The schizophre-nia that separates institution from charisma, though well-mean-ing in its desire for the location of charism and for the clarity of structure, ends by uncritically embracing institution and by merely tolerating charism.

Bernard Cooke accepted the fundamental charismatic struc-ture of the church's ministry but distinguishes between temporary and permanent charisms. He accepts the line that moves from Spirit through charism to ministry.

> Ministerial role is the expression of charism. Not only such manifestly "charismatic" activities as prophecy are rooted in

this empowering by the Spirit, but also regularized teaching and structured governing. This means that one cannot simply contrast "charism" and "institution" in the life of the church. Institutions themselves are meant to be the organs through which the Spirit-animated community expresses its life.[3]

Office (or a commissioning thereto) does not alone create ministry and charism but rather is a formulation of the ministry into a public legal status. An ordination, as we will see below, is the public designation of the Christian to public ministry. Cooke finds a harmony between Spirit and human spirit that seems to agree with Paul's recurring telos for charism: the building up of the church in the world.[4]

Charism ultimately is grace; as such it is a dialogue, a conversation between the Spirit and an individual Christian. The Spirit holds within its being infinite possibilities, and so the individual members of the community have their own pneumatic identities. Each Christian receives from and responds to the Spirit out of his or her own clear, limited identity. Since the Spirit and the Lord Jesus are one with the Father-Creator, there can be no conflict between my God-given biological and psychological identity and the personal gift of the Spirit. My charismatic identity is not utterly different from my personality. Charisms find in people potentialities they can draw forth, for the Spirit does not ask people to be what they cannot be, to exist as they do not in the mind and plan of God. Charism will not lead me in a way that is destructive of my given personality, nor will spiritual gifts utterly transform my one identity. *Gratia perficit naturam* ("Grace brings nature to completion")—Thomas Aquinas's theological axiom of extraordinary ordinariness throws light upon the theology of charism, for when charism is placed within the Body of Christ, that metaphor implies ordinary activity.

What is charism, that silent, interior, active facet of grace, and what is its relationship to ministry? Charism's action is not a flamboyant theophany. Charism mediates between Spirit's grace and service. Charism is not the creation or possession of the individual Christian, because charism is God's gift, the active presence of the kingdom of God permeating an individual, and charisms respect the sovereignty of God and the individuality of the person. Although the charismatic activity of God is for the good of the church, it is never fully fashioned or controlled by the church (although the community's charisms may be asked to discern the charismatic life of individuals and full-time ministries). Ideally church ministry to grace should not be mainly automatic or purely institutional, and Christians without signs of vocation or gift should not be established as public ministers.

Professional, central ministry in the church—teaching, preaching, leadership—does not form a second, ordinary, and official structure over against the rare charismatic. Charism is the source and foundation of every ministry whether this be temporary or lifetime. Charism is diaconal. Every vital ecclesiology draws its inspiration from the Spirit working in the world, and structure is the bridge from divine charism to real service. "Our competence is from God, who has made us competent to be ministers of the new covenant" (2 Cor 3:5, 6). So ministry is not an institutional product of the church but a realization of the pneumatic life of the community; the church is the center but not the sole agent in the call and development of ministry.

Sometimes both visionaries and hierarchy picture the Christian community in a schizophrenic way: for the visionaries, charism displays supernatural powers and proclaims a God-appointed alternative to the offices of a too powerful church; for hierarchs ministry is conceived as office and may end up as an ossified institution because it has separated itself from the Spirit. Without a close and direct relationship of charism to ministry the very source of ministry is diluted. Its openness and responsibility to the Spirit is lost.

We have established "charism" and "service" as normal aspects of community life and have joined the two. Every ministry is grounded in charism; some charisms in individual Christians lead to ministry. Diaconal charisms come to baptized men and women in various modalities during their lives. Now we can turn to further characteristics of the fundamental ecclesial structure of the early churches and ask about the diversity and arrangement of ministers, men and women whose work is so wondrous that they are called coworkers with God (Col 4:11).

In a commissioning to ministry in liturgy, church leaders

are prominent, but their roles do not compete with other presences of the Spirit: baptism, charism, call, and community. The church with its leaders calls forth ministries out of the community so that the church might live. The process of training and evaluating the new ministers tests the validity of the personal call. Obviously multiple influences of the Spirit are no less important than the decision of the community's leader, and we will look at each below.

II. The Activity of God and the Vocation of the Individual

First of all, it is God—now active in earth's salvation history through the risen Christ and his Spirit—who unites and builds the church. It is God who calls (Rom 1:6); it is God who enables people to believe (1 Cor 3:6); it is God who establishes some as apostles, others as prophets and teachers (1 Cor 12:28).

A tendency toward reductionism appears over the past centuries in the sources of ministry, as unconsciously the bishop drew to his office symbolically the different powers that are at work in bestowing ministry.[5] He called, trained, ordained, assigned. Inadequate theologies of ministry resulted from the insistence that there is only one source of ministry. A monocausal theology of ministry neglects the Spirit as active and personal. Not only the community of the church but God and Trinity are neglected by this episcopalization of the source of ministry. The Holy Spirit is conceived in a nonincarnational way, for the *Pneuma* enters life apart from matter, psyche, and history.

Public commissioning to church work neglects the incarnational core of the Gospel, when its style is mechanical and even magical. In the ordering of church life, we do not need to be afraid of diversity. We cannot have too much visibility, too much sacramentality, for the Spirit accepts our animal nature and it delights to come among our tones, lights, gestures, colors, embraces, and applause. It is not the sacramental that is to be feared—here every iconoclasm and puritanism is set aside—but the idolatrous. A single ministry, a monoform leadership of a passive community, an absence of ordinations or commissionings of ministers other than presbyters, or a glorification of the bishop often imbues a church not with lofty worship but with boring sparseness.

Vocation is traditionally understood as a call to a special, usually religious mission. Vocation involves our life of grace as a presence of the Spirit. Vocation in the broadest sense is my taking part in God's plan for me. A personal vocation does not mean struggling for every achievement, nor is it the search for one intensely religious mission clearly given by God.

What is a vocation? God's presence liberates men and women. Among the various prisons that could entice and entrap me is a false image of myself or of my abilities. A false self would lead me to a false vocation and life; it might suggest a life as a composer of symphonies or an extroverted teacher in a foreign county—vocations my personality cannot fulfill. Discovering a vocation is not accepting what is difficult and unpleasant. Finding myself and my future begins with hearing humbly God's call for me to move toward his future and to escape what are for me the false paths and the distorted faces that we call sin.

A vocation is a call, but before that call I am not purely passive. I bring something personal to God's call. The genes and drives that make me to be me are not a burden or a responsibility. I am not called only to listen to the call, just to bow down before a vocation: I am my vocation, for the God who created my individuality out of finite potentialities is the same God who has introduced me into his wider plan of meaning and life. It is out of this interweave of my personality and my promise that my vocation, God's various calls, emerge. Thomas Merton wrote:

> For me to be a saint means to be myself. Therefore the problem of sanctity and salvation is in fact the problem of finding out who I am and of discovering my true self. Trees and animals have no problem. God makes them what they are without consulting them, and they are perfectly satisfied. With us it is different. God leaves us free to be whatever we like. We can be ourselves or not, as we please. But the problem is this: Since God alone possesses the secret of my identity, he alone can make me who I am.[6]

At this point we encounter that theological puzzle that will not yield a solution: the mystery of my free contribution amid

God's influential grace. My vocation, within my life, is a dialogue between the presence of God (who in his powerful vastness cannot be set aside) and my freedom. God's meticulous plan for billions of people is wise, flexible, yielding to change, ultimately efficacious, but always enacted as love.

In the past the theology of vocation was given a cold component of guilt feelings. Since my personality is itself a gift from the love of God, his signals to me will not be ugly or strange. It is a dangerous and destructive theology that rejoices in suffering and imagines that holiness comes from contradiction rather than, as it does, from harmony. Life, nonetheless, is not uninterrupted joy, but happiness and growth are signs that we have found ourselves, that is, found our vocation. Of course, no life escapes the cross, but internal conflicts or neuroses of suffering and compulsion are signs that my created personality, a gift of God, is out of harmony with the unfolding of my life. If our image of God is one of a distant master planner or judge, then we may imagine that there is an abstract or oppressive vocation for us—computer produced, unrelated to our self, commanded by the Almighty. God will not crush us by his vocations/charisms for us, but we through a pagan view of God can enfeeble ourselves by guilt.

Mobility is a keynote of our society; mobility touches each personality. Career development, career change, the setting aside of a career that really never worked—this too is part of an ongoing view of vocation. Without sacrificing permanency in ecclesial ministry, along with so many aspects of social stability embattled by today's values, we must ponder in theology, psychology, and spirituality how the charisms of the Spirit can be developmental as well as stable. Some lives and some vocations are better than others in the abstract, but in an individual life comparisons about good and better are not helpful. Jesus, in his portrayal of a last judgment based upon simple acts like feeding the hungry, and Paul, in his hymnic summation of all charisms in love, direct us to the ordinary. I cannot be called to what is "better" than myself. My concern is to find my call from God, not to choose the most difficult ministry or life, or to try to capture a charism that ends in prestige but also in an addiction to sustain that prestige. Vocation is the call accompanying charisms and leading to ministry.

"Everyone has a vocation!" With our deeper understanding of baptism not as an initiation into a frozen state of life but as implying discipleship and ministry, we can expand that old slogan as a call to ministry for every Christian. Every Christian has a vocation to ministry, to serving the kingdom of God. Some are called to give more and more of their time and energies to spreading the kingdom. This is a special call (but not the only special call) for those to whom it is existentially suited. To be an educator for the Christian community, to be a deacon, to be in social justice, to preach, to prepare those to be baptized—these ministries are serving the future of God. Today the great expansion of ministry leads us to have a wider, and yet more personal, view of vocation. There are ministerial vocations other than those to religious life and priesthood.

III. First Entry into Ministry: Baptism

Christian vocation is begun in baptism (Eph 1:4 ff.). In baptism the early Christians experienced not only a beginning or a confirmation of their charisms but also a ritual with priestly overtones. In the baptismal liturgy and theology of the ancient church motifs of priesthood are connected with the rite, particularly postbaptismal anointing. Within the ceremony of Christian initiation, particularly in the anointing, there may have been by the second century an allusion to the Old Testament initiation of priests.[7] But this "priestliness," as we saw, became not a sacral cult but, rather, centered around service to the Gospel. The current renewal of the theology and liturgy of Christian initiation highlights the discrepancy between a mature theology of baptism into ministry and an immature theology of passive laity.[8] Godfrey Diekmann saw the greatest achievement of Vatican II to be "the restoration of the baptismal dignity of the laity, an achievement even greater than episcopal collegiality."[9]

A theology of ministry on behalf of the community begins with baptism. The rite of Christian baptism has spoken of the sacrament as rebirth and regeneration, but that is linked to the coming of the Spirit and to further life: it is not the bestowal of a talisman. Aidan Kavanagh writes: "It must be remembered that the baptism of Christians was not johannine but christic: it was a baptism not of water but of the Holy Spirit. The water bath is a function of the Spirit."[10] As sacramental initiation bestows new life and confirms faith, baptism also initiates a person into charism and diaconal action, into a community that is essentially ministerial. In baptism the early Christians experienced not only a beginning or a confirmation of their charisms but also a ritual with priestly overtones. In the baptismal liturgy and theology of the ancient church motifs of priesthood are connected with the rite, particularly postbaptismal anointing.

> In baptism by water and the Holy Spirit...one is anointed with as full a sacerdotality as the Church possesses in and by the Anointed One himself. Ordination cannot make one more priestly than the Church, and without baptism ordination cannot make one a priest at all. Becoming a Christian and becoming a sacerdotal being are not merely correlative processes, they are one and the same.[11]

This "priestliness," as we saw, became not a sacral cult but service to the Gospel. Kavanagh, after observing that Jesus, the one priest, was himself baptized in the Jordan, writes:

> While every presbyter and bishop is therefore a sacerdotal person, not every sacerdotal person in the Church is a presbyter or bishop. Nor does sacerdotality come upon one for the first time, so to speak, at one's ordination. In constant genesis in the font, the Church is born there as a sacerdotal assembly by the Spirit of the Anointed One himself. *Laos* ["laity"] is a priestly name for a priestly person.[12]

A deeper understanding of baptism corresponds to (and has caused) the expansion of ministry beyond clergy and religious, and all forms of initiation should be understood in the context of a renewal of church life.[13]

So divine and human forces work to give birth to ministry. Even if it seems normal and traditional, the idea that ordination creates passively in the material of a human being a quasi-divine form is theologically immature. The church should not treat ministry as its creature, magically dispensing it into a void. People are never purely receptive: their dignity as images of God and temples of the Spirit makes them much more. The recipient of a commissioning is not purely passive; for instance, a bishop may at times lack good judgment and so should not be alone in discerning charisms.

IV. Further Liturgical Entries into Ministry

Writings from the early church indicate a distinctions of ministers and their commissionings. The church understood itself as involved in a mission based upon an apostolate wider than that of the Twelve and, in proclamation and conversion, proceeding according to tradition. An entry into ministry is a humble entrance into this world of the church.

The place of ministry is the local church. Whenever we speak of local church, we become aware of the fact that neither large North American parishes nor very large dioceses throughout the world are able to be local Christian communities. The local church should be large enough to contain within itself the resources for central ministries, and it should be sufficiently limited so that its ministers and communities can have contact with each other. Its local nature is not only geographical and sociological, but it is also liturgical and ministerial. Because the dimensions of some local churches have changed little since Christianity's appropriation of Roman and Germanic structures, many European dioceses have for centuries been too large to have any local identity or real cohesion. Large American urban archdioceses have been created in the same pattern. Western Roman Catholic ecclesiology is less episcopal than it seems, for the bishops can never enter very deeply into the personal and ministerial life of their dioceses. The real ministerial structure is presbyteral: a network of pastors. While the Roman Catholic local church suffers from being caught between two large assemblies, urban parish and diocese, Protestant parishes offer real communities. Many parishes, however, are too small, and the Protestant synod, district, or diocese may be a cluster of small parishes and not an ecclesial organism in itself. The addition of ministries into the world, the enhanced liturgy, and the expanded ministry have given to both parish and diocese a new situation, one that renders them more a church and less a monastic chapel or a cafeteria of devotions and sacraments. Ordination comes out of the local church. It should be more than an act of witness by the local community. The Spirit turns the diversity of the Body of Christ into an active community where ministry can emerge and be judged.

The bishop is the leader of the local church and solicits and constitutes ministry in the church (the nature of the episcopacy casts doubt upon the spiritual and theological life of a bishop who discourages other ministries and is hostile to Christians who are not priests). History shows that usually the bishops (and especially the bishop of Rome) drew ministries into their orbit for laudatory reasons, for instance, to save the ministry from control by the state or by transient movements. The bishop is not the only minister, nor does he personify the Platonic fullness of each and every ministry. That theology has a post-Tridentine devotional history but is not supported by the theology or ecclesiologies of the first centuries. The theology of the fullness of ministry residing in the bishop (and then in the priest) flourished under Platonic and Aristotelian metaphysics. As one ministry had absorbed the plurality of ministries, it soon returned to redistribute parcels of ministry out of its own fullness. As it rejects the idea that there is only one ministry (the priesthood shared by presbyter and bishop), a theology of ministry looks critically at the idea that ministries are shares in the episcopacy, in a potentiality of ministry residing in the leader of the church. Does episcopal ministry contain in itself "virtually" (to use a neo-scholastic term indicating a fullness awaiting extraction and animation) all other ministries? If so, then a description of ordination is rather simple, for it is thoroughly episcopal. All other Christians, including the ones to be commissioned to ministry, have a passive role. In this theology of a single ministry, whose participation is dispensed by the bishop, only the bishop is publicly and effectively a charismatic and a minister; before him, not only the "laity" but the "clergy" are passive, for all depend totally upon the bishop's causality.[14] The bishop, however, is not the sole teacher in the local church, not in the second century and not now: he is a teacher who organizes and examines teaching. Catholic schools and their teachers do not share in the bishop's ministry of teaching but in the local church's ministry of teaching (one has only to think that most Catholic schools were the gifts of religious orders who acted more or less independently of the bishops who came and went). Does every ministry come from the ministry of leadership? Does the pope share his ministry with bishops? Does a bishop share facets of the one priestly ministry with other Christians? This is a question of considerable import, for it touches upon whether the ministry is an objective reality, whether it can expand, and whether ministry is charismatic in origin and diverse in form.

The ministry of leadership stimulates, discerns, and orders the charisms of the Spirit. Each ministry of a diaconal charism in the community seeks incarnation. A theology that encourages excessive control of ministry can only pretend generosity in the theology of shared ministry.

What was the source of the theological opinion that episcopacy creates and bestows rather than recognizes and enacts all ministry? Monarchy, Neoplatonism, and the organization of the Baroque encouraged such a theology, and in a ministerial void where only priesthood and its episcopal form existed, it triumphed. Our world of diversity and independence renders such a theology of episcopal ownership of ministry questionable. Just as it appears less and less real to claim that the reality of a Brazilian or Ugandan church is derived totally from Rome, so a bishop, by clinging to total possession of ministry, risks being threatened by the expansion of the ministry; thereby he prefers dividing his church into two groups, "lay" and "ordained," to sustain an elite from which he came and which supports him psychologically.[15] A center of unity both organizational and evangelical, the bishop is the stimulus, commissioner, and center of local ministry. Ministers in the diocese and parish have their own identities. Full-time ministers are not pawns or parcels of the bishop but rather coworkers with different services. While the bishop and pastor have rights with and over them, their birth and being come from a variety of causes, of which the church leader is one.[16]

The Holy Spirit's perspective on ministry is generous and creative. No doubt the bishop's ministry remains at the center of

other ministries, but it belongs to the Spirit to initiate and direct
the process of a call to public ministry and to its inception at
ordination. If this seems too charismatic in the pejorative sense
of being at the whim of nonempirical forces of psyche and Spirit,
we should add that charism and call are subject to strict judges:
to performance (Is this person capable of and interested in this
ministry, clearly capable of preaching or consoling well?), to the
community (Can this person be an effective minister to others?),
and to the ministry of leadership.

A. *The Constellation of Ordination*

We have looked at the three forces where ministry begins
and acts: the Spirit, the human personality, and the local church
with its leadership. Now we want to look at other actors in the
ceremony of admission to ministry, to spotlight movements and
people who have traditionally formed the event of sending into
ministry. Ordination is a constellation of actors and actions, and
ecclesiology is its theological background. The church's liturgy,
which is a symbolic, representative mosaic of rich and sane theology, has preserved sparks of this multiple event. We are not introducing new causes of ordination to ministry but rather coaxing
channels of the Spirit's grace back onto the historical stage and
turning the klieg lights up to discern the diversity that traditionally surrounds admission to ministry. The Spirit always enters
and speaks through many, and so it is not only the solitary mystic
but the social consciousness of the church that prays, "Do not
extinguish the Spirit" (1 Thes 5:19).

People and actions prepare a Christian to enter ministry in
the church. For public, full-time ministry especially, but also for
other part-time or assisting ministries, symbols, words, people,
and movement come together in the constellation of public commissioning, a moment that is both climax and beginning, both
charism and the source of further charism. A new theology of
ministry cannot (as some Reformation traditions intended) turn
ministry into laity nor eliminate ordination liturgies as excessively
cultic. Just the opposite is needed. The social and animal facets
of our human nature call for sacramental liturgy. Ordination is a

visible invocation and affirmation of charism, a celebration of the church's diverse life and mission, a symbol of the Spirit present in the church. Ordination is sacrament with celebratory liturgy and communal structure. Ordinations should be enhanced, not diminished; expanded, not reduced.

If the actions of the leading minister, his prayers and sacramental gestures (laying on of hands, anointing, entrusting with book or cup, robing), are central, focusing the attention of the community and join Spirit with matter, ordination is more than an act by a church leader. Community and Spirit meet in solemn commissionings. Ordination is an ecclesial act involving the entire community. The community's diversity—preserved in principle by tradition and liturgy—is still visible in the ordination ceremony when it is given modest voice and recognition. Liturgy symbolizes polity. The event of ordination is not the apotheosis of a sacred personage but is a sacramental reminder to all Christians of their ministries and a presentation of all leading ministries such as teaching, oversight, and evangelism. The liturgical act of ordination is a community event among Christians whose baptized lives are for a moment focused by the bishop. Just as the leaders of the local church, bishop or pastor, are not monopolizers of ministry but catalysts and coordinators, so all those in ministry, whether limited or full-time, take part in the public life of the community. Part of that life is the discernment of charisms of service in other Christians, the education and approval of new ministers, and the ordination of ministers. The present laying on of hands by the presbyters attending stands for the welcome of the full-time ministers; the voiced approval of the congregation resounds not as polite social applause for a relative but as the climax of a long discernment process within the local church with the new minister. Today these elements of a richer community life are weakly present in the venerable ordination ceremony.

Initially drawn from Jewish (and perhaps from Greek) custom, a laying on of hands expressed public commissioning in the church. Drawing on the Books of Deuteronomy and Numbers, in which Moses established Joshua in leadership, the Mishnaic literature expresses the importance of a laying on of hands for rabbis.[17] In later Judaism the scribes of the first century B.C.

received into their group and confirmed the wisdom of ready pupils by the laying on of hands. If this approach toward communal commissioning entered the wider churches through Jewish Christians, similarly the New Testament signifies the advent of charism with a laying on of hands. In the Acts of Apostles Paul and Barnabas were prepared for a missionary trip by fasting, prayer, and the imposition of hands (13:1 ff.). By prayer and the imposition of hands the Twelve constituted seven deacons for an office of service (6:6). Paul and Barnabas in Asia Minor designated elders in each church through prayer and the imposition of hands (24:23). Those texts show a commissioning to serious church office based upon prayer and a symbolic-sacramental action related to Judaism. As presented in First Timothy, the leaders of communities through the imposition of hands accept worthy candidates into ministry; indeed charism is said to have been given through the hands of the church leaders, given through prophecy (here meaning perhaps the gift of leadership) (4:14).[18]

From a linguistic perspective, ordination constitutes someone in a new position in the order of a society. In Latin Christianity the "laying on of hands" yielded to "ordination," and, as we saw, the ordo of the Roman empire bespoke public power, fixed office, social status and implied a mode of being along with a permission to function.

So the Latin ordo grounding the theology of ordination and orders contains linguistic, theological alterations: an activity has become a social state; a term of group relations has replaced a network of activities; one word has replaced many powers. To the extent that the derivatives of this ordo represent legitimate arrangement and variety, they are sound, but at present, within this word lies a static sociology that has largely faded. In the Western church, ordination was visually a liturgical ceremony involving signs like the laying on of hands, but the word itself introduced an ecclesiology neglectful of service and charisms. We cannot ignore the influence that the linguistic metamorphosis from apostolate and commissioning to order and ordination exercised upon the church.

An ordination cannot only be characterized by a priestly or a ministerial class welcoming someone into a brotherhood. It must

signify a diverse community placing its hopes upon someone designated for a specific work. The community does not just witness a
ritual of initiation but creates a sacramental event of mission. The
community's active presence in selecting and educating its ministries comes to a climax in the liturgy of ordination. *Ordination is a
sacramental liturgy performed by a Christian community and its leaders
during which a baptized, charismatically called, and professionally prepared Christian is commissioned into a public ministry within and on
behalf of the local church.* The elements of this definition sum up a
theology of ministry. The sacramentality of ordination exists in a
multifaceted liturgy assuming a background of baptism and
charism, of education and discernment; the candidate for ministry
will join a community with its full-time ministers and leadership
and engage in public service in the two realms of church and society. Ordination cannot assume any appearance of casual secularity; nonetheless, it should possess in its liturgical sacramentality a
realism of dedication and service.

Ordination brings together several forces. First, one must
discern theologically the prologue to the sacrament: a symbolic
declaration of a ministerial charism and a petition for grace to
enact that ministry. Ordination should not be a pure beginning
ignoring baptism and charism. Second, this particular ordination and ministry exist within a diversity of ministries and ordinations. In some way, the community ordains and all the
baptized ordain but also the focus of ordination, the leader,
ordains. As Yves Congar expressed it:

> A vocation to ministry is not only a personal attraction, con-
> trolled and verified by superiors, and then consecrated. It is
> the recognition by the community and by its leader of a per-
> son's gifts and it designates someone to receive a mission
> from the ordination by a bishop....Since the Middle Ages,
> with its scholastic analytic and its canon law, things have
> been separated which were previously moments of an
> organic whole.[19]

Ordination is a sacrament: it brings, presuming faith, freedom and a more or less intense receptivity in the individual, the
powers of service and the grace of ministry. It is not a creation of

grace ex nihilo but a prayer for grace, a communal celebration of graces promised and received. Karl Rahner wrote:

> The conferring by God of the office of administering the sacraments (which is only possible in the context of bearing witness to the faith) must therefore also necessarily imply the gift of grace, without which the carrying out of the functions of the office would be impossible. Otherwise God would be requiting something to be done, and at the same time making it impossible, by refusing the necessary means. The gift of ministry is therefore necessarily a proffer of grace to exercise the office....But this conferring of ministry is, in fact, always a fundamental act of the indefectible Church and therefore is and remains a valid and true transmission of office, and can never be emptied of its significance and become outward show of such a transmission of power; the gift of grace on God's side in the rite of handing on of ministry is absolutely promised, it is *opus operatum,* a sacrament.[20]

The leader, the bishop, proclaims and sacramentalizes grace through the belief that a charism has been discerned and a ministry prepared; it is also the community's liturgy, a liturgy that is an act of faith by the one ordained and those to be served.

B. Diversity in Ordinations

Is ordination one or many? Which ordination have we been discussing? Should some liturgical acts be "commissionings" or "installations" and others be "ordinations"? Does the diversity now found in ministry extend to ordination? Can the tradition of different orders reaching back to the third century support ordaining traditional ministers such as reader and acolyte and newly begun ministers of healing, counseling, liturgy, and social justice? Marcel Metzger, studying the *Apostolic Constitutions* and the traditions before it, notes that in the early church all ministries, precisely in their variety and difference of importance, received an ordination, or a commissioning or blessing. The members of the baptized community, quite aware of their baptism, saw access to ministry to be linked to a sacramental act. Second, the present arrangement of giving the baptized roles in liturgy and jurisdiction but referring to them as "laity" would be seen in the church of the first centuries as a contradiction. Clergy were not a caste but people who acted in ministries.[21]

Ordination is a symbolic event, a liturgical, public commissioning that points to some deeper, more stable reality, because a sacrament is a causal sign of a deeper reality both in the person and in the church. Ordination is the correlate of ministry since the commissioning event recognizes and begins a significant ministry. Ordination is a recognition not that a Christian will heretofore exist in a different essential and metaphysical mode, but that this individual manifests a charism for service that the church needs. The difference between the pastor and the reader is not one of religious dignity or personal holiness and not one of service or jurisdiction versus secular activity; it is a sacramental (both liturgical and ministerial) distinction in that the activities of a bishop or of a reader are extensively, indeed, essentially, different.

Because there is a variety of ministries in a healthy Christian community, there is a variety of ordinations. Ordination is not an abstract constitution of a Christian for a ministry universal. The verb *to ordain* is incomplete—someone is always ordained to something. As correlates, ordination and ministry cannot be defined alone; ordination is the liturgical and communal bridge between personal charism and a particular ministry.

Three ministries have survived the storms of centuries—bishop, presbyter, deacon—but are they really such impressive travelers? History shows that the role of presbyter (priest) had changed its identity; another (deacon) had been informally suppressed; and a third (bishop) was in sacrament and role partly absorbed by its junior partner, the priest, or by membership in the feudal nobility. Nevertheless, under the guise of these three sacred names (whose etymologies were forgotten or altered) services for the community have been exercised. The third century pursued its historical alterations of ministries. The reality signified by the role of deacon, for instance, varies comparatively in the first, third, thirteenth, and twentieth centuries; moreover, a diaconal reality existed among many men and women who were not ordained to this office.[22]

Documents from the early third century confirm the privileged place that Ignatius, a century earlier, had given to three ministries—overseer, elder, and servant—and to their ordinations. It seems that the roles of bishop and presbyter came to include duties that Christian communities had earlier assigned to ministers called prophet, apostle, shepherd, or teacher.[23] In the writings of Ignatius of Antioch the bishop is described as priest, and elders and deacons are portrayed as performing diverse ministries that assist him.[24] Hippolytus's *Apostolic Tradition* gives us two groupings of ministers: there the first triad receive an important laying on of hands; the others (readers, widows, etc.) do not receive one. In the third century there were still distinctions among ministries and their public commissionings: for example, different churches valued the roles of presbyter and deacon and deaconess[25] differently, while the nonordained ministries differed from region to region, expanding and diminishing according to regional conditions. The *Didascalia* urged:

> Honor the bishop as God, for the bishop sits for you in the place of God Almighty. But the deacon stands in the place of Christ and you are to love him. And the deaconess shall be honored by you in the place of the Holy Spirit; and the presbyters shall be to you in the likeness of the Apostles; and the orphans and widows shall be reckoned by you in the likeness of the altar.[26]

The third century church in the Roman Empire can appear to be one of curtailment of the ministry, but Bernard Botte cautioned against such a conclusion:

> What is the church in the theology of St. Hippolytus? It is first of all a charismatic church. We must not forget that the *Apostolic Tradition* was preceded by a tract, "On Charisms." We do not know much about this treatise except that it spoke of the gifts by which God returns to the human person's resemblance to the creator lost by sin. The *Apostolic Tradition*, which begins by the consecration of a bishop, evidently presents the institutional aspect of the church. We must not oppose these two forms as irreconcilable....It

would be erroneous to see in the institutional church only
an arbitrary juridical organization....In virtue of the prayer
of ordination, the bishop is a charismatic just like the priest
and the deacon; each has received a gift adopted for his
proper function. The church of Hippolytus is truly a church
of the Holy Spirit for both faithful and hierarchy have been
inspired by the same Spirit. The Christian receives the gift
of the spirit in the rites of initiation....The Christian people
(receive it) after the Eucharist."[27]

The early third century generally shows us a transition to
selecting some ministries for special status, a selection based
no doubt upon personal training, upon the importance given
to work, and upon permanence in the ministry. The community still introduced baptized men and women into ministry.
More and more, the members of the community rather than
the bishop evangelize; his ministry is becoming liturgical; he
teaches by sermon and catechesis, summing up this ministry of
the word by baptizing and by focusing the Eucharist of the
entire community.[28]

The three ordained ministries are not survivors of Jesus'
institution of forms maintained in a pristine state, but are, rather,
the remnant—through the centuries polyvalent in identity and
imprecise in purpose—of a larger group. Ministry is not three
eternal offices but a fullness given to the church. History draws
out of the potentiality of a ministerial pleroma (sustained by
incarnational charism) three or six or nine particular ministries.

A theology of active potentiality understands ministry to be
established by Jesus in a global way: with a depth open to various
realizations, with an organic richness that can offer ministries for
different cultures and times, with varying degrees of importance,
and with some roles transitory depending on need. This gives an
institutional form to ministry but allows the churches to escape
being limited by a small number of offices meagerly described or
conceived. Ministry begins normally with public and liturgical
recognition. Since there are already distinct ordinations for distinct
ministries, as ministry expands, public commissionings—some of
which are ordinations—should be increased and enhanced. There
are certainly important distinctions between ministries based upon

duration of service, objective, and significance for church and kingdom. These characteristics will influence the seriousness of the commissioning (which is part of every ministry) and the expansion of the number of ordinations. We already have three distinct ordinations; it is possible to have a few more. The distinction between baptismal ministries and ordained ministries is not fully satisfactory, but, unlike the other pairs, it does avoid the difficulties inherent in the clergy-laity distinction and allows baptism to ground ministries differing in import but having a common nature and theological etiology. Baptism is the opening for all ministry; but because church is a celebratory and sacramental community, various kinds of admissions to ministry should be encouraged.

Our interest, however, is not only the expansion of the ministries within the community (although that is an important aspect of the general expansion of the ministry and challenges past theologies of the ministry), but the expansion of the full-time ministry. Churches are asking how the energies of many Christians can be channeled through their baptismal and diaconal charisms, for we have thousands of Christians entering into full-time ministry not as presbyters and deacons but as teachers, workers in peace and justice, and potential preachers. If through theology and preparation, through tested charism and action, they are in the ministry, they too should enter ministry through some form of ordination.

Essentially an ordination is a communal liturgy of public commissioning to a specific ministry. If one who occasionally reads at the liturgy or bears the Eucharist to the sick can be publicly designated for that limited ministry, cannot teachers and ministers, whose preparation and personal sacrifice, whose parochial and diocesan employment also bespeak ministry, also be ordained? When new ministries assume importance and permanence in the eyes of the church in a particular area or nation, they should begin with ordination. For ordination does not create the ministry, but a Christian prepared and approved for ministry calls for, at the onset of service, an ordination.

It may be that different levels of service should be distinguished by levels of ordination. As with baptismal and ordained ministries there is a problem of terminology. Words such as *installation* and *ordination* ultimately reflect not rules and sacral states but degrees of service, all grounded in baptism. Perhaps one should speak of three kinds of activities by which an individual is commissioned in the church: ordination, installation, and presentation. The three ordinations of deacon, presbyter, and bishop in their separateness are no longer understood as forms of one priesthood; rather, each points to diverse identity (in theory, other ministries could be begun by ordination). Some parishes speak of "installation" and "presentation." Installation is for ministers who have an extensive education and whose ministry is full-time in the parish and diocese, while presentation is for readers, acolytes, visitors of the sick, assistants to other ministries. Nonetheless, there would be some sacramental inception for each ecclesial service.[29]

7

THE SPIRITUALITY
OF MINISTRY

Ministry lives out of the theology of a ministering community, out of a church's tradition of Christian life and faith, and
out of a minister's silent conversation with grace. As we have
seen, a theology of the ministry begins with deep questions rising up out of the faith-reflection of the community. Why does
the church exist? What does it serve? Who is a minister? It ends
with questions about how the church will survive and how it will
flourish in the immediate future. A fundamental theology concludes by offering some directions concerning the individual
Christian in ministry. Theology drawn from and offered to an
individual person is a spirituality, and so spirituality for ministry
is a bridge between the baptized and their services.

I. Disciples of Jesus, Servants of the Reign of God

The reign of God is the background, milieu, and goal of the
church: its ministry under the kingdom and the Spirit effected a
revolutionary metamorphosis in religion. Religion moved to
something new and mature involving all of humanity united in
community, future hope, and divine work. Convinced that they
were the temple of the Spirit of God, a group of evangelists
emerged calling themselves "a people," "the saints," or "brothers
and sisters." In Greek, the elect community was called "gathering," *ekklesia,* and this reality has come down to us in a different
word, *church,* the Lord's household. This people's mode of living
locally and around the world is described metaphorically as an
organic body of active members whose head is the risen Christ.

Christian communities grasped that no Christian ministry

225

can be greater than the ministry of the Lord of ministers. Precisely as the incarnate word of God, Jesus is not an example of divine magic but is for men and women paradigmatically—in his birth, ministry, Crucifixion, and Resurrection—God's plan in a human being. Jesus was a minister to God's reign in various ways. Not a cultic priest but a prophet of the new advent to all who could perceive it (Mk 1:4), he described himself as a minister saying that he had come to serve others. Moreover, he insisted upon his followers discarding ambition and dominance because loving service would transmit the values of the kingdom of God (Jn 12:26). A church interprets its relationship to God's reign in different ways: some are correct and some are debilitating. Ministry follows upon particular theologies and psychologies fashioning a ministerial spirituality in daily life.

The church rejoices in being a servant of the kingdom, and so the church and its ministers ceaselessly try to avoid two extremes: identifying God's kingdom with church offices, or asserting the ministry to be only an efficient organization and not a presence of grace. If the church identifies itself with the kingdom, the ministers claim too much, becoming fanatical ascetics or overbearing pontiffs, asserting that they are always the voice of the will of God. Scandals and missionary failures, the result of such an identification, are detectable in too many periods of church history. Roman senators, Germanic princes, English lords, modern businessmen—the ministers of Christ have ended up behind these masks. It has been not just personal ambition or a weak theology of ministry that led them to embrace these *personae* but a false theology about the proximity or distance between the kingdom of God and its community and ministry. The self-satisfied presumption that "the Church" is perennially and automatically the instrument of the divine will is the danger typical of the Roman Catholic and Orthodox churches, large and ancient. The universal church is the center, directing all of its ministry into a campaign for itself, demanding only obedience and offering only rituals. God's grace is not permitted much freedom, and there are no contingency plans for history. This ecclesiology of glory may include, too, a spirituality of contempt for the world: people are not trusted, society is bad, and whatever is new is sinful. The opposite of Pentecost holds sway: the Spirit is locked up within one set of church forms or sent back to heaven unwanted, and the church's mission is static and exclusively internal. But St. Paul said, "Do not extinguish the Spirit" (1 Thes 5:19).

At the opposite extreme the church, fearful of sacramentality or magic, asserts that it has almost no contact, in a supernatural and ontic mode, with the horizon of God. The ministers may lose themselves in ambiguity and secularity and dare not preach the presence of God in history; they may substitute psychological renewal for improved structures in the parish and diocese. In a church of the real absence they focus upon organization and programs, not realizing that these need a divine grace (which is not in heaven) to succeed.

A third mode of being-the-church is a sectarian movement separating itself from the larger church and claiming to be a sole, miraculous location of God's work today. These groups protest against the larger church's tendency to identify itself with the kingdom of God, but eventually they fall into a similar identification. This inevitable new movement alone is the place of salvation: outside of its purity of Gospel and enthusiastic membership are only theological error and sin. What was at first a burst of healthy ministries recalling the New Testament becomes miraculous, antiworld, and triumphalistic. The sectarian church leadership turns evangelization's success to its own profit: money is a sign of divine calling.

Before and within the reign of God, ministry has three healthy stances toward the milieu that is its source and its goal. In these modes of service ministry flows through the ministering personality into a spirituality of ecclesial life.

As Servant. Ministry approaches the reign of God not as high priest or banker but as servant. When the church replaces the kingdom of God with its organization, adorns itself with unwarranted divine prerogatives (which are not the same as tradition and sacraments), or develops ecclesiastical life in neurotic searches for disfigured power, the church is giving up its modality of being a servant of grace and striving to be an agent of control. But that is impossible. Ministry serves the divine life itself—and a human being cannot control or create grace. Can the servant be the master in God's present reign? Jesus' insistence on the mode of servant is very clear. Ambition, display, and dominance are not human failings but enemies of Jesus' gathering. "They do not practice what they preach....Everything they do is done to attract attention....The greatest among you must be your servant (Mt 23:4, 5, 11). Every minister from reader to archbishop is obliged to serve in the mode of love, a love that is neither niceness nor public discipline. Alexandre Faivre notes Paul's theology of paradox: "A spiritual gift that is the least well defined and the most general, a gift bestowing on the person who possesses it not special place or dazzling function and not status or special recognition within the assembly—that is the gift that is placed above all other gifts, love."[1] There is no activity, role, or position in the church that is not a service, and services that are done apart from love and that oppress others are fraudulent. Authority, seemingly removed from service, exists to serve the unity and the true teaching of the church, to serve thereby the members.

As Universal Servant. The church is finite. It is publicly identifiable amid the human family; its members and its structures are known. Theologies of grace outside the church and explicit faith, which theologians have called "invisible," "implict," "latent," or "anonymous," are important in today's world. They suggest that ministry needs a macroanalysis of grace.

First, there is a theological analysis of God's presence in each individual, a humble and perceptive pondering of how grace is present at this time in this person. Ministers need some proficiency in understanding and discerning grace in Christians but also in those seeking the reality of Christ but not the name. There is grace outside of weekly church life, and ministry involves discerning in those approaching Christianity and those leaving it the presence of grace in a particular person. The minister contemplates how God is working in the mystery and mutable depth of an individual life. Awed by the relentless mercy of God, ministers serve the mysterious point of intersection between a single personality and the unknown God. The goal of ministry is not ultimately membership in the church or doctrinal orthodoxy, although these are important, but the individual's relationship with God, the process of becoming that which God's creative love intends in a life, particularly membership in the reign of God now and in the future. Christian ministry does not intrude on the religious identity of people nor on their personal dialogue with God.

The minister seeks to discern grace outside of the church. If Catholic faith holds that generally and abstractly the Christian community is the center, the explicit expression, and sacrament of the kingdom of the church, a recognition that it is not coextensive with God's presence leads the minister to be modest in perceiving degrees of religious quest. The kingdom of God flows through the entire human race—all are called to be saved (1 Tm 2:4), and the blood of the cross has objectively redeemed not only the baptized but the entire race—and each man and woman at each moment is drawn by God. The horizon in human consciousness that we call grace is present in some modality or another—as offered, received, rejected—within everyone. Christian ministry exists to make this presence explicit: in short, to serve the kingdom of God wherever it may be. This demands theological depth and pastoral sensitivity. Motivated by love and enabled by grace, ministry serves others.

Thus a condition so close to the service of ministry as to be hardly separate from it is to seek to know something about the people in the church, a knowledge of disclosure rather than definition.

As Sacramental Servant. The church and its ministry point to the reign of God and serve what is invisible. Together, they are more than a preacher of the advent of what is unseen; they announce a God who has entered history in the past as well as today. If the church and its activities were not more than words and symbols, we would still be waiting not for more words but for the Word made flesh. In an incarnational faith, ministry exists at the intersection of the human and the divine, at the invisible horizon where grace seeks to become concrete in word, celebration, and person. The ministry not only in its preaching and liturgy but in its myriad of services cannot escape being flesh and blood.

The church should bring reality and power and not be just a library of religious information nor an assembly of cloistered and self-congratulatory devotees. The Spirit finds in the interplay of discussion, mutual service, celebration, and activity its strongest (if far from perfect) realization on earth. Businesses, universities, factories, and the federal government do not intend to concretize the life or values that Jesus declared to be his Father's interpretation of human life. The church does intend that, but it also makes grace—more abundant and accessible after Good Friday and Pentecost—concrete in word, sign, and personal meeting. And the transcendental nature of God and the eschatological nature of the kingdom are balanced by a second dynamic: that of the Incarnation. The religious reality that is the underlying structure of all reality is incarnational, theandric, an interplay of the human and the divine. The church is not divine, but it does partake of the intersection of creation and grace confronting sin.

The great traditions of the churches, East and West, have never accepted the idea, developed among some Protestant churches, that the church is only a voice, or only a servant waiting upon its Lord. The church is servant and voice, but the church is also reality, a sacrament of the kingdom of God. By sacrament we do not mean a liturgical service such as the sacrament of baptism. The sacramental is the interplay and mix of human and divine horizons. There is an incarnational nature to the church and ministry because ultimate reality is a dual presence of the human and the divine. "In times past, God spoke in fragmentary and varied ways to our ancestors through the prophets; in this, the final age, he has spoken to us through his Son" (Heb 1:1 f.). The preface of the Christmas Eucharist proclaims that the Incarnation leads us to move to the unseen through the seen. Neither Christianity nor local church should aim at reproducing the divine logos or Jesus Christ. It is *after* the events occurring at the end of his ministry that Jesus lives on in history in a pneumatic way. What Matthew and Mark call the kingdom of God and what John and Paul call the Spirit express the great theme of Scripture—of all revelation and religion—namely that God is intimately present in people's lives, drawing them forward to an unseen destiny.

The church's ministers really do express, extend, and incarnate the reign of God. Ministry, while ultimately and totally the work of the Spirit, is also truly the work of the minister and even depends somewhat not for its graced results but for its realization on the life of the minister. The ancient conviction of the sanctity of the minister contributing to the efficacy of the service cannot be set aside. Of course, spirituality and holiness cannot effect grace automatically or replace intelligence and natural gifts, education and maturity. In a spiritual life and in a ministerial life grace and nature are both at work. The spiritual life aids the zeal and voice of the minister, while the professional and theological preparation of the minister offers the means for charismatic service. Yves Congar spoke of bishops and priests as "sacrament-persons," and recent French theology has seen that such a theology must be true of all who are significant public ministers.[2] The minister through word, service, and silence, is not only an occasion of God's presence but an intersection of the human and the divine: by this the church continues the life and message of the incarnate Word existing now for us as risen Lord and Spirit. At the same time, all that is accomplished for the reign of God is totally a result of God's grace active in the community, and the church and ministry are subject to the limitations and paradoxes of nature, sin, and grace in every man and woman. Thus the spirituality of the minister is not passivity before a miraculous charism nor a suffering attempt to minister in ways for which she is not suited. It is, first of all, the Christian life but as a background; it is a life of grace focused upon a particular service suggested by both the human and the divine. Ministries are inevitably the result of grace active in people, and their individual struggle to be minister is their spirituality.

II. Spirituality as a Source of Ministry

What is a "spirituality"? What do we mean by a spirituality? The word is only a century or so old, but it has attained in recent decades a usage beyond that of the Catholic Church, where a spirituality is a group's particular arrangement of and emphasis upon aspects of Christianity. A spirituality is a way of life and a way of seeing life; a spirituality is doctrine in praxis. A spirituality is a tradition and a school, a cluster of beliefs about God and self. Where does a spirituality come from? A person living in a cultural era selects and emphasizes out of his or her faith ways of encountering the realm of the holy and of the revealed. That arrangement of gospel truths into a pattern is stimulated by a particular person and time. Life's and love's preferences lead one to select, to arrange, to emphasize a coherent gathering of teachings and images. That cluster, very much one's own, is a spirituality.

A spirituality is, then, a theology of grace personalized. History and psyche create a spirituality. Christianity is too rich to be fully presented by any one monastery or school, by one age or culture. Out of a cultural period and a life, a spirituality appears in a moment of history to present a vision or a path to grace. A spirituality comes into existence not to dismantle or critique the content of the Gospel but to apply dynamically those facets of revelation that appear powerful and usable for this world or this psyche. The thought-forms of a genius, of his or her disciples and community, do not create the gospel Word but they, tuned into the epochal *kairos*, do contribute patterns and stimuli. In a sense, there is one spirituality of Christianity, but within the inexpressible depth of the Christ-event there are distinct spiritualities. The spiritualities that attract disciples and communities are charisms of God embodied first in the individual and next in schools and traditions.

Why do we speak here of a "spirituality" and not of a "theology"? First, there is a freshness in the word that lacks the abstraction of stolid orthodoxies or ephemeral liberalisms. Second, spirituality *is* a theology—but one that is, through its personal selection, focused and limited, a theology personalized. Spirituality does not mean only monasticism, asceticism, pietism, or psychologism. Not only medieval or pietist times created spiritualities; the Spirit is always leading believers to concretize their faith. Spirituality is the subjective side of theologies of grace and freedom: as a personal and psychological comprehension of ecclesiology and liturgy, and as a spiritual life describing a personal and communal life born of the cluster of selected reflections and charisms born of Christ's Spirit.

The expansion and diversification of the ministry cannot mean a diminishment in the rigor or mystery of service to grace and church. New spiritualities must arise, new ascetic forms of

education must be developed, and proven traditions of discipleship must remain. The expansion of the ministry should have not
only form but depth, for the New Testament makes it clear that
ministry is crippled unless the minister is a healthy branch of the
vine, a true focus of the Spirit's presence.

John Donahue offers a spirituality of ministry in light of St.
Paul. Paul had a strong sense of vocation and a sense of being
related in love and friendship to a number of communities; he
spoke of his background and personality, and of the presence of
the Spirit and of Jesus in his activity. The ministry of the word was
central, but he also addressed the problems of the communities
he knew—he was a slave to all so that he might win more to Christ
(1 Cor 9:19) and he had a constant "anxiety for all the churches (1
Cor 11:28). Ministry for Paul was certainly not dictatorship or
self-glorification. "Though often viewed as a rugged individualist
moving feverishly from one city to another, Paul's pastoral strat-
egy involved close association with various coworkers."[3] Paul's
ministry contains doctrine and authority, but it is also collabora-
tive and affective. He longs to see his communities, and his con-
cerns are never separate from genuine affection and real prayer
for them. While he knows great difficulties of schism and sexual
scandal, he never tires of explaining the lofty calling of the saints,
of those who build up the Christian temple.

III. Spiritualities for Ministry

The spiritualities of ministry today, unlike those in the Middle Ages or the Baroque period, are less and less going to be
derived from a religious order. There have developed many spiritualities in the church, and we have no lack of volumes on Jesuit,
Carmelite, or Theatine spirituality; the great spiritualities remain
valuable, for their survival indicates their wisdom. Each of these
can contribute to the life of the minister, although the person
within a particular religious community is immersed and formed
in that one particular spirituality. Certainly it is a sign of spiritual
maturity to have had some contact with a great tradition of spirituality, and to draw from it and compose variations that enrich
one's own spiritual life. One can, as Michael Buckley does, draw a

traditional spirituality into the new ecclesial and ministerial situation. "The church's own relationship with Christ becomes the embodiment and paradigm according to which and within which the person [following the Spiritual Exercises] realizes her or his own relationship to Christ. In being what it is, the church itself indicates what the exercitant can become."[4] The follower of Ignatius pursues not only the union of the person with Christ but the mission of the Spirit at work for the salvation of the human race. The mysticism of the *Exercises* combines a critique of the actual church with an openness for the church to become more effective, thus embodying an interplay of the mystical and the institutional. We very much need a reversal of some of the great spiritualities. Now they would no longer only draw the baptized into their more or less monastic milieu but would go out to the varied ministers of parish and diocese to assist spiritual growth and enable reflection on ministerial life. The mode of life and prayer for today's baptismal ministers is very important, but one cannot look only to the Benedictine monastery or the French oratory for its forms. Why should we not presume that the great spiritualities of the past (like those of Catherine of Siena or Meister Eckhart) can undergo metamorphoses and contribute to the new life of the laity. Just as wider ministry, like every ministry, flows first from baptism and charism, so the most basic forms of the spirituality of ministry come from the dynamics of the Gospel: a critique of superstitious religion, a primacy placed upon individual life, the diaconal goal of grace, a public image and activity by all disciples, an importance of baptism, a call to holiness and the sacramentality of people as well as liturgy. These are some first principles for discovering a ministerial spirituality (we can find behind each one an opposing, self-centered blocking of ministry), and from them would flow more precise spiritualities of ministry.

In recent centuries newly founded congregations have been largely active and ministerial, and one can find in their foundation and life, in the story of their founders and the collective service of the community, an example of a spirituality born of and contributing to ministry. The many vowed groups founded in the great explosion of religious life since 1830 have brought forth spiritualities in action. This recent form of religious life offers a spirituality that is something other than the liturgical and monastic spiritualities of the monks and friars. Often these modern schools of spirituality and religious congregations have spoken of ministry sustained mainly in terms of prayer, but a contemporary spirituality must integrate prayer and ministry.

Another central issue is the spirituality of the diocesan priest. This spirituality was for centuries not an inner backdrop to directing the local church but a form of the spirituality of some religious order and held little that was distinctive about it. Often even the writers and mentors of the spirituality of the priest and bishop were members of a religious order, like Louis de Montfort or Dom Marmion. As we saw at the end of chapter 3, Vatican II goes beyond the spirituality of the French Baroque—it can still offer valuable insights and methods—to a more realistic, communal ministry. Perhaps as part of the reemphasis on the local church by Vatican II and as part of the more focused role of the pastor in a community of ministers, there has been extensive consideration of the spirituality of the community leader in an evangelical life that is, nonetheless, not occurring within the vows of religious life. Introducing a volume of essays on this topic, Donald Cozzens writes:

> The ordained pastor exists for the empowerment of the community. In acting as shepherd, the presbyter experiences his own transformation in the image of the One he represents. This is how he becomes holy. In calling forth the gifts for the whole community, he also experiences himself being loved, cared for, and supported by the embrace of a shepherding Church.[5]

Writers today emphasize the centrality for pastors and priests of preaching, that is, of preaching within Eucharist and sacramental liturgies. Preaching is in turn formed by daily contemplative prayer.

> In these periods of silent prayer [the diocesan priest] finds the grace to name what it is that he is experiencing at this particular point in his journey. In turn, this spiritual self-knowledge allows him to listen to God from his heart. Not only does he find the direction God wishes him to take per-

sonally but he finds himself able to discern what it is that
God is asking of him in his ministry as priest.[6]

The presbyter is a servant-leader, and ordination must be the confirmation of mature and intellectual preparation, and of a conviction that the priest is part of the community of ecclesial ministers.
He finds his identity in the imitation of the zealous Christ and in
the service of others and not in antiquarianism, sensuality, or
quasi-blasphemous claims of controlling the divine.

In terms of the ordained ministries for the local church
there should be too a spirituality of the permanent deacon who
today bridges liturgy and service, ordinary life and ministry. The
spirituality of the bishop over the past century has also been neglected, weakened by an overemphasis placed upon administrative authority, by an attempt to isolate and elevate the will of
authority, and by an exaggerated guarantee of teaching the faith.

Developing a spirituality of Christians involved in ministry
who are not members of religious orders and not ordained presbyters has certainly begun, but it remains the task of the coming
decades. This is a spirituality of people in ministry who are important and active in the church. Bishop Kenneth Untener writes:

> Theirs is the original spirituality—the spirituality of the
> Christian community, the fundamental spirituality of every
> book of the New Testament. Lay people have access to the
> total riches of the Church. Before the coming of monasti-
> cism the spirituality of Christians was simply ecclesial. It was
> founded in discipleship of Jesus, securely rooted in the com-
> munity where the word was preached, Eucharist shared.[7]

Happily there is a great interest today in spiritualities, traditional and new, but we should not think that a general Christian
spirituality is fully adequate to the active ministerial life of pastoral ministers in education and liturgy. The spirituality of ministry will itself be diverse depending upon the social context of
ministry, whether the ministry is peace and justice or health
care; whether the minister is married or single, man or woman
will influence the Christian life from which ministry is done.
Ministry brings chastity but not celibacy for all, commitment to
the eschaton but not poverty, responsibility but not blind obedi-

ence. Just as there have been many spiritualities of monastic life, so there will be a number of spiritualities for contemporary ministers, and the church will learn again the lesson that no one spirituality or mode of community life is the sole ideal.[8]

There can be no spirituality of baptized ministers that is primarily and mainly "lay" and only secondarily and condescendingly ministerial. One cannot imply that reading at the Eucharist is a secular activity because the reader is married and works for a living; any exclusion of the baptized from a sacral realm of rites and vessels is anti-Christian. The baptized can read, organize the liturgy, and distribute the Eucharist, while the Eucharistic prayer in its words is clearly the prayer of the entire community through its ordained leader. The ordained, as we have seen often, function within a community of ministers where different ministries have different activities and roles. But the differences exist within an ecclesial communion of a basic equality in grace. Of course, today any identification of a "lay" world with the secular, the nonsacramental, is self-contradictory and alien to the New Testament. Since Vatican II the structure of the vital diocese and parish has rendered that theology untenable.

Beyond the religious orders, beyond the permanent ministry of presbyter and bishop, the American church and other churches need a spirituality for the full-time or part-time people in church ministries. Richard McBrien speaks of the accountability presumed in a church of ministers:

> Every parish and every diocese has a plurality of ministries. Those who exercise those ministries do so in service of the church. As such, they are accountable to the church. But the church also has obligations to its ministers....If the parish and diocese are authentic manifestations of a local church, then the church's full missionary spectrum must provide the critical standard by which we measure everything the parish and the diocese do: the budget process, the allocation of ministerial resources, the time and care invested in various parish and diocesan projects and programs, the public presence and lifestyle of parish and diocesan ministers, the parish's and diocese's relations with other religious community, with the national church, with the church universal, and with the political community.[9]

If, he concludes, ministry is service to the missions of the Trinity on earth and that ministry is the whole purpose of the church,

> then we have the right and duty to demand, within reason, the highest standards of ministerial performance..., the best in recruitment, formation, and certification of the church's ministers, especially those who present themselves for the ministry of ordained pastoral leadership.[10]

The American ecclesiologist suggests "qualities," traditional virtues, needed by ministers in terms of a basic human wholeness where grace "builds upon nature." Clearly a person needs a faith strong enough not only to withstand disappointment in the ministry but also to withstand imprudent and short-sighted decisions within the church; a hope enabling one to look to the future and take some responsibility for fashioning it; a charity that leads to zeal, to spontaneous creativity, to service, to abilities to work with others. Since so much of ministry is making decisions, prudence (which, along with justice, temperance, and fortitude, form a particular quaternity for life) is of the greatest import. Thomas Aquinas placed prudence at the control center of our personality and our Christian life, and McBrien emphasizes a realism for each minister. "A minister without prudence is a danger to the church. Good judgment is not a luxury in ministry; it is an absolute necessity."[11] McBrien helps us see how virtues have not only a public dimension but how their social and ecclesial modes can be ministerial. He concludes that virtues in ministers should be tested by working in a community of ministers and people.

Richard Gaillardetz brings together Trinitarian theology and parish ministry by presenting the minister as prophet, as source of mature experience and compassion, and as person of hope. When the ministry is viewed within the relations of Trinitarian life, the minister emerges as nourished by the relations, as demanding as they are, of the community.

> This image of ministry is multi-dimensional but gives primacy to the affirmation and nurturance of authentic human relationships which are inclusive, mutual, reciprocal, and

generative, and the condemnation of relationships of manipulation, domination, and subordination as sinful perversions of the call to human communion.[12]

Certainly the difficult field of church relations, in which each minister, pastor, and youth minister alike lives, needs both psychological assistance and a Christian vision drawn from the Trinity or from Jesus' attitude toward his own coworkers.

IV. Ministerial Spirituality: Facets and Dangers

Through its chapters this book proceeds (as has been obvious) from a certain view of nature and grace, one reaching from Thomas Aquinas to Karl Rahner. It espouses a theology of independence and interplay, an approach where grace does not repress nature nor promise miracles of impossible fulfillment.[13] Not all Christian churches espouse this theology, and there is no lack of Catholic spiritual writers since the Reformation offering a counter-theology of blind obedience, or one that seeks out suffering and encourages failure and contradiction, one that trusts metaphor over reality. Does not pastoral experience show that some harmony of personality and grace, both gifts of one God, has positive effects in the local church?

Discernment. We spoke of the discernment of grace at work in men and women. Ministry begins with an openness to the "other," with a sympathetic attitude toward the aspirations and vicissitudes of life. Rather than being frightened by the ambiguities of life, by histories of sin and failure, by hopes and aspirations, the minister seeks ways of learning to be a prophet and an apostle rather than a successful or failed entrepreneur. The abilities to listen and to serve require, as recent writings on the spirituality of the ordained and baptismal ministers mention, time apart, times of reflection and prayer. These nourish the analysis of grace in people and establish the point of departure for ministry.

Generosity. At the core of any life-work touching other people is generosity. While we may view love, the charity and *agape* of the New Testament as the milieu and goal and mode of

Christian life and service, nonetheless, behind and prior to love itself is generosity. It is generosity that, according to Thomas Aquinas, prompted God to create the universe and to become a human being, to redeem the human race. Is generosity a virtue, or is it a psychological trait? Is generosity able to be cultivated or is it partly the result of heredity and family? Regardless, church office and ministry, because they have no ultimate purpose except the service of the unseen God and the seen neighbor (1 Jn 3:14ff.) must presume a spontaneous and cheerful generosity. Service, difficult assistance, extra hours, disinterest in honor and possessions are not to be summoned up in rare moments of pressure but are the atmosphere of the minister. A broad generosity that leads gifts of nature and grace to be with people in some success and enjoyment is unavoidable for the ministry. A pastor, a teacher, a bishop, a cardinal who prefers solitude to people, who is marked by isolation and self-absorption, who has long suppressed in anger any interest in others is in the wrong work, and no amount of ecclesiastical honors will alter that condition. The ethos of the hermit and monk is spiritual but it is not the spirituality of the ministry.

Zeal. Biblical and spiritual writers often speak of zeal. The minister needs to be something of a self-starter, developing a spiritual life that acknowledges the importance of grace for living the Christian ideal, that recognizes energy and instruction, but that also accepts the limits of the personality. There must be an enthusiasm for the ministry, a willing and happy interest in being with other people and speaking to them of God's work in Christ and his Spirit. Zeal need not be, year after year, filled with emotional exuberance. Zeal understands that ministry in the church involves effort and fatigue but also spontaneous commitment. Zeal is a spontaneity, a lack of depression, a positive attitude toward people. Zeal involves nature and grace, psychological content and charism. It manifests a joy in, day after day, working with people in the world of the church. The opposite of zeal is, first of all, laziness: interest and energy are lacking, and projects and plans either do not come to mind or are not completed because they lose their attraction. This apparent "diffidence" may actually indicate a lack of interest in the invisible realm of the reign of

God or a psychological disinclination toward working with people. A lack of zeal may be not a religious vice but simply the natural psychological result of a person's lack of suitability for and interest in the extroverted world of ministry. A withdrawal or depression that results in a habitual rejection of all work may be more than a psychological disinclination to ministerial service. It may become not only a flight into inactivity rooted in a weak self-identity but spurred on by selfishness, lazy sensuality, a subtle idolatry of the self and a contempt for others. One of the paradoxes of church life and seminary education is that ministry attracts personalities that are introverted, slow to act, and enamored of libraries and books—but the ministry is activity, service of other people, an extroverted speaking and preaching.

* * *

There are natural gifts and graced virtues and powerful charisms and there are—here we are thinking of the minister—destructive opposites to nature and grace that must be avoided. Shall we call them dispositions, subtly insinuating characteristics of behavior, habits, even vices? Reducing zeal and diminishing ministerial efforts, they render ministry difficult, as they bring to the person aspiring to ministry distraction and depression. We are thinking of the desire to control, of ambition, of discrimination; and now we turn to some of these anti-elements of a spirituality of ministry.

Control. Human beings like to control their surroundings and activities. Some personality types must have a great deal of control over all that touches them, and they seek a rigid control over others. History shows how religion encourages some to magnify the desire for controlling God. Priestly castes and magic have for millennia manipulated people through claims of human power over divine power. Control can take place through words, laws, and bad theological principles. Control is particularly insidious when that vice pretends to be a virtue: then control demands support from claims to be God's will. The controlling ecclesiastic in the Roman Catholic Church has too grand a sweep of authority—indeed potentially it is the grandest sweep of power—because it claims to be divine and mysterious and lacks counterbalancing institutions. There is at present no counterbalance to solitary authorities. The landmarks of ecclesiastical control remain with us in various forms: aesthetically ugly churches, unneeded church buildings, the reduction of vital parishes, expensive lawsuits concerning sexual misconduct, a cult of ignorance. Controlling personalities' disdain of others explains bad pastoral decisions, insulted coministers, and charismatic initiatives suppressed.

Neither church nor ministry is called to be lord of the reign of God. Hermann Hauser observes: "Christ has explicitly condemned the exercise of directive power in the manner of a royal power: no potentate, no ascending careerist, no course of honors and of material gains in the church....The model for the one responsible for the community must be the Supreme Shepherd (1 Pt 5:4) who gives his life for his sheep" (Jn 10:11).[14] Christian ministry always begins with the equality of the baptized and never loses some sense of working with others; its goal is not to pontificate (sadly, the origin of that pejorative verb is ecclesiastical) but to help everyone in the church in their vocation to be followers of Christ. There is no place for arrogant authorities: "The greatest among you will be your servant" (Mt. 23:11).

Ambition. The message and example Jesus gave to his followers was to become servants. The biblical word *deacon* does not designate primarily an office in a religion. The Gospels are replete with Jesus' teaching about service of others, about avoiding public display, and about choosing a different law and atmosphere for the kingdom of God than political and economic dominance. Before the dynamic presence of the Ineffable, one's only sane stance is that of servant. The church's ministry is healthy to the extent that the church models its activity upon service. Service here does not mean only repeating biblical rhetoric or presiding at too lengthy liturgies. If service includes the preservation of tradition as well as unity and fidelity to the Gospel, a spirituality of the ministry is first and foremost a religious psychology of serving others. The opposite of service is ambition for display and power.

"Ambition for display and power"—nothing could be more removed from the work and destiny of the head of the church,

Jesus. He rejected honors, was crucified among thieves by the powerful of religion and state, and rose from the dead. Sadly, ambition is frequent in the history of the church: from Simon Magus in the Acts of the Apostles through medieval and Renaissance prince-bishops to the embarrassing perdurance in this century of mediocrities clinging to ecclesiastical honors and clothes.

St. Augustine wrote that ambition can dominate a person and that it was the sign of a driven person.[15] He interpreted the "hirelings" of the Gospel according to John (10:12) as church leaders

> who do not love Christ freely and who do not seek after God for his own sake. They are pursuing temporal advantages, grasping after gain, coveting honors from the public. When such things are loved by an overseer and when he serves God for those things, whoever he is, he is a hireling who cannot count himself among the children of God; he is one about whom the Lord said, "I say unto you, they have their reward."[16]

Thomas Aquinas posed the question, Why did the Messiah choose a lowly state of life, being a craftsman and a traveling preacher? He answered: If Christ had lived in wealth, power, or great dignity, it could be construed that his doctrine and miracles had been accepted by people out of deference or ambition.[17] Further, turning to the clergy, he said that an ambitious leader will be a bad and inept ruler-leader, for his overarching purpose is not the benefit of others but that of his own person.[18]

Ambition is a kind of obsession about a goal, a compelling will to posses that goal and so the pursuit of any means to reach it. The desired goal dominates life, and one must seek out and find favor with those who can bestow ambition's quest; their will and attitude must be accepted without any question. An acceptance of not just the will but the mentality of the higher office-holder who can fulfill ambitions must be total and preclude any other allegiance—there can be no independent voices or desires, even those of the Gospels. Conversely, the rejection of those outside the sphere of ambition is necessary; even to be seen in the company of people who represent a freedom or a faith not like the operative, narrow ecclesial ideology of the powerful inner circle is not tolerable (we see the point of the biblical incidents where Jesus associated with the disreputable). Hence the importance of clerical clothes, of sanctuary rubrics, of Latin phrases and devotional clichés, for these externals are the signs of sympathy between promoter and promoted, and of the exalted separation of the officeholder from the laity. Allied to this is the rejection of all intellectual life, of theology. Genial interpretations of the Gospel, and free thinking itself must be given up. One's very faith becomes the faith of another.

Ambition, the means to an end, distorts a personality, and the person who has acquired a church ministry through ambition will remain fixated on the self even when ambition is fulfilled. Church ambition in modern times is supported by the bad theology of God's will being often and easily found in a superior's desires, by the ontology that ordination makes Christians essentially different from each other, and by the disdain of the baptized and their charismatic life in grace. Clearly, ambition is such a destructive fault because it strikes directly at the pastoral life of the church, at the dignity of the Christian, and at the power of the Spirit.

Serving God or Money. The ministry of the people of God cannot be limited to the adulation of one elite or another. Jesus' ministry includes all—the wealthy and the marginalized—but he criticizes the former and embraces the latter. The minister, tired of poverty and work, may find association with the wealthy and powerful an interesting distraction, but their plans and priorities should not determine the ministry (already in the third century Origen complained that bishops preferred being entertained by wealthy pagans rather than associating with poor Christians). Seeking financial help for ministries is necessary, but experience shows it is also the road to neglecting the needy. Too close contact with a rich elite begins to impede the freedom of the Gospel and its *diakonia,* for the preaching of the Gospel and the recognition of the poor tell the world that economic injustice and political discrimination exist. The tendency of elites of wealth and power will inevitably be against change, against ministerial improvement, against institutional service of the poor. From these false ideologies church ministers, like Jesus, must be free.

Fine buildings have ended up compromising the church. Each ministry is a ministry to all the people of God and for their improvement. In the postconciliar church, diocese and parish are increasingly involved in recognizing not that there are a few poor people but that systems of neglect produce people who end up abandoned by society but who, not abandoned by grace, await the church's service.

Antiquarianism. By 1980 there were numerous and well-financed movements of reaction (but with meager popular and ministerial support) opposing what Vatican II renewed and set in motion. That restoration has been one of recent devotional phrases and forms, of superficial aspects of a church that only older people have actually experienced. It is understandable that a few believers (or outsiders identifying Catholicism with change-lessness) would be frightened at the creativity of the future and the reanimation of the early church. Restorationists aim at superficial gestures and oppose the dynamic renewal of the local church. In the baptized they see secularity; in liturgical participation they find modernism replacing mysticism; in the degrees of the presence of grace or church authority they find ideas too difficult to grasp. A longing for the church to stay as it was is a longing for the recent past, for the nineteenth-century version of the Baroque is an ecclesiastical refuge for people who cannot imagine or face a vital Catholicism.

One cannot restore a culture or an age. In the past decade certain ecclesiastical policies and reactionary journals have furthered moves backward and discouraged the impetus of the postconciliar period. In some of this there is a current that is antitheological, antiwoman, and antijustice. A rote creed, an arcane devotion, a handbook of propositions, unintelligible symbols, and ecclesiastical isolation are doomed by the diversity of peoples and by the quest for vital liturgy, ministry, and theology by active Catholics. The cult of the antiquarian is antiministry, for it serves a museum of the past and not the grace of the present. Its theology knows only one ministry: a priesthood of sacral things. Moreover, complaints that the sacral character of the priesthood is being obscured simply cover up discouragement among Catholics that the presbyter and bishop have not exerted enough effort to improve preaching and liturgy and to draw baptismal and ecclesial roles into the local church. The imagination of a sacral character manifest only in a withdrawn life, odd clothes, and some intangible ontological accident is usually an excuse for the absence of helpful ministry.

Neurosis. Because grace builds upon the human personality, psychological disorders will impede charism and its realization in ministry. There are ways of living that demean or impede the power and dignity of the ministry. Depression, anxiety, addiction, or passive-aggressive or schizophrenic patterns hinder grace. God does not withhold his saving and healing ministration from anyone. However, realistically considered, it must be admitted that the problem-ridden personality is limited in the ways that it can be a channel of grace among men and women. Deeply neurotic grooves of living will ultimately impede ministry.

The elitist person who denigrates human beings or classifies them in a hostile way, the promiscuous person who cannot live chastely, the insecure person who must either dominate others or flee from them—none of these are fit for ministry. Ministry reveals itself as immature or neurotic when it seeks to replace the divine or to engage in a self-serving charade. Among human endeavors religion is particularly susceptible to neurosis: ministry can be a refuge for pathology as priesthood had been a refuge of the ambitious. If one espouses a theology or spirituality wherein God works mainly through miracles mobilizing the inactive or inept, and where the education and supervision of ministry is impossible because God is always preparing some surprise, then neurosis may be judged to be no impediment to ministry. An addictive personality is not simply an indicator of problems that more willpower can erase. The syndrome of addiction repeats itself in the personality that cannot function freely and actively without a freedom-negating stimulant. Zeal, insight, and self-dedication are difficult for the addict because the ordinary trials of life are difficult to sustain. One sees the exaltation of the neurotic in the individual who falsely claims to be prophetic or charismatic. She substantiates those claims mainly by being radical and hostile; she denounces the ordinary work of daily ministry and finds in a small group or sect the right milieu for self-importance. From the churches of the New Testament on we see a human tendency to produce prophets who are not verified by their helpful service of others but by arrogance and self-importance. There follows the unhappy dialectic of narcissistic leaders and wounded followers: both need and find each other. Religious groups and society can attract ministries that never have much success. Some collect money; some are supported by the money of others because their gospel supports the status quo. Some spend a lifetime of trumpeting their excellence and the damnation of others; imprisoned in a strong, unyielding personality, they spend years injuring themselves and others.

Deformed ministry often masks some form of narcissism; religion mixes with narcissism, and the minister, liberal or reactionary, escapes self-preoccupations with difficulty.[19] Public activity on behalf of religion, with its distinctive clothes and rituals, boarders on theater. Theater is the backdrop for the sectarian founder or apocalyptic prophet or guru of the self-help circuit. The theology that God works through liturgy and sacraments only intensifies the desire for these performances. Far from being a servant, a confidant, or a shepherd who enhances other Christians, this particular type of minister focuses on performance. Ministry as theater includes distance, superficiality, and elitism; it is the opposite of service, for it is centered on self rather than on God, on externals rather than on the life of grace, and it excludes others or reduces them to an attending choir or chorus. How far that kind of bishop or liturgist is from Jesus, who found himself ignored by the wealthy and powerful, who attended Temple rites from afar, and who faded easily into the crowd of the poor and oppressed. The expansion and diversification of ministry can only challenge ministry too caught up in external formats, because the activities and ideas of others are a threat inasmuch as they distract from the central ecclesiastical figure. The young, women, the poor, the educated, the zealous, the diversity of the church, the collegiality promised by Vatican II must be avoided, for they can all raise questions and enterprises that might prompt anxiety, anger, and flight.

These few examples of styles of life render sustained service to visible people and invisible grace very difficult. The unhealthy personality wars against the rigors of full-time dedication, and the Spirit cannot plant charisms of prominent ministry in a psychological labyrinth of deception.

Nominalism. Nominalism lets words and ideas determine realities: mental, textual, and legal arrangements state what is what. Through Thomism and other theologies and philosophies, the church has been resolutely opposed to nominalism, but this virus can infect church leaders because nominalism brings control—unverifiable and unrealistic control. The triad of God's will (rarely known clearly and easily), church authority (in a monarchical form), and rules and terminologies conspire to support autocratic ecclesiastical power and to repress all other voices. A too strong influence of canon law, a reduction of liturgy to rubrics, a simplification of the Gospel to a catechism—these support nominalism. Nominalism in the church is the incorrect and fanciful reversal of reality and church rules; in the realms of the human and the divine a mental logic dominates. Sacramental grace is blocked or constrained because of a human rule and not because of sin obstructing the divine. Nominalism introduces the ridiculous when it calls a sermon by one baptized Christian a homily and then insists that a sermon by another is an instruction, or when it attempts to draw many and serious consequences from the biological fact of being a man or a woman, or a European, or an African. For a truly Catholic (in the tradition of Thomas Aquinas) theology of ministry, church authority, while it certainly has the right to give organization through administration and law, must be very slow to claim this or that arrangement is of divine constitution. As ministry serves grace, church order discloses the divine: it should not control it unjustifiably or render it trivial, incredible, or absurd.

Psychological health in ministers is not a luxury, and psychology in the preparation and selection of ministers is unavoidable. What are the implications of finding in those preparing for the ministry a disparity between the interests and actions of the candidate and the high calling of church ministry? Formation programs exist to let charismatic inclinations or, negatively, a "phenomenology of incongruence" surface. Inevitably the candidate's own real interests display his or her true personality.

Chronic depression, fear of people, reluctance to learn are signs of how a candidate reacts to ministry. When someone has difficulty dealing with married people, children, heterosexual males, the poor, it is questionable whether that person has been called to public life in the local church. Behavior must be permitted to speak its message.

* * *

Like life in contemporary society, life in the church increasingly involves education. A spirituality of ministry includes the desire to learn about the Gospel, about the history of the church's expression of its faith, and about contemporary theology. The church is always living between past interpretations and forms, and future incarnations. It is difficult to be a Catholic today without some education. Christianity does not lend itself to brief black and white answers: that was true in the third and fourth centuries, in the thirteenth century, and it is true in the twenty-first century. Whether there were ever "simple Christians" or only Christians who never recognized the need or opportunity to think about their faith, they do not exist today and cannot exist in an age of media and education. Telecommunications brings theology into everyone's life, and yet never before have there been such extensive resources in books, journals, and schools, and personnel for learning about revelation and church. Areas prominent at the intersection of faith and life clamor for attention and do not go away; more and more people in the church are asking about them in one way or another.

One of them is the subject of the book: the expansion of ministry.

A *second* is: How is Jesus of Nazareth the Logos, the Son, and the Word of God? How, too, is Jesus a completely human being? The Christian teacher and preacher needs to have thought through a Christology which does not imply that God replaces the humanity of Jesus Christ, nor gives the impression that God only inhabits the shell of his body (not a few Christians, unconsciously docetist or monophysite, think in those unacceptable ways). Jesus' full humanity and true divinity raise questions about his self-awareness. Passing beyond imagining Jesus' mind as a screen displaying at once the totality of the universe, all who explain or proclaim Christianity need to ponder how Jesus knew his intimate, ontological relationship to the Word of God and how he came to understand his identity as the religious prophet par excellence of the kingdom of God. The Gospels show that he, out of his experience, changed directions in his ministry, expanded its horizons, and came to see that not only success but condemnation lay ahead of his preaching of the reign of God. What were the purpose of his rare miracles and how do they always relate to faith and the arrival of the kingdom? The Crucifixion is not an accident drawn from a sadistic heavenly script but is what happens to the Word of God teaching and confronting human society sunken in sin; and Jesus' Resurrection is that of the firstborn of the new human race, the anticipatory event of the resurrection of men and women already destined and empowered by their grace. So the location of the Christ in human nature and human history does not diminish the incarnation of the Word but explains and makes vivid the divine presence.

A *third* area lies in moral theology, particularly bioethics. The moral teaching of the church cannot be presented only as rules found in various documents whose authors may have been poorly educated or inexperienced. What principles does the teaching of Jesus offer? How are new ethical discoveries viewed in light of the Gospel? Christian morality cannot be derived solely from natural law, but human nature, in general and in the individual, remains an important source for the Catholic Church. Should people expect instant answers to every new topic from the church? Social issues seem to be treated differently from marital issues, but there are church positions about social issues that could improve society. Moral theologians, bishops, the pope, the Vatican, experts in all fields, the baptized, and individual consciences—all have their distinctive roles in deciding these issues. Their contribution is not of the same import, but all make a contribution to discerning the views of the Spirit.

Fourth, what is the Catholic interpretation of Christianity? A preacher representing the Catholic Church should be able to explain the "essence" or "heart," the underlying aspects of the

Catholic spirit. Is it a Marian vision or a glimpse of the pope? What is the difference between Catholic devotions and fundamentalisms of all sorts? Catholicism lives amid the great motifs of sacramentality and mediation, community and history. Deep religious orientations, central to Catholicism, continue Jesus' Incarnation in our own time. A positive approach to human life, the ordinariness of grace, delight in sacraments and liturgy, hope for grace working in society, both mysticism and church membership—these ground papacy and saints, devotions and political attitudes. Catholicism is ultimately a way of seeing self and world, and to be a Catholic is a way of being human as well as a way of being a Christian. This faith is more than propositions and numbers (seven sacraments, four moral virtues). The Catholic mind and life are drawn from sacramentality and mediation, community, and a family of traditions. The sacramental vision finds God in and through things; the visible, the tangible, the finite, the historical bear the divine presence. Mediation extends sacramentality. Not only human beings and their communities but also word and matter, action and liturgy signify and cause grace. Human nature is not always ugly, decrepit, or at war with God's grace. Catholicism is an active symbol-making church, and the church community explains the prominence of local churches, different ministries, liturgies in a hospital room or in a cathedral, the contours of the sacramental in architecture or social action. To the surprise of many, Catholicism is not particularly monoform or authoritarian but is composed of many groups and movements: different religious orders, an international panoply of theological schools, many liturgies and ethnic devotions. All these characteristics explain the extended family of the church worldwide and its ability to adjust to new cultures.

A *fifth* area is the history and breadth of human religion. There is today not just academic dialogue but personal contact—in the media, on campuses, on vacations or business trips—with people from other religions. The Catholic Church teaches that grace can be present in other faiths and in other lives. How, then, is Jesus Christ the center of God's plan of salvation for all human beings? The history of grace on earth, born of the loving plan of God, apparently can extend to billions who have no personal contact with Jesus Christ or the church. But what is the purpose of Christ and the Gospel in the long history of religions? Here we return to the theology of circles, circles of grace, not just of ministry in the local church but of sacramentality in a world of grace.

Finally, there is the area of authority: decision-making in the church, the authority of bishops and popes, authority and freedom in theological discussion. Clearly not everything central to Christianity has been formally defined as a dogma. What are the dogmas of the church; how many are there and where do we find them? Some dogmas touch upon an aspect of Christianity that is not at the most central core of faith. Distinguishing degrees of church authority seems a technical topic, but it is an unsettling public issue for Catholics. This technical question is discussed in classes ranging from college to adult education, in television talks shows and rural coffee shops whenever a Roman congregation publishes something controversial. The activity of the Vatican is frequent, but the statements of church authority are not always convincing. Since authoritative statements about ethics attract individual concern and media attention, it is imperative that Catholics be educated not only to respect the various offices of church authority but also to distinguish among various levels of authoritative teaching.

In the spirit of Dominic, Ignatius Loyola, Dorothy Day, and others, theological reflection is a component of the minister's life.

V. Doing and Being: Ministerial Modes of Life

"Doing" is a necessary stage in the liberation of ministry and we have been balancing that aspect with "being," with the spiritual life, which is a proximate source of all ministry. If psychology grounds spirituality where charism draws forth nature, there should be no conflict between psychological profile and readiness for ministry just as there need not be any conflict between the created person and grace. The development of an adequate psychological profile of the personality entering into and enduring a life of ministry is not easy but it is important.

Philosophers tell us that the dialectical problem of being and doing pervades our entire life. Certainly it raises old and new issues for a theology of ministry. Affirming the active dimension as essential to ministry is much like holding a sailing ship's wheel steady in a storm, for people naturally gravitate toward stability. The spiritual life is not a substitute for public service but its ground.

Modes of being have entered into the fiber of ministry in many ways. The church has yet to free itself from the step of Christian bishops entering the Roman imperial bureaucracy in the early fourth century—a moment when the waters of salary, insignia, and power (all warned against by Jesus) flowed into the wine of preaching the Gospel and coordinating the ministry. Rome, Constantinople, Aachen, Paris, Würzburg, New York—centuries and civilizations have not been able to imagine the ministers of the church without their status, their clothes and mansions, their marginal roles in society and politics. There are also less glorious roads by which being infiltrates service. At times ministry itself became mainly a state of life, a mode of being.[20] Lifestyle at times absorbed the ministry. A particular style of being had to be maintained while the ministry of doing seemed to be highly desirable but not essentially necessary. We see this exemplified in the evaluation of a priest, whether by bishop or people, as someone who is bound by clerical style. The church tolerates ministers who are ineffective in ministry, men who cannot preach, counsel, or celebrate the liturgy except with ineptitude; the official church does not, however, tolerate the minister whose clerical mode of being is compromised. If one must choose, right clothes seem preferable to zeal and ministerial ability; *figura* over *diakonia*. Offenses against the essence of ministry were tolerated—communities suffered for years under ministers who were incapable of any ministerial work and whose guidance in private and from the pulpit was both heterodox and scandalous. Offenses against the lifestyle, however, were not tolerated. The alcoholic survived, the incontinent did not; the inept preacher was promoted, the dedicated slum worker who had set aside clerical clothes was forgotten. Both being and doing, however, are aspects of the healthy personality. Christian being is the atmosphere of ministry but not its substitute.

An important aspect of letting ministries stand forth, of letting their activities and goals and spiritualities be unencumbered by unwarranted suppression or permissiveness is to distinguish between a specific ministry and a mode of human life. Both are facets of being-a-Christian. Each has its own identity. By ministry we mean not every Christian activity but those done on behalf of the church, and our theology speaks mainly (but not exclusively) of professional, full-time ministry while including a variety of other true but part-time ministries. By a modality of living, on the other hand, we mean a stable way of being a human person. The conditions that give a mode to individual life can come with birth (race, sex) or they can be freely chosen (marriage, vowed celibacy, divorce). There are also ambiguous (manic-depressive) or anti-Christian (promiscuous) ways of living. All ways of living awaiting our choice are subject to the dialectic of sin and grace. Living out one's life can be ethically and existentially at the service of charismatic ministries or it can impede them by sin, error, scandal or neglect.

We are biologically determined by birth. Male and female, of different races and cultures, sprung from various economic and social classes—these are modalities of human life. But they do not spring from our choice. Can we argue convincingly that ministry cannot join with one or more of these natal styles of existence? What inner dynamic in the kingdom of God would exclude through an aspect of birth the baptized from a particular ministry? Could ontic and biological modalities of life given at birth impede the exercise of ministry in the church? If so, then the theology of freedom and universality of the kingdom of God, so richly exemplified in the Gospels and proclaimed in Paul (Col 3:11), is brought into question. God's Spirit has brought about a revolution in human religion: the Word invites acceptance by all people and this was effected in the teaching and in the sacrificial death of Jesus bringing a universal end to barriers between people (Eph 2:19). The potentialities offered by a universal and eschatological people must be open to each human being. The exclusion of biological groups bespeaks the old time religion of humanity that Jesus came to end.

Social consciousness in the past did exclude certain groups—feudal peasants, American Negroes—from some ministries. The ministry is not a prize or a club but an integral aspect of following the Gospel, and yet it has a rich diversification reaching from archbishop to liturgical reader according to the charism of the individual and the needs of the church. It is hard to grasp how biological aspects could exclude people from ways of serving the Body of Christ animated by the universal Spirit who challenges any a priori exclusivity and elitism in the ministry. The accompanying chart displays the different modalities of life which meet baptism and ordination.

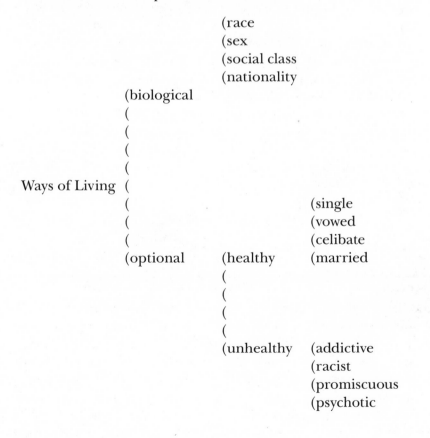

For some reason, the acceptance of differences among human beings is a difficult task. A cultic rejection of another is a mark of sin. Still, the realization that more than one or two modes of life may unite with being a minister should not begin a rush to embrace any lifestyle. While there may not be biological or ontic states intrinsically opposed to ministry, there are freely chosen lifestyles, for instance, addiction, materialism, and sensuality, that are not compatible with charismatic activity for the Gospel. Some churches have excluded marriage as being incompatible with ministry, but this exclusion has been based upon spirituality and positive law rather than dogmatic assertion. There are profound reasons for the preference of celibacy as a lifestyle in the West for the past millennium. Whether that way of living is as suitable to men and women in Asia, South America, and Africa as it was to the Celts and Germans remains to be seen. Nevertheless, the admission of ministers to marriage in churches that now exclude it could happen when a regional church desires it and the universal church permits a change in current law. This would not mean that all celibate ministers would marry, because many of them are celibate not by reason of their priesthood but by reason of their vowed entrance into a religious community like the Franciscans or the Benedictines. Protestant Christians know that a reduction of mandated celibacy for Roman Catholicism would bring new dangers; for marriage brings not only benefits but modern obstacles to pastoral ministry.

It belongs to the spirituality and ecclesiology of an age to select optimum modes of Christian life that will enhance Christian ministry. This choice has its own hope and its own risk, and is based not only upon what seems normal but upon the charisms and eschaton of the kingdom, which ministry serves. Do culture and history suggest that regions rather than the universal church should make decisions about manners of life compatible with ministry as long as these ways of living display clear fidelity to the Gospel? Yet, this seemingly easy argument for regionalization would bring new difficulties in a world whose size media and travel have reduced. As they did in a church of ministries, unity and diversity enter here at the level of being. The Christian ways of life that the public ministers of the church assume are of the greatest importance, because diaconal action cannot flourish where the exemplary Christian life is absent or obscured.

Through most of history the church focused on combinations of life and ministry in terms of gender, legitimate birth, sexuality and sexual continence, or social class. Today we look more deeply at human life, not so much at biological conditions but at proximate, psychological conditions. When we come to remarriage after divorce and homosexuality, new problems and legitimate questions emerge. The ministry is concerned not simply with a private lifestyle after work hours but with the public life of those who are professing the values of the Gospel. The Roman Catholic Church is now preserved from some decisions by its strict requirement of celibacy. Some Protestant churches, with surprisingly little discussion, accepted some debatable lifestyles. Does this imply that they view any manner of living as compatible with ministry? Ministry, however, is not a hobby for everyone but a permanent decision to be both servant and sacrament. Chosen styles of life influence not the external makeup of the person in ministry but the entirety of life at every moment.

The minister's manner of life in its ethical structure and public image is not only an individual decision but an ecclesial decision. Life is the ground of service, and Christian life is, as we said, ministry as sign. The church's approach to life joined to ministry should lie somewhere between the remote decision of a seminary to admit a relatively unknown person to ministry and the similarly gnostic insistence by an individual of an infallible call by the Holy Spirit. The community is not simply an object of ministry for ordained church leaders whose private lives are monastic or libertine as the individual minister determines. The community is not a sick person before a medical team; it is a source of ministry. The charisms of the Spirit, since they are not magic nor extrinsic to personality, will speak through individual lives, and they will be muffled by sin and illness. When a Christian's life is contrary to the Word and sacrament of revelation or contrary to the community as sign (for even the unbelieving and contemning world has expectations of the church and Gospel), there occurs an appropriation of the values of the "world"—the ambition, avarice or sensuality that Jesus opposed even as he evangelized and saved our fallen race. Desacralizing the ministry cannot mean secularizing it; nor can it mean reducing it to vulgarity or immorality, neglecting the cost of discipleship and the contemplative asceticism expected by the kingdom. As ministry expands, formation and spiritual life must become deeper, more intense.

The entire church must come to major decisions, although we should expect more independence for local and regional churches. While the call for an expanded ministry can be prophetic, a solipsistic act is schismatic. The forcing of ordination, the marginal ordination apart from the wide church, can only be a display of an immature theology: such a constitution in orders calls upon a rigid theology *ex opere operato* of external acts, a media event vibrating apart from the living church. Entry into ministry cannot bypass the wider church whose servant the minister is. Nor may ministry claim to lie outside the cross or outside a mature, dedicated spirituality of discipleship.

The challenge is to let there be distinction but also a constant dialogue between the ministry and the Christian spiritual life. This silent interplay in which both forces and voices assist each other is simply a dimension, a mode of that deeper dialogue of grace. Rahner wrote that each of the sacraments of orders and marriage is "a vocational sacrament"[21] in which the inner core of the personality is opened to act under God's influence, to witness, to teach, and to preach. But, like all grace, diaconal charism is neither automatic nor overpowering, but works through the maturity and spirituality of the minister.

* * *

Western Catholicism has a considerable richness and variety in spiritualities—but they have been the spiritualities of nuns, monks, friars, sisters, and priests. Spiritualities of the bishop and pastor, of various teachers, and of the baptized in ministries need to be expressed and lived. The spirituality of the dedicated religious educator, the contemplation of the pastor, the identity of a bishop who is present to the diocese are only beginning to emerge, but their journey to fruition is assisted by the great interest in spirituality and by the number of writings joining spirituality today to ministry.

CONCLUSION

This book is not the last word in a theology of ministry, but it may still be a first word for an ecclesiology which, in imagination and tradition, would attempt to respond to today's opportunities.

To respect the Holy Spirit and the community of the baptized is to presume that the church has resources for the aspects of its life in every age. When it lacks ministries, this comes not from a divine curse or from selfish people in a corrupt age. To be the church in time is to see with courage, intelligence, and hope where adequate energy can be found. Bursting forth and dying away, ecclesial forms come out of an encounter as the grace of the Spirit meets the patterns of human life.

A few principles emerge from these chapters:

1. The dynamic of a theology of ministry for today is not decline but expansion: the expansion of the Christian population, the expansion of their needs, the expansion of the number of Christians interested in various levels of ministry.

2. The context of ministry is grace, that multifaceted, active presence of God that Jesus calls God's "kingdom." In a time of rapid change, theology must be rooted in realities, or it becomes absorbed in conflicts over past and present words. Grace brings reality and realism to ecclesial issues, for ultimately grace is the source and the goal of all that the church is and does.

3. The church is ministerial. Ministry is not a rare vocation or a privileged office but belongs to the nature of the new covenant; God's religious destiny happens in community but is intended for the entire human race. As with its universal source, baptism, ministry exists in the churches as an aspect of every Christian's life.

259

4. The context of ministry is contemporary life. Diversity within the church (and there is considerable diversity) comes not from states of membership or biological modes of human life but from the choice of levels of ministerial activity. Christians are invited to degrees of ministry according to their particular charism, and charism looks both to the Spirit's plan for each Christian and to the needs, structures, leadership, and discernment of the community.

5. The ministry of leadership in parish, team, and diocese exists to serve ministry as catalyst and coordinator. This leading ministerial role, within similar but diverse ministries, grounds the responsibility of presiding at Eucharist and of focusing and maintaining union with the church's tradition and universality.

Our conclusions may, in fact, go little beyond the five trajectories sketched at the opening of the book, where the expansion of population and the migration of groups meet a rediscovery of the Body of Christ and the universality of ministry. It does not take great imagination to see that the immediate future should bring education, spirituality, and financial and professional justice for all ministers in the Catholic Church; a return to a high standard for future priests and bishops in terms of understanding theology and working with pastoral experience and success on behalf of the ministering church; a preparation for the exit over the next decade or more of a large number of religious women active in the ministry, particularly ministries to the poor. Furthermore, there should be open conversations at the national and international level on the ordination of married men and on the public ministries of women.[1]

There are limitations in expression in the previous pages, and ideas that are incomplete. From my fallible perspective, there is nothing that is contrary to the New Testament nor to the tradition of the church. Whatever its deficiencies, this book does present a theology of the ministry that is coherent, realistic, and evangelistic.

History has its own schedule. In the long run, incapable of being easily blocked, time is on the side of the expansion of ministry because of the modern churches' large numbers of parishioners. A reemphasis of facets of the early church, like wider ministry, will take longer than a few decades, and the ministering church must be patient. If we are in the midst of an unprecedented change in parish and diocesan forms and in an emerging return to the diaconal charismatic revolution in religion enacted by Jesus' followers, we cannot expect history and church to race forward. We have today still the first generation: the first generation of this new era to be lay theologians, to be religious educators, to be directors of the RCIA, to direct new ministries, the first generation of pastors to move easily from Tridentine solitariness to a broad parish staff, and the first generation of pastoral associates.

More ministers are needed for the great number of believers and non-believers: for ministering to their graced lives with some individuality, for meeting heightened levels of education and cultural diversity in the world, and for engaging the great works of mercy and evangelization that a large global population needs. We might conclude that ahead will be new religious orders. Will there be a fourth form of religious life ranking with monks, friars, and active orders (The unimaginative imitation of religious life in the 1940s, which has produced a few groups since 1980 is not significant.)? It is possible that such a future is not the plan of the Holy Spirit. The new family of religious orders seems to be the baptized. For the numbers of people and their ministerial needs even tens of thousands of vowed men and women would not be adequate (although religious will remain, in smaller numbers, significant). The end of the recent cycle of religious life—from 1530 or 1830—is indeed leading ahead. But it may be leading into broader modes and kinds of ministry: in short, into a church of ministers, many with the same education as priests and religious.

We should hesitate to glorify our own age or the first century. Nevertheless, there seems to be an affinity between our times and the first decades of Christianity from the point of view of ministry. The similarity comes from the awareness that Christ sent his followers to be ministers of the good news to all the earth. After Pentecost, the church came to the startling conclusion that it was destined not for Jews alone, nor for just Antiochenes or Corinthians, but for all the world. There have been centuries when that insight was paramount in the church's consciousness, and centuries when it was forgotten. The transformation of ministry—not a revolution or a modification—has in fact occurred several times and is now joined to the emergence of a varied world-church.

We should not be surprised that questions remain to be answered (the expansion of ordinations), that issues of image and ethos are challenging (the ordination of married men), that issues of tradition are unsettling (the public ministries of women), or that language itself does not reflect well the present situation. Klaus Schatz concludes his sweeping study of papal primacy by noting that Vatican II permitted a variety of theologies to speak. There is the past theology of the pope and bishops ministering alone, and the new theology of each placed in a context of communion or collegiality; there is a theology of an almost divine priesthood and that of baptismal ordination; there is the tension between jurisdiction and ordained ministry, the collapse of clergy and laity as the basic ontic format for Christians, and the emergence of local church and ministry in many countries outside of Europe.[2] The past seven hundred years indicate many times when small groups offering the older theology of baptismal and evangelical ministry were silenced by church authority or diluted by being forced to enter the priesthood or convent. But now in a new century we are dealing not with small movements but with the form of the local church, not with a few hundred people but with a hundred thousand. It is a question of how to shape an engaging church, a local church, and a church for the world.

NOTES

PREFACE

1. Michael McGinniss pointed out what the author did not perceive during the writing of *Theology of Ministry*, namely, the formal relationship of the book's pattern to the theology of Karl Rahner: "The theology of grace within culture is distinctly Rahnerian. Church and ministry serve grace, the presence of God, the in-breaking Kingdom. Grace is the prior reality; church and ministry are servants, heralds, and sacraments of the presence of God drawing so close to the world in love as to be the very environment in which we live....The church is uncentered in that its mission and structures (language, law, ritual, organization, and so on) are always to be understood in light of, and to be critiqued by, the Kingdom of God....The historico-cultural forms are principles of self-interpretation which the Church employs as it seeks those particular forms which will enable it to be a vital and credible sacrament in the present" (Review of *Theology of Ministry* in *Theological Studies* 45 [1984]: 384).

1. MINISTRY: BETWEEN CULTURE AND GRACE

1. The restored diaconate is an awkward but valuable intermediate stage; it is a traditional sacramental order and a part of the "clergy," but it changes the image and phenomenon of such ministry by admitting married men.

2. *Origins* gives, over the past decades, the documents of bishops and of the National Conference of Catholic Bishops as a documentary history of the emergence of an expanded ministry; this process is continuing in special committees of the NCCB.

3. It is worth noting that the expansion of the ministry within the Roman Catholic Church has not at all led to accusations of becoming Protestant. Those who do not agree with roles for the baptized and for women in the life of the church have, nonetheless, been perceptive

enough to see that the presence of youth ministers and acolytes does not imply the ecclesiology of other Christian traditions. Indeed, the initial expansion of the ministry occurred within the liturgy and then quickly poured out into evangelism. The reemphasis upon the theology of baptism by the precursors of Vatican II is a factor here, as is the Catholic ability to draw realities into the realm of the sacramental. Indeed, it is the traditional praxis of having in the church only one minister, the pastor, which resembles some Protestant ecclesiologies.

4. Cardinal Montini, *Discorsi al Clero, 1957–1963* (Milan: Studi, 1963) cited in Yves Congar, "Moving towards a Pilgrim Church," in A. Stacpoole, *Vatican II Revisited* (Minneapolis: Winston, 1986), 142.

5. Y. Congar, *Lay People in the Church. A Study for a Theology of Laity* (Westminster: Newman, 1957), xvi; Congar speaks in the 1950s of lay people taking part "in the hierarchical apostolate, that is, in the sacred activity...which defines the church's proper task and mission." *Lay People in the Church*, xxiv.

6. Y. Congar, "Congar, "My Path-Findings in the Theology of Laity and Ministries," *The Jurist* 32 (1972): 169, 181. "The *responsibility* of witness and service flows from the Christian quality as such: thus there is mission in the broad sense, and this mission is equally incumbent on every Christian. All the disciples received the Holy Spirit and the gifts which render them responsible for God's cause" (Y. Congar, *Le Concile au jour le jour* [Session IV] [Paris: Cerf, 1966], 61); for another journal of the course of the Council in terms of ecclesial issues, see Joseph Ratzinger, *Theological Highlights of Vatican II* (Mahwah, NJ: Paulist, 1966).

7. Y. Congar, "My Path-Findings": 176, 178.

8. Y. Congar lists words of the conciliar documents not found in those of Vatican I: *love* (113 times), *evangelization* (31 times), *layperson* (200 times), *ministry* (147 times), *to minister* (31 times), *service* (80 times), and *to serve* (17 times).

9. See Dennis Castillo, "The Origin of the Priest Shortage: 1942–1962," *America* 168 (1992): 302–4.

10. Y. Congar, "Reception as an Ecclesiological Reality," in Giuseppe Alberigo and Anton Weiler, eds., *Election and Consensus in the Church, Concilium* 77 (New York: Herder and Herder, 1972), 60; see B. Stubenrauch, "Tradition und kirchliche Erneuerung," *Stimmen der Zeit* 214 (1996): 478–83; Michael Himes, "The Ecclesiological Significance of the Reception of Doctrine," *Heythrop Journal* 33 (1992): 146–60.

11. H. Legrand, "Le Développement d'Église-subjets, à la suite de Vatican II," *Les Églises après Vatican II. Dynamisme et Prospective* (Paris: Beauchesne, 1981), 149–84. Clearly, a restoration of an ethos of Vatican

control and diminution of the episcopacy to a reward for ecclesiastical service has direct consequences for the ministry in the local church.

12. *Dogmatic Constitution on the Church*, n. 30.

13. H. Pottmeyer, "A New Phase in the Reception of Vatican II: Twenty Years of Interpretation of the Council," in G. Alberigo, *The Reception of Vatican II* (Washington: Catholic University of America, 1987), 43.

14. R. McBrien, "The Ecclesiology of Vatican II," *Catholicism* (San Francisco: HarperCollins, 1994), 682–87; see Dennis M. Doyle, *The Church Emerging from Vatican II* (Mystic: Twenty-Third Publications, 1992); G. Alberigo and J. Komonchak, *History of Vatican II* (Maryknoll: Orbis, 1995).

15. The ecclesiology of the neo-scholastic manuals can be found in a textbook by Gerard Paris, widely used in the *studia* of the Dominican order, *Tractatus de ecclesia Christi ad mentem S. Thomae Aquinatis* (Malta: Muscat, 1949), which presents the four causes of the church in Aristotelian language: the formal cause is the bishops; the efficient cause is Jesus, the Holy Spirit, and the bishops; the final cause is heaven; the material cause, like clay for a statue, is everyone who is not a bishop, provincial, or pastor.

16. Hermann Pottmeyer writes: "The difference between this and neo-ultramonatane ecclesiology is immediately evident. In that earlier view the church appears as the mature, one-sided teacher of humanity....The theologically grounded liberation of world and society for the development of its own proper realities, the recognition of a proper and specific religious role in this society, which is understood as a service to human development, the acceptance of a dialogical relationship between partners whose pluralism one expects, and finally the affirmation of the gain that individual self-determination can bring—all this is characteristic of a progressive, if also critical-reflexive modernization of the church which is found in the ecclesiology of Vatican II." Hermann J. Pottmeyer, "Modernisierung in der katholischen Kirche," in F. X. Kaufmann, ed., *Vatikanum II und Modernisierung* (Paderborn: Schöningh, 1996), 131.

17. The ecclesiology of "priest, prophet, and king" is a transitional theology. It has some rich biblical and patristic sources, and permitted Roman Catholic thinking to move away from an isolation of all activity in the ordained. But it remains a theology that has considerable limitations and is not adequate for today's local church. Since its ministerial application is rather recent, coming from Bucer and Calvin, it is first of all a theology of three metaphors: neither the baptized nor the ordained are literally priests, prophets, or royal rulers. So these terms must be interpreted, and the interpretations vary as they seek tenuous links with

parish life. A theology of active ministries in the Body of Christ is not easily derived from the roles of prophet and king in the community, roles
which have little existential meaning. Congar points out that Vatican II
"operated with the category of the people of God and of communion in
Christ; it emphasized a baptism which was the means of belonging to this
people. It is this people, it is the church, which is prophetic, priestly, and
royal. Vatican II says many times that the participation of the ordained
ministers in the *munera Christi* is a participation indeed in Christ, but in
Christ as the head of the Body, *caput*." Congar goes on to observe that the
three metaphors have "a 'circumincession' flowing into each other....The
Council works within the inspiration of the history of salvation; it is a
question of the people of God, of actualizing its mission and the functions
of Christ through a plurality of ministries. Certainly there are sacramentally ordained members, but this is a service ordained for the people of
God by activities which correspond to the three offices of teaching, sanctifying, and leading" (Y. Congar, "Sur la trilogie: Prophète-Roi-Prêtre,"
Revue des sciences philosophiques et théologiques 67 [1983], 106: 112).

18. Y. Congar, *Une passion. L'unité* (Paris: Cerf, 1974), 109. Y.
Congar, "A Last Look at the Church," in A. Stacpoole, *Vatican II Revisited*, 351. "It is astonishing how the postconciliar period has so little to
do with the Council....The postconciliar questions are new and radical,
and *aggiornamento* [now] means changes and adaptations to a new situation, assuming the principles of the original institution" (Private letter
of 12. 9. 70).

19. G. Lafont, *Imaginer l'église catholique* (Paris: Cerf, 1995), 15.

20. Y. Congar cited in J. Puyo, *Une vie pour la vérité* (Paris: Centurion, 1975), 149.

21. "Situation ecclésiologique au moment...," *Le Concile de Vatican II* (Paris: Beauchesne, 1984), 27.

22. H. Küng, *The Church* (New York: Sheed and Ward, 1967), 437.
"We can and should recognize the seriousness and depth of a spiritual
change in a culture; for the consequences of such a shift in the limits and
range of experience and understanding for the life of (Christian) faith
call for a state of preparedness and give a mandate for a new interpretation of it....When our ways of understanding reality, our models, our
whole intellectual and spiritual equipment begin to shift and alter, the
way we think about the faith as a whole will be different too." E. Schillebeeckx, *Jesus* (New York: Seabury, 1979), 579 f.; see also P. Chirico,
"Dynamics of Change in the Church's Self-Understanding," *Theological
Studies* 39 (1978): 55 ff.; M. Fahey, "Continuity in the Church amid Structural Change," *Theological Studies* 35 (1974): 415 ff.

23. For a theology of the relationship of ministry, church, and

office to the Trinity, see Gisbert Greshake, *Der dreieine Gott. Eine trinitärische Theologie* (Freiburg: Herder, 1996), 411 ff.

24. See Joseh Komonchak, "Clergy, Laity and the Church's Mission in the World," *The Jurist* 41 (1981): 422–47.

25. For a lengthier version of these remarks, see T. O'Meara, *Together in God's Service: Toward a Theology of Ecclesial Lay Ministry* (Washington, DC: USCC Office for Publication and Promotion, 1998), 70–86.

26. "Christian ministry is the public activity of a baptized follower of Jesus Christ flowing from the Spirit's charism and the individual personality on behalf of a Christian community to witness to, serve, and to realize the Kingdom of God" (see chapter 4).

27. Y. Congar, "Laïc et Laïcat," *Dictionnaire de Spiritualité* 9 (Paris: Desclée, 1976), 79.

28. Teachers and advisers like Meister Eckhart and Johannes Tauler indicate a high level of education, preaching, and spiritual direction within women's monasteries, and Thomas Aquinas mentions women preaching in their own communities (*Summa theologiae*, II–II, 177, 2).

29. "Not a hierarchology," Y. Congar, *Ministères et communion écclésiale* (Paris: Cerf, 1971), 10. Congar described the institutionalized ecclesiology that had lasted almost four centuries. "We can note the ecclesiological aspect of Roman centralization, which is linked to a further important aspect. Trent had affirmed in the face of Protestantism that Christ is not solely a redeemer but that he is also a lawgiver. In this line, even in its work at sustaining and demanding a kind of bishop who was truly pastoral, it favored the construction of a hierarchical order, but not one arranged around the Eucharist but around the 'regime' of which Rome occupies the center and summit. Despite the admirable expansion of Christian life and pastoral ministry, an era of legalism began, replacing a somewhat theoretical ecclesiology. Finally an orthodoxy, not only of faith but of theology, is fixed by a kind of canonization of the conceptual and verbal system come down from scholasticism, which from then to our own times has incorporated itself into Catholicism." *L'Église de saint Augustin à l'époque moderne* (Paris: Cerf, 1970), 368. One often finds what seem to be new ideas in unlikely sources. Not long after 1500, Thomas de Vio, Cardinal Cajetan wrote: "The faithful, because they are moved by the Holy Spirit to the works of their spiritual life,...act as parts of one totality....Each faithful believes they are members of the church, and as a member of the church believes, hopes, ministers the sacraments, receives, teaches, learns, etc., and on behalf of the church does these things as a part of the whole to whom they [the activities] all belong." *Commentaria Cardinalis Caietani* on *Summa theologiae*

II–II, 39, 1, in Sancti Thomae Aquinatis, *Opera Omnia* , Leonis XIII, P. M., edita, vol. 8 (Rome: Typographia Polyglotta, 1895), 307.

30. Paul VI, "Allocutio Secunda SS. Concilii Periodo Ineunte," *Acta Apostolicae Sedis* (Sept. 29, 1963), 55; (1963), 895.

31. Gustav Thils, *L'Après-Vatican II. Un nouvel âge de l'église?* (Louvain-la Neuve: Faculté de Théologie, 1985), 81 ff.

32. Cited in *La Documentation catholique* 66 (1969): 765.

33. C. Dagens, "Le christianisme dans l'histoire. Le temps des origines et notre temps," *Nouvelle Revue Théologique* 114 (1992): 801 ff.; see "The Parish in the Year 1000," *Chicago Studies* 37 (1998).

34. Pauline theology presented what became, with difficulty in theological expression and practical realization, the ecclesial, traditional theology of the church and its actions. Charism was a communal reality, and the community—Christians in other ministries, as well as the community leader—had roles in discerning the presence of the Spirit. For Catholicism, verification of the presence of the Spirit includes signs of evangelical discipleship, perdurance and success in service over time, and personal holiness. How these phenomena are verified in the long history of the church, examples of ecclesial and personal successes and failures in discerning the Spirit, requires precise historical analysis; for a survey of recent theologies see Daniel Donovan, *What Are They Saying about the Ministerial Priesthood* (Mahwah, NJ: Paulist, 1992).

2. PRIMAL MINISTRY: SPIRIT, FREEDOM, CHARISM, AND MINISTRY

1. *Summa theologiae* III, q. 22, a. 1; q. 8, aa. 2, 5, 7; q. 2, a. 10, 2; q. 7, a. 9.

2. On the Gospel according to John and cultic religion, see R. Schnackenburg, "Worship in Spirit and in Truth," *Christian Existence in the New Testament* (Notre Dame: University of Notre Dame Press, 1969), 2, 85 ff.; E. M. Braun, "In spiritu et veritate," *Revue Thomiste* 52 (1952): 245ff.; 285 ff., G. Sloyan, *Is Christ the End of the Law?* (Philadelphia: Westminster, 1978); W. Trilling, "Amtsverständnis bei Matthäus," *Mélanges...B. Rigaux* (Gembloux: Duculot, 1970), 39 ff.

3. *Dialogue with Trypho....Patrologia Graeca* 6, 74 ff.

4. See J. M. R. Tillard, "La 'qualité' sacerdotale du ministère chrétien," *Nouvelle revue théologique* 95 (1973): 481 ff.; Albert Vanhoye, *Old Testament Priests and the New Priest according to the New Testament* (Petersham: St. Bede's Publications, 1986), 213 ff.

5. "Its (Hebrews') starting point is the insight that all human

sacrifices, all ritual and cultic attempts to reconcile oneself to God, have remained helpless and futile works of man....The hour of the cross was the cosmic day of reconciliation. There is no cult other than this one and also no priest other than the one who fulfilled this liturgy, Jesus Christ....Whoever reads the New Testament attentively will see that it is— despite the differences that it otherwise exhibits—at all points character- ized by a deep knowledge of the radical termination of the foregoing history of religion signified and effected in the Christ-event. What was said about Jesus, who was, juridically speaking, a layman, and about the profane character of his death appears here once again: that day (the day of his death) manifested the holiness of the apparently profane and the nonholiness of the previously religious....From a historical point of view, Christ's death was not a cultic activity or event but an occurrence belonging very much to the realm of the profane." J. Ratzinger, "Priestly Ministry: A Search for Its Meaning," *Emmanuel* 86 (1980): 250 ff. On the fulfillment of sacral religion see J. Blenkinsopp, *Celibacy, Ministry and the Church* (New York: Herder and Herder, 1968); G. Schrenk, "Iereus in the NT," *Theological Dictionary of the New Testament* 3 (Grand Rapids: Eerdmans, 1967), 263; Y. Congar, "Situation du sacre en régime chré- tien," *La liturgie après Vatican II* (Paris: Cerf, 1967), 385 ff.; J. Colson, "Ecclesial Ministries and the Sacral," *Concilium* #80 (1972): 74; H. Wen- schkewitz, *Die Spiritualisierung der Kultusbegriffe. Tempel, Priester und Opfer im Neuen Testament* (Leipzig: Olms, 1932); G. Klinzing, *Die Umdeu- tung des Kultus in der Qumrangemeinde und im Neuen Testament* (Göttin- gen: Vandenhoeck und Ruprecht, 1971); J. Jungmann, *The Place of Christ in Liturgical Prayer* (New York: Alba House, 1965), 146 ff.

6. "The nature of the subject and the canonical character of the New Testament gives [the topic of ministry] contemporary import. Every look at the organization of modern ecclesial life must be attentive to the directives and impulses coming from the apostolic tradition wit- nessed to by the writings of the New Testament. Certainly we do not find there either a receipt totally fixed or precise and immutable canon- ical data which forbids every change and condemns us to a sterile uni- formity in structure. We believe in the existence of permanent data and in a dynamism of the Spirit which takes part in the inheritance received from the Apostles. They should be present in any restructuralizing of ministry." Hermann Hauser, *L'Église à l'âge apostolîque* (Paris: Cerf, 1996), 169; on ministry in the first decades, see E. Schillebeeckx, *The Church with a Human Face* (New York: Crossroad, 1985), 42–50, 74–115.

7. See Raymond Brown and John Meier, *Antioch and Rome* (Mah- wah, NJ: Paulist, 1983); Jerome Murphy-O'Connor, *St. Paul's Corinth* (Wilmington: Glazier, 1983); *Paul. A Critical Life* (Oxford: Clarendon,

1996).

8. Daniel Donovan, *The Church as Idea and Fact* (Collegeville: The Liturgical Press, 1988), 25.

9. L. Goppelt, *Apostolic and Post-Apostolic Times* (London: Black, 1970), 56; relating an interpretation of the Pauline letters that joins charism and office to Vatican II is Albert Vanhoye, "The Biblical Question of 'Charisms' after Vatican II," in R. Latourelle, ed., *Vatican II: Assessment and Perspectives* 1 (Mahwah, NJ: Paulist, 1988), 439–68.

10. See E. R. Dodds, *Pagan and Christian in an Age of Anxiety* (London: Cambridge University Press, 1965). "On the basis of theological criteria I think that preference must be given to the first Christian millennium as a model for a future shaping of the church's ministry—albeit in a very different, modern historical context—and in particular to the New Testament and the pre-Nicene period." Schillebeeckx, *Ministry* (New York: Crossroad, 1981), 67.

11. Ingo Hermann, *Kyrios und Pneuma* (Munich: Kösel, 1961), 140.

12. Ibid., 145.

13. A. Kavanagh, *The Shape of Baptism: The Rite of Christian Initiation* (New York: Pueblo, 1978), 30.

14. Josef Hainz, *Ekklesia* (Regensburg: Pustet, 1972), 335; see Hermann von Lips, *Glaube - Gemeinde - Amt. Zum Verständnis der Ordination in den Pastoralbriefen* (Göttingen: Vandenhoeck und Ruprecht, 1979), 222. "Three elements seem to emerge from this exposition on the charisms of the state of life. The charisms of the Spirit in light of the Gospel and the Kingdom find a certain model, while transfiguring it, in the constitutive realities of human existence. They do not substitute for the humanity of people but suppose and ordain it in a direction which accomplishes it. The exercise of a charism supposes and provokes a thought and an organization of practical theology...[concerning] the manner of being a Christian in a particular situation. Perhaps the person responsible in the church must listen first to what the Spirit says to people, to respect their incertitudes...to accept a certain plurality....The stability in a state of life comes too from the gift of the Spirit which is not a perpetual change and dissatisfaction but gives force to continue in a line taken" (G. Lafont, *Imaginer l'église catholique* [Paris: Cerf, 1995], 170).

15. See Gisbert Greshake, *The Meaning of Christian Priesthood* (Dublin: Four Courts Press, 1982), 42–51; "The Priesthood, a Thorny Question for the First Christians," and "Jesus Christ, The New Priest," Albert Vanhoye, *Old Testament Priests and the New Priest*, 39 ff., 61 ff.; *Ministère de Jesus-Christ et le sacerdoce de l'évangile* (Paris: Beauchesne, 1966); J. P. Audet, *Structures of the Christian Priesthood* (New York: Sheed

and Ward, 1968); H. Schlier, "Grundelemente des priesterlichen Amtes im NT," *Theologie und Philosophie* 44 (1969): 168 ff.; Y. Congar, "Le sacerdoce du NT," *Les Prêtres* (Paris: Cerf, 1968); "The Different Priesthoods. Christian, Jewish, Pagan," *A Gospel Priesthood* (New York: Herder and Herder, 1967), 74–89; D. Donovan, *The Levitical Priesthood and the Ministry of the New Testament* (Münster: Akademieverlag, 1970); on the permanence of the sacred in Christian life, H. Mühlen, *Entsakralisierung* (Paderborn: Schöningh, 1970).

16. Greshake, 48.

17. See S. Lyonnet, "La nature du culte dans le Nouveau Testament," *La Liturgie après Vatican II* (Paris: Cerf, 1967), 357–85.

18. See C. Weiner, "*hierourgein*," *Studiorum Paulinorum Congressus 1961* 12 (Rome: Pontifico Istituto Biblico, 1963), 393–401; C. Wiéner, "Excursus 1" in *Les Pretres* (Paris: Cerf, 1968), 257 ff.; H. Schlier, "Die 'Liturgie' des apostolischen Evangeliums," in Karl Rahner, ed., *Martyria, Leitourgia, Diakonia* (Mainz: Matthias-Grünewald, 1968), 251; P. van Bergen, "La vie quotidienne vecue comme culte," *Sainteté et vie dans le siècle* 2 (Rome: Herder, 1965), 81 ff.

19. See Ernst Käsemann, "Worship in Everyday Life: A Note on Romans 12," *New Testament Questions of Today* (Philadelphia: Fortress, 1969), 188–95.

20. "For Paul, ministries are charisms, gifts of God for the good of all; the ministries of apostles, prophets and teachers come at the head of the charisms given to the church...essentially ministries of the Word. These ministries do not, however, exhaust the gifts made by God to his church. There is still place for a multitude of other gifts and functions for which language and vocabulary remain quite flexible." J. Delorme, *Le ministère et les ministères selon le Nouveau Testament* (Paris: Seuil, 1974), 62. In the context of the new discussion of office, ministry and charism, the exegete E. Hahn observes the intention of Paul to join "spiritual gifts" and "activities" with *diakonia*. "He (Paul) spotlights the spiritual gifts not because of their particular mode of appearance but because they are to be, at the same time, *diakoniai*; for this reason he lists gifts and tasks as charisms which until now were not viewed as the activities of the Spirit" (Rom 12:8; 1 Cor 12:28). "Charisma und Amt," *Zeitschrift für Theologie und Kirche* 76 (1979): 424. Supporting the linear linking of *charisma* and *diakonia* are Hainz, Hasenhüttl, Cooke and Lemaire.

21. Y. Congar, *Power and Poverty in the Church* (Baltimore: Helicon, 1964), 38 ff.

22. See F. J. Cwiekowski, *The Beginnings of the Church* (Mahwah NJ: Paulist, 1988); Jean Marie Tillard, *Church of Churches: The Ecclesiology of Communion* (Collegeville: Liturgical Press, 1992).

23. On ministry in the early church see (with their bibliographies) A. Lemaire, *Les ministères dans l'Église* (Paris: Le Centurion, 1974); *Les ministères aux origines de l'Église* (Paris: Cerf, 1971); J. T. Lienhard, *Ministry* (Wilmington: Glazier, 1984); Hermann Hauser, *L'Église à l'âge apostolique* (Paris: Cerf, 1996).

24. "Paul naturally does not want to describe a complete, differentiated hierarchy of offices, circumscribed according to assignments and law, but to speak of the fullness and variety of the gifts of the one *Pneuma*, and for this he lists charisms of which have the character of institutions, fixed or becoming fixed, and others of spirit-led activities of believers giving witness in the midst of the community." Otto Kuss, *Römerbrief* (Regensburg: Pustet, 1957), 556.

25. Hauser, *L'Église*, 12 f.

26. Ibid., 56 ff.

27. Cf. G. Hammann, *L'amour retrouvé. Le ministère de diacre du christianisme primitif aux Réformateurs protestants du XVIe siècle* (Paris: Cerf, 1994); A. Faivre, "Origine et réforme," *Revue des sciences religieuses* 71 (1997): 104 ff.; see R. Alastair Campbell, *The Elders: Seniority within Earliest Christianity* (Edinburgh: T&T Clark, 1994).

28. Hauser, *L'Église*, 92 ff., 132 ff.

29. J. Delorme, *Le Ministère et les ministères selon le Nouveau Testament* (Paris: Seuil, 1974), 59.

30. The early triad of prophet, apostle, and teacher is still witnessed to by the *Didache* with unclarity and overlapping; see É. Cothenet, "Le prophetisme et le Nouveau Testament: La Communauté Primitive," *Dictionnaire de la Bible, Supplément*, 8 (Paris: Letouzey et Ané, 1971), 1264 ff.; J. Panagopoulos, ed., *Prophetic Vocation in the New Testament and Today* (Leiden: Brill, 1977).

31. See A.F. Zimmermann, *Die urchristlichen Lehrer* (Tubingen: Mohr, 1984).

32. Ulrich Neymeyr, *Die christlichen Lehrer im zweiten Jahrhundert* (Leiden: Brill, 1989), 233–40; see A. Faivre, *The Emergence of the Laity in the Early Church* (Mahwah, NJ: Paulist, 1990), 64 ff., 78 ff.; H. Greeven, "Propheten, Lehrer, Vorsteher bei Paulus," *Zeitschrift für die neutestamentliche Wissenschaft* 44 (1952/53): 1 ff.

33. Franz Schnider and Werner Stenger, "The Church as a Building and the Building Up of the Church. Static and Dynamic Features in a Set of Images of the Church," *Concilium* 80 (New York: Herder and Herder, 1972), 21 ff.

34. Chapter 3 returns to the theme of the house church.

35. Catholic Biblical Association, "Women and Priestly Ministry: The New Testament Evidence," *CSR Bulletin* 11:2 (1980): 45; see E.

Schüssler-Fiorenza, "Women in Pre-Pauline and Pauline Churches," *Union Theological Quarterly Review* 33 (1978): 15; "Neutestamentlich-frühchristliche Argumente zum Thema Frau und Amt," *Theologische Quartalschrift* 173 (1993): 173–85; G. Dautzenberg, *Die Frau im Urchristentum* (Freiburg: Herder, 1983); Pheme Perkins, "Women and Ministry," *Ministering in the Pauline Churches* (Mahwah, NJ: Paulist, 1982), 49–71.

36. See A. Faivre, *The Emergence*, 97 ff.; Peter Drilling, *Trinity and Ministry* (Minneapolis: Augsburg, 1991), ch. 4.

37. R. Brown suggests that "a more plausible theory is that we have here a reflection of two strains of Judaism which came into Christianity. The synagogues of Pharisaic Judaism had a group of *zegenim*, 'elders'....In addition to such *zegenim* the Dead Sea Scrolls community of the New Covenant had officials who bore the title *mebagger*...supervisor, overseer." Brown concludes his recent study of the office of bishop in the different communities of the New Testament by pointing out a difference in manner and exercise of supervision in different places and different periods as well as in official terminology. The American exegete views the vacuum left by the death of the great leaders of the first decades after Jesus as exerting pressure for a more uniform structure of the church. "By the '80s–90s' the presbyter-bishop model was becoming widespread, and with the adjustment supplied by the emergence of the single bishop that model was to dominate the second century until it became exclusive in the ancient churches." R. Brown, "Episkope and Episkopos," *Theological Studies* 41 (1980): 333. Some exegetes offer an opinion that the "deacons and bishops" in Philippians do not represent two distinct offices but stand for all of those in ministry and leadership in the community. It may well be that at the time of Peter and Paul these were not specific ministries like teaching and healing but were global names for all or some ministries, perhaps for those who held directional ministries. The core of full-time ministers would be addressed as "ministers" and "overseers." Paul attached little importance to titles and he was not preoccupied with consistency in titles. The more important ministries would be ones of leadership and direction in a community of ministry. This would help explain why in the later letter to the Ephesians the diversity of ministries stands out but no mention is made of bishops, presbyters, or deacons (4:4), while Acts speaks of presbyters in Ephesus (Eph 20:17). J. Gnilka writes: "Individual holders of ministry and administration do not stand out in a special way in Paul's letters. From this we conclude that the communities first bear responsibility for themselves, that each person living in the community was considered to share in the responsibility of the community...that the various 'community-offices' are effects of the Spirit,

and that both ministers and leadership roles are within these effects of the Spirit." Gnilka, *Der Philipperbrief* (Freiburg: Herder, 1968), 33.

38. In the theology of ministry there was a subtle shift: whereas Paul speaks of the power-source of ministry to be the Spirit of Jesus, a few decades later Clement and Ignatius speak of the authority of ministry flowing from the awesome authority of God.

39. J. Delorme, *Le Ministère...*, 23 ff.

40. Ibid., 57 ff.

41. Ibid., 27.

42. E. Schillebeeckx, *Ministry*, 23 ff.

3. THE METAMORPHOSES OF MINISTRY

1. Cited in O. Clément, *Transfigurer les temps* (Neuchâtel: Delachaux et Niestlé, 1959), 136.

2. See T. O'Meara, "The History of Being and the History of Doctrine," *American Catholic Philosophical Quarterly* 69 (1995): 351–74.

3. G. La Piana, "The Church of Rome at the End of the Second Century," *Harvard Theological Review* 18 (1925): 201 ff.

4. C. S. Lewis, "De Destructione Temporum," *They Asked for a Paper* (London: G. Bles, 1962), 23.

5. "Consequently the mystery of Christ's Incarnation was to be believed in all ages and by all peoples in some fashion—but in diverse ways according to the differences of times and peoples" (Aquinas, *Summa theologiae*, II–II, 2, 7); for papal and theological texts on culture, see Joseph Gremillion, ed., *The Church and Culture Since Vatican II* (Notre Dame: University of Notre Dame Press, 1985).

6. Y. Congar, "Situation écclésiologique au moment de 'Ecclesiam suam' et passage à une église dans l'itineraire des hommes," *Le Concile de Vatican II* (Paris: Beauchesne, 1984), 27; *Fifty Years of Catholic Theology: Conversations with Yves Congar*, B. Lauret, ed. (Philadelphia: Fortress, 1988), 8.

7. E. Schillebeeckx, "De Sociale context van de verschuivingen in het kerkelijk ambt," *Tijdschrift voor theologie* 22 (1982): 26.

8. E. Schillebeeckx, "The Catholic Understanding of Office," *Theological Studies* 30 (1969): 568.

9. E. Schillebeeckx, "De Sociale context," 58. "In the history of the church's structure it is clearly not a question of the history of a decline but of a first line of development, of a pursual of certain principles and points of departure which made possible the 'incarnation' in the church in that time. The problem for the student of the New Testament

today lies not in the fact of this development (which is affirmed) but in any emphasis upon exclusiveness. The New Testament is open for other forms of 'incarnation' for other possibilities of development even for those which were never tried....That church 'office' sucked up so many, various functions (prophet, teacher, evangelist, leader of the Eucharist) is not unbiblical but only postbiblical. All these functions can of course be drawn anew out of this office." W. Pesch, "Kirchlicher Dienst und das Neue Testament," *Priesteramt* (Stuttgart: Huber, 1970), 23.

10. See Y. Congar, *L'Église de Saint Augustin à l'époque moderne* (Paris: Editions du Cerf, 1970).

11. See A. Lemaître, *Les ministères dans l'Église* (Paris: Le Centurion, 1974); T. O'Meara, "Philosophical Models in Ecclesiology," *Theological Studies* 39 (1978): 3 ff.

12. P. du Bourguet, *Early Christian Art* (London: Weidenfeld and Nicholson, 1971), 32; R. Krautheimer, *Early Christian and Byzantine Architecture* (Baltimore: Penguin, 1975); G. Norberg-Schulz, *Meaning in Western Architecture* (New York: Praeger, 1975); Pierre du Bourguet, "The First Biblical Scenes Depicted in Christian Art," in *The Bible in Greek Christian Antiquity* (Notre Dame: University of Notre Dame Press, 1997), 299–326.

13. Minutius Felix, *Octavian* 32:1.

14. J. Petersen, "House Churches in Rome," *Vigiliae Christianae* 23 (1969): 265 ff.; P. Stuhlmacher, "Exkurs: Urchristliche Hausgemeinden," *Der Brief an Philemon* (Zurich: Einsiedeln, 1975); A. Malherbe, "House Churches and Their Problems," *Social Aspects of Early Christianity* (Baton Rouge: Louisiana State University Press, 1977); H. J. Klauck, "Die Hausgemeinde als Lebensform im Urchristentum," *Münchener Theologische Zeitschrift* 32 (1981): 1 ff.; K. Gamber, *Domus Ecclesiae* (Regensburg: Pustet, 1968); L. M. White, *Domus ecclesiae–domus Dei: Adaptation and Development in the Setting for Early Christian Assembly* (Yale Univ. Diss., 1982); Del Birkey, *The House Church. A Model for Renewing the Church* (Scottdale: Herald Press, 1988); Vincent Branick, *The House Church in the Writings of Paul* (Wilmington: Glazier, 1989); H. Hauser, *L'église*, 79 ff.; S. Wiedenhofer, "Die Tradition in den Traditionen. Kirchliche Glaubensüberlieferung im Spannungsfeld kirchlicher Strukturen," in K. Gabriel, *Wie geschieht Tradition? Überlieferung im Lebensprozess der Kirche* (Freiburg: Herder, 1991), 130 ff.

15. On forms which the church adapts after the time of Trajan and Diocletian, see H. P. L'Orange, *Art Forms and Civic Life in the Late Roman Empire* (Princeton: Princeton University Press, 1965); P. Nautin, "L'evolution des ministères au IIe et au IIIe siècles," *Revue de droit canonique* 23 (1973): 47 ff.

16. See Christine Trevett, *Montanism. Gender, Authority and the New Prophecy* (Cambridge: University Press, 1996); Matthias Wunsche, *Der Ausgang der urchristlichen Prophetie in der frühkatholischen Kirche* (Stuttgart: Calwer, 1997).

17. Eusebius, *Hist. Eccl.*, VI, 45, 11; see R. Grant, *Early Christianity and Society* (San Francisco: Harper & Row, 1977).

18. See James A. Coriden, *The Parish in Catholic Tradition. History, Theology and Canon Law* (Mahwah, NJ: Paulist, 1997).

19. See M. Fahey, *Cyprian on the Bible* (Tübingen: Mohr, 1972); M. Poirier, "Vescovo, clero e laici in una communita cristiana del III secolo negli scritti di S. Cipriano," *Rivista di storia e letteratura religiosa* 9 (1973): 17 ff.; J. Jacobs, *Saint Cyprian of Carthage as Minister* (Boston University Diss., 1976); John D. Laurance, *The Priest as Type of Christ. The Leader of the Eucharist in Salvation History according to Cyprian of Carthage* (New York: Lang, 1984); Richard Seagraves, *Pascentes cum disciplina* (Fribourg: Presses Universitaires, 1993).

20. *Contra Celsum*, 8, 73; 8, 17; *Homilies on Leviticus*, 3, 5; 10, 3; 24, 2; 9, 9; cf. A. Vilela, *La condition collégiale des prêtres au IIIe siècle* (Paris: Beauchesne, 1971), 43–156; J. Lecuyer, "Sacerdoce des fidèles et sacerdoce ministeriel chez Origène," *Vetera Christianorum* 7 (1970): 253 ff.

21. On the changing role of the bishop, cf. C. Vogel, "Unité de l'église et pluralité des formes historiques d'organisation ecclésiastique du IIIe au Ve siècle," *Episcopat et l'Église* (Paris: Cerf, 1962), 591 ff.; J. Lynch, "The Changing Role of the Bishop: A Historical Survey," *The Jurist* 39 (1979): 289 ff.

22. There is no noun in English drawn from the Greek word for *priest*, although the adjective *hieratic* exists.

23. *De Exhortatione castitatis* 7, 3; G. Otranto observes that Tertullian's text indicates a common priesthood which does not exclude or attack the role of the presbyters and bishops; "Nonne et laici sacerdotes sumus?" *Vetera Christianorum* 8 (1971): 46. On the priesthood of the Christians in the first centuries cf. D. Donovan, *The Levitical Priesthood and the Ministry of the New Testament* (Münster, 1970).

24. H. Legrand, "The Presidency of the Eucharist according to the Ancient Tradition," *Worship* 53 (1979): 427. Schillebeeckx argues that the centrality of the Eucharist alone does not explain the development of the community leader into priest. E. Schillebeeckx, *Ministry: Leadership in the Community of Jesus Christ* (New York: Crossroad, 1981), 48 ff.; see J. P. Audet, *Structures of Christian Priesthood* (New York: Macmillan, 1968).

25. See E. Schillebeeckx, *Ministry: Leadership in the Community of Jesus Christ*, 48 ff.

26. P. Du Bourguet, *Early Christian Art*, 140.

27. R. Nowell, "Why Did the Deacon Disappear?" *Ministry of Service* (New York: Herder and Herder, 1968), 34.

28. "Concilium Romanum I pro Reformando Ecclesiae Statu," *Patrologia Latina* 148: 771 ff.; see A. Fliche, *La Reforme grégorienne* (Louvain: Spicilegium sacrum Lovaniensis, 1924), 3 vols.; C. Dereine, "Vie commune, règle de S. Augustin et chanoines reguliers au XIe siècle," *Revue d'histoire ecclésiastique* 41 (1946): 365 ff.; *L'Église de Saint Augustin*, 112.

29. K. J. Conant, *Carolingian and Romanesque Architecture, 800–1200* (New York: Penguin, 1979), 34; cf. J. Evans, *Romanesque Architecture of the Order of Cluny* (Cambridge: Cambridge University Press, 1938); R. de Lasteyrie, *L'architecture religieuse en France a l'époque romane* (Paris: Picard, 1929).

30. J. Leclerq, *The Love of Learning and the Desire for God. A Study of Monastic Culture* (New York: Fordham University Press, 1961).

31. G. Dix, "The Coming of Monasticism and the Divine Office," *The Shape of the Liturgy* (London: Dacre, 1945); R. Zinnbohler, "Die mönchischen Strukturen des Priesterbildes," *Priesterbild im Wandeln* (Linz: Schmidt, 1972), 73 ff. On the clericalization of the liturgy and the distancing of the people, L. Bouyer, *Liturgy and Architecture* (Notre Dame: University of Notre Dame Press, 1967), 70 ff.; on the privatization of the minister in the Middle Ages see E. Schillebeeckx, *Ministry*, 52 ff.; O. Nussbaum, *Kloster, Priestermönch und Privatmesse* (Bonn: Hanstein, 1961), and A. Häussling, *Mönchskonvent und Eucharistiefeier* (Münster: Aschendorff, 1973).

32. A. Borras, L. Thier, *Ursprung und Entwicklung der Priesterkleidung* (Linz: Schmidt, 1970), 353 ff.

33. "Ad S. Bernardi Epistolas, Appendix," Epistula 472, *Patrologia Latina* 182, 677; see M.-D. Chenu, "The Evangelical Awakening," *Nature, Man and Society in the Twelfth Century* (Chicago: University of Chicago Press, 1968), 237; see H. Grundmann, *Religious Movements in the Middle Ages* (Notre Dame: University of Notre Dame Press, 1995), and a bibliography in Congar, *L'Église de Saint Augustin*, 112, 198 ff.; also, Pierre Mandonnet, *St. Dominic and His Work* (St. Louis: Herder, 1944), 132 ff.; Chenu, "Monks, Canons and Laymen in Search of the Apostolic Life," *Nature*, 202 ff.

34. *L'Église de Saint Augustin*, 174; on an ecclesiology of order culminating in the twelfth century, Y. Congar, "Les laïcs et l'ecclésiologie des 'Ordines' chez les théologiens des XIe et XIIe siècles," in *I Laici* (Milan: Verita, 1968), 83 ff.

35. M. D. Chenu, "Nature and Man—the Renaissance of the 12th Century," *Nature...*, 1ff.

36. R. Roques, *L'univers dionysien* (Paris: Aubier, 1954), 131; see J. Stiflmayr, "Über die termini Hierarch und Hierarchie," *Zeitschrift für katholische Theologie* 22 (1898): 180 ff.; Interestingly, J. Meyendorff criticizes Pseudo-Dionysius for removing church role from the community and locating it in mysticism, *Christ in Eastern Christian Thought* (Crestwood: St. Vladimir Press, 1976), 91ff., while Congar argues that the Western churches resisted such a dominance of gnostic hierarchy until the twelfth century (*L'Église de Saint Augustin*, 224 ff.; Faivre, 283–85). Thomas of Ireland, Aquinas's first teacher at Naples, wrote: "The Blessed Dionysius came to Paris so that he might make of this city the mother of studies after the pattern of Athens." M. D. Chenu, *Towards Understanding St. Thomas* (Chicago: Regnery, 1964), 24.

37. See *Towards Understanding St. Thomas*, 172; G. Tellenbach, *Church, State and Christian Society in the Time of the Investiture Contest* (Oxford: Blackwell, 1948), 8; cf. Y. Congar, "The Sacralization of Western Society in the Middle Ages," *Concilium* 47 (Mahwah, NJ: Paulist, 1969), 67; also Y. Congar, "Les Ministères de l'Église dans le monde féodal jusqu'à la reforme grégorienne," *Revue de Droit Canonique* 23 (1973): 82.

38. Roques, *L'Univers Dionysien*, 92–100.

39. Faivre, 174; see R. Roques, 99–100. Orthodox theologian John Meyendorff has called Pseudo-Dionysius's hierarch a gnostic because his spiritual power was not a function of the inner structure of his ecclesial community but his personal possession. Meyendorff goes further, attributing the "magical clericalism" of the West to the later influence of Pseudo-Dionysius on medieval speculations about the progressive powers of the ecclesiastical hierarchy. He suggests that further research is needed in order to establish the measure of considered and of unreflective Pseudo-Dionysian influence on the development of Western ecclesiology in both the scholastic and post-scholastic periods. J. Meyendorff, *Christ in Eastern Christian Thought*, 79–82; see G. Théry, "L'entrée du Pseudo-Denys en Occident," *Melanges Madonnet*, 2 (Paris: Vrin, 1930), 23–30.

40. Cf. Y. Congar, "Aspects ecclésiologiques de la querelle...," *Archives d'histoire doctrinale et litteraire du moyen age* 36 (1961): 72.

41. Faivre, 174.

42. *2 Sent.*, 9. 1, 1; *De Divinis Nominibus* 1, 2.

43. *4 Sent.*, 24, 3, 2; cf. J. Lecuyer, "Les étapes de l'enseignement thomiste sur l'episcopat," *Revue Thomiste* 57 (1957): 29 ff.

44. *Summa theologiae* II–II, 184, 5. "He who preaches should have

what he preaches permanently and integrally." *Summa theologiae* III, 41, 3, 1. On Denys as a source of hierarchy through illumination, cf. Congar, *L'Église de Saint Augustin*, 226 ff.; Aquinas, *2 Sent.*, 9, 1, 1; *4 Sent.*, 5, 2, 1; *1 De Veritate*, 9, 1.

45. Aquinas, following Gratian and Lombard, admitted an influence from pagan sources upon the monarchical aspect of the church, 4 Sent., 24, 3, 2, qa. 2, ad. 2; see *L'Église de Saint Augustin*, 154.

46. *Summa theologiae* II–II, 184, 4. It is common to speak of the hierarchy or the hierarchical structure of the church as if this term was of divine revelation or ecclesial essence. As the history of theology shows, words and thought-forms coming from this "sacred principate" are a Neoplatonic theology of some centuries after Pentecost. One must understand that in common parlance "hierarchy" is standing for "authority," and so belongs indeed to the constitution of the church. But any unfortunate connotations coming from the hierarchical theologies of Pseudo-Dionysius and others implying that a fixed, descending, pyramidical structure of a single authority possessing all being and activity is Jesus' will and sole model for the role of church authority is untenable.

47. *Summa theologiae* II–II, 183, 1, 3.

48. *Summa theologiae* II–II, 184, 3–6; cf. P. Michaud-Quentain, "Aspects de la vie sociale chez les moralistes," *Miscellanea Medievalia* 3 (Berlin: de Gruyter, 1964), 37 ff.

49. See Y. Congar, "The Idea of the Church in Thomas Aquinas," *The Mystery of the Church* (Baltimore: Helicon, 1960); H. Krings, *Ordo* (Hamburg: Meiner, 1981); Avery Dulles, "The Church according to Thomas Aquinas," *A Church to Believe In* (New York: Crossroad, 1982), 149 ff.

50. Y. Congar, *L'Église de Saint Augustin*, 239. Aquinas never wrote a treatise on ministry for the *Summa theologiae*. From his commentaries on Paul, though, we can glean some further views on ministry. Paradoxically, Aquinas thought that the ministry actually had expanded since the first century, when the lesser ministries like the office of reader were all contained in the diaconate (*4 Sent.*, 24, 2, 1, ad 2). Explaining Romans, Aquinas saw that there existed ministerial diversity, and, as in the body, the goal of diversity was sought by "diverse activities." *Super Epistulas S. Pauli Lectura* 1, *ad Romanos* (12:4) (Turin: Marietti, 1953), 181. These ministries, however, were something other than ordained, ecclesiastical offices. They were in fact charisms, and for Aquinas charisms were temporary, personal graces lacking stability and so not ending in public office. Charisms ("gratuitous graces") inspired an individual transitorily to a specific work in the church. Aquinas interprets the Pauline metaphor of Body of Christ as a communion of varied graces for lives in the church

rather than as ministerial offices (*Summa theologiae* II–II, 171–78). To be a bishop or a priest, called in Scripture "ministers of God," was different; they had "a grace and an office." (*ad Romanos* 12:7, 182). Office is distinct from charism, possibly separate from grace. What distinguishes these ministers? What brings them the dignity of office, the stability of status? It was their relationship to the sacraments, especially the Eucharist. Aquinas interprets the list of ministers in Ephesians in this way: The "apostles" were the Twelve; the "evangelists" were the four authors of the New Testament Gospels; the "teachers" were the bishops whose main task was to teach and nourish with the Eucharist (*Super Epistulas S. Pauli Lectura* 2, *ad Ephesios* (Turin: Marietti, 1953), 52 f.). What gave stability to the religious side of medieval society was the bishop, around whom, as with a magnetic pole, the diversity of charismatics, monks, nuns, friars, lawyers, and cardinals found their orientation.

51. Sabra, *Thomas Aquinas's Vision of the Church* (Mainz: Matthias-Grunewald), 66. Aquinas mentions as a minority opinion the view that the apostles and not Jesus instituted some of the sacraments like confirmation and anointing (*Summa theologiae*, Supplement, 29, 3).

52. *The Sermon-Conferences of St. Thomas Aquinas on the Apostles' Creed*, N. Ayo, ed. (Notre Dame: University of Notre Dame Press, 1988), 125.

53. *Summa theologiae* I–II, 97, 1; II–II, 184. In the age of the apostles the basic ministries were present, but their names and descriptions were not the same then as those appearing in later ecclesial organization. "Since in one city there are not many bishops, this expression in the plural must include the presbyters....In the beginning, although the orders were distinct, still the names of the orders were not" (*Super Epistulas S. Pauli Lectura* 2, *ad Philippenses* (Turin: Marietti, 1953), ch. 1, lect. 1, 91). "In the early church, because of the small number of faithful, all lower ministries were confided to deacons....All those powers were contained in the single diaconal power. But with time, divine service was expanded and that which the church possessed in one order it has distributed in many." *In 4 Sent.*, d. 24, q. 2, a. 1, ad 2. Still, Aquinas spoke of the beginnings of the church and its completion but also of its progress which is the subject of the apostles' letters in the New Testament. *Breve Principium Fratris Thomae de Commendatione Sacrae Scripturae, Opuscula theologica* 1 (Turin: Marietti, 1954), 439.

54. *Summa theologiae*, Supplement, 37, 1, 2.

55. Y. Congar, *L'Église de Saint Augustin*, 232 ff. On the structure of the curia as a pyramid see G. Zizola, "Le pouvoir romain," *Lumière et Vie* 26 (1977): 25; W. Bassett, "Subsidiarity, Order and Freedom in the Church," *Cross Currents* 20 (1970): 141 ff.; E. Panofsky, *Gothic Architec-*

ture and Scholasticism (Latrobe: Archabbey Press, 1959); T. O'Meara, "Paris as a Cultural Milieu of Thomas Aquinas's Thought," *The Thomist* 39 (1974): 689 ff.; O. von Simson, "Die Kunst des hohen Mittelalters— 'Lichtvolle Geistigkeit,'" *Propyläen Kunstgeshichte* 6 (Berlin: Propyläen, 1972); cf. W. Dettloff, "Der Ordogedanke im Kirchenverständnis Bonaventuras," *Ecclesia et Jus* (Munich: Schöningh, 1968), 25 ff.

56. Aquinas, *Summa theologiae*, II–II, 184.

57. *On the Babylonian Captivity, Luther's Works* 36 (Philadelphia: Fortress, 1966), 116; cf. H. Schutte, *Amt. Ordination und Sukzession* (Düsseldorf: Patmos, 1974); G. Haendler, *Luther on Ministerial Office and Congregational Function* (Philadelphia: Fortress, 1981).

58. A. Ganoczy, *Calvin. Théologien de l'église et du ministère* (Paris, 1964), 245. For the United States, cf. D. Hall, *The Faithful Shepherd: A History of the New England Ministry in the Seventeenth Century* (Chapel Hill: University of North Carolina Press, 1972); D. Scott, *From Office to Profession: The New England Ministry, 1750–1850* (Philadelphia: University of Pennsylvania Press, 1978).

59. P. Portoghesi, *Roma Barocca* (Cambridge: MIT Press, 1970), 4 ff.

60. Cited in William M. Thompson, "Introduction," *Bérulle and the French School* (Mahwah, NJ: Paulist, 1989), 55 f.

61. J. E. Bifet, "Presbytérat [Les Écoles sacerdotales]" *Dictionnaire de spiritualité* [fascicules 80–82] (Paris: Beauchesne, 1985), 2092 ff.

62. The organic life of Baroque eccelesiology depended, like Baroque art, on a tension between a central focus and independent pieces. "The Counter-Reformation ecclesiology can be seen, in retrospect, to have begun a time of juridicism which dampened its vitality. Theoretical study was replaced by law, and the concepts and words of scholasticism were canonized. There was an insistence on obedience in theology and not just in faith." Y. Congar, *L'Eglise de Saint Augustin*, 368. Baroque ecclesiology was not the only theology of church and ministry existing between 1600 and 1900. An ecclesiology of national conciliarism, one of whose forms was Gallicanism, competed with the papal organization for dominance and was at times of great importance.

63. R. Drummond, *A History of Christianity in Japan* (Grand Rapids: Eerdmans, 1971), 58, 112, 115.

64. F. Schlegel, *Dialogue on Poetry and Literary Aphorisms* (University Park: Pennsylvania State University Press, 1968), 143; see Bernard Plongeron, "Archetypal Christianity: the Models of 1770 and 1830," in R. Aubert, *History: Self-Understanding of the Church* (New York: Herder and Herder, 1971), 78–92. The liturgy is always a mirror and realization of church and ministry, and the history of ministry is intimately linked to it; for this period see Keith Pecklers, "History of the Roman Liturgy

from the Sixteenth until the Twentieth Centuries," in A. Chupungco, *Handbook for Liturgical Studies* 1 (Collegeville: Liturgical Press, 1997), 153–75; Thomas O'Meara, "The Origins of the Liturgical Movement and German Romanticism," *Worship* 59 (1985): 326–41.

65. T. O'Meara, *Church and Culture* (Notre Dame: University of Notre Dame Press, 1991), chs. 8 and 9.

66. See Michael Himes, *Ongoing Incarnation. Johann Adam Möhler and the Beginning of Modern Ecclesiology* (New York: Crossroad, 1997); T. O'Meara, *Romantic Idealism and Roman Catholicism. Schelling and the Theologians* (Notre Dame: University of Notre Dame Press, 1982).

67. Y. Congar, "Laïc et Laïcat," *Dictionnaire de Spiritualité*, 9 (Paris: Beauchesne, 1976), 98 f.

68. P. Claudel, "The Development of the Church," *Poetic Art* (Port Washington: Kennikat Press, 1948), 145.

69. Y. Congar, *L'Eglise de Saint Augustin*, 467. For a history of the church in the United States during this period see Peter Drilling, "Inculturating Ministry in the United States," *Trinity and Ministry* (Minneapolis: Augsburg, 1991), ch. 6.

70. See C. Moletter, "Breve histoire de l'action catholique," *Lumière et Vie* 12 (1963): 45 ff.; P. Guilmont asked if, when we look at the discourses of Pius XII on Catholic Action, one sees a wide variety of activities under this umbrella, and an (unsuccessful) attempt to relate these actions to past times. Yet, the church is not solely clerical and sodalities illustrate that, but Pius XII's writings in no way offer any new consideration of the problem of the laity (*Fin d'une église cléricale* [Paris: Cerf, 1969], 5, 292 ff.). "Our conclusion is simply: if, in our age, the problem of the laity has arisen with a particular sharpness, that is because the conception the church had of itself was, in a way, unilateral, found in two images: the flock and the army....At the same time, the term lay is full of ambiguities" (349). On the history and nature of lay movements as "papal solutions to secularism" (5) see Theodore Hesburgh, *The Theology of Catholic Action* (Notre Dame: University of Notre Dame Press, 1946). It is instructive to compare Rahner's classic defense of the laity briefly participating in the work of the bishops in 1963 ("Notes on the Lay Apostolate," *Theological Investigations* 2 [Baltimore: Helicon, 1963] with his later "A Declericalized Church," in *The Shape of the Church to Come* (New York: Seabury, 1974), 56 ff. See the article cited below by Gary MacEoin.

71. Vatican II, *Lumen gentium*, #33.

72. "Le Sacerdoce du nouveau testament. Mission et culture," *Les Prêtres* (Paris: Cerf, 1968), 238.

73. Ibid., 239 f.

74. On the ways in which American lay movements prepared for the expansion of ministry (as the accomplishments of women religious did) see Gary MacEoin, "Lay Movements in the United States Before Vatican II," *America* 165 (1991): 61–65.

75. "La Théologie du presbytérat de Trente à Vatican II," *Les Prêtres*, 206–26; see Hubert Jedin, "Das Leitbild des Priesters nach dem Tridentinum und dem Vaticanum II," *Theologie und Glaube* 60 (1970): 102–24.

76. Hervé Legrand concludes: "*The nonordination of women to pastoral ministry is an undeniable historical fact, but it is not 'Tradition' in the strong sense of the term.* [Our considerations] do not allow us to conclude resolutely that the nonordination of women was a Tradition which revealed the will of God for his church....We find ourselves faced with a constant custom which represents an appropriate way of acting to the conditions in which the church has lived until now. She has not examined critically this way of acting, as she was not faced with the parameters which are characteristics of it today." Hervé Legrand, "*Traditio perpetuo servata?* The Nonordination of Women: Tradition or Simply an Historical Fact?" *Worship* 65 (1991): 504.

77. St. Jean Perse, *Chronique* (New York: Pantheon, 1961), 44.

4. A MINISTERING CHURCH

1. See K. Rahner, "Notes on the Lay Apostolate," *Theological Investigations* 2 (Baltimore: Helicon, 1963), 319 ff.

2. The two codes of canon law in this century speak of church offices. What this originally Roman term, with its original sense of function and responsibility for public activity is intended to mean today, and whether it communicates well a sense of service and activity, for today's church must be studied (see R. Naz, "Offices ecclésiastiques," *Dictionnaire de droit canonique*, fasc. 35 [Paris: Letouzey et Ané, 1957], 1074–84).

3. J. Hainz, *Ekklesia: Strukturen paulinischer Gemeinde-Theologie und Gemeinde-Ordnung* (Regensburg: Pustet, 1972), 362.

4. See Mary Collins, "The Public Language of Ministry," *The Jurist* 41 (1981): 261–94.

5. On *ordo*'s relative absence in Cyprian but wide usage in Tertullian, see Richard Seagraves, *Pascentes cum disciplina* (Fribourg: Presses Universitaires, 1993), 23 ff.; see also the treatment of *ministerium* (335). See P. van Beneden, "*Ordo*," *Vigilae Christianae* 23 (1969):

175; A. Michel, "Ordre, Ordination," *Dictionnaire de théologie catholique* 11 (Paris: Lebouzey et Ané, 1932), 1194–1393.

6. See J. Folliet, "Les trois categories de chrétiens..." *Augustinus Magister* (Paris: Études Augustiniennes, 1954), 631–140.

7. See B. Coffey, "The Notion of Order according to St. Thomas Aquinas," *The Modern Schoolman* 27 (1949): 1 ff. In the opening of the *Summa contra gentiles*, the wise person discerns that order and goodness in the universe results from divine Truth.

8. See T. O'Meara, *Thomas Aquinas Theologian* (Notre Dame: University of Notre Dame Press, 1997).

9. Y. Congar, *Power and Poverty*, 64.

10. During the first centuries of the church, the notion of local church was so prominently linked to diverse ministry that there could be no idea of ministry existing apart from the "building up" of a particular church. Then by the fourth century we have indications of bishops moving from one church to another, and absolute ordinations (bestowals of office without community as source, milieu, or goal) are unequivocally condemned by the Council of Chalcedon. Despite this, under the influence of the imperial organization of an expanding church, and then of monasticism, absolute ordination in practice if not in theory attained a strong foothold.

11. *Summa theologiae* II–II, 1, 2, 2.

12. K. Rahner, "Intellectual Honesty and Christian Faith," *Theological Investigations* 7 (New York: Seabury, 1974), 67 f.

13. K. Rahner, "Meaning of Ecclesiastical Office," *Servants of the Lord* (New York: Herder and Herder, 1968), 21 ff.

14. K. Rahner, "Notes on the Lay Apostolate," *Theological Investigations* 2 (Baltimore: Helicon, 1963), 319–52. See "The Sacramental Basis for the Role of the Layman in the Church," *Theological Investigations* 8 (New York: Herder and Herder, 1971), 51–74; "The Position of Women in the New Situation in Which the Church Finds Herself," *Theological Investigations* 8, 75–93.

15. K. Rahner, *Das Dynamische in der Kirche* (Freiburg: Herder, 1958), 14–38.

16. K. Rahner, "The New Image of the Church," *Theological Investigations* 10 (New York: Herder and Herder, 1973), 11. "To the extent that humanity really accepts this absolute self-sharing of God offered in an eschatologically irrevocable way in Christ through his grace effecting from this sharing that acceptance and makes present historically in word of the confessing proclamation of this self-sharing and in sacramental cult this eschatological event, and in social unity, are human

beings church." *Handbuch der Pastoral Theologie* 1 (Freiburg: Herder, 1964), 119.

17. For texts on these themes see Ulrich Möbs, *Das kirchliche Amt bei Karl Rahner* (Paderborn: Schöningh, 1992), 87 ff. and 145 ff.

18. K. Rahner, *The Shape of the Church to Come* (New York: Seabury, 1974), 56.

19. Ibid., 57.

20. K. Rahner, "The Role of the Layman in the Church," *Theological Investigations* 8 (New York: Herder and Herder, 1971), 52.

21. Ibid., 53 f.

22. Ibid., 57, 72 f. An uncharacteristic avoidance of reality is the following: "In the secular sphere *layman* means one who cannot take part in the discussion, who has nothing to contribute, who is excluded from a specific area of life and responsibility. But when the term *layman* is used in the theological context it means the opposite of this." (Ibid., 72).

23. K. Rahner, *Das Amt in der Kirche* (Freiburg: Herder, 1966), 11.

24. K. Rahner, "On the Theology of Revolution," *Theological Studies* 14 (New York: Seabury, 1976), 324 f.

25. K. Rahner, *Das Amt in der Kirche*, 33.

26. K. Rahner, *Selbstvollzug der Kirche, Sämtliche Werke* 19 (Freiburg: Herder, 1995), 83.

27. K. Rahner, "Der theologische Ansatzpunkt für die Bestimmung des Wesens des Amtspriestertums," *Concilium* 5 (1969): 196.

28. K. Rahner, "Vatican II and the Diaconate," *Theological Investigations* 10 (New York: Herder and Herder, 1973), 227 ff.

29. K. Rahner, "Pastoral Ministries and Community Leadership," *Theological Investigations* 19 (New York: Crossroad, 1983), 80; Möbs has drawn together the observations of Rahner and other German theologians on the directors of parishes without presbyters (*Das kirchliche Amt bei Karl Rahner*, 218–34).

30. K. Rahner, *Theology of Pastoral Action* (New York: Herder and Herder, 1968), 26.

31. See Michael Skelley, *The Liturgy of the World: Karl Rahner's Theology of Worship* (Collegeville: Liturgical Press, 1991); J.T. Farmer, *Ministry in Community: Rahner's Vision of Ministry* (Grand Rapids: Eerdmans, 1993).

32. Y. Congar, "My Path-Findings in the Theology of Laity and Ministries," *The Jurist* 32 (1972): 178.

33. Ibid., 178, 181.

34. Offering an alternative from the preconciliar mentality is Hans Urs von Balthasar. With an ecclesiology avoiding difficult renewal by describing the church mainly as a mystery and by locating roles in the

church as pious imitations of New Testament figures, the laity is not permitted to leave its constraints for fear that the clerical state will be qualified. "It should not be forgotten, however, that the lives of the laity will always be directed toward goals proper to themselves and that any attempt to burden them with an ecclesial ministry...in imitation of the apostolate of those in the states of election will soon prove to be impossible not only because of the practical difficulties involved, but also because of the realistic boundaries that separate the lay state from the states of election. Lay persons are obliged to practice Christian love of God and neighbor as perfectly as possible....The popular attempts being made in France and elsewhere to remove the distinction between laity and clergy by a continual interchange of services, ministries, and even offices and functions...seem to me to be...unbiblical." Hans Urs von Balthasar, *The Christian State of Life* (*Der christliche Stand*, 1977) [San Francisco: Ignatius, 1983], 16, 383. This is not an ecclesiology or systematic theology but a spirituality, never escaping a Neoplatonic ethos and a Barthian sympathy; inevitably, freedom and growth, life beyond post-Baroque spiritualities, within a wider range of grace, sacrament, and ministry bring anxiety.

35. H. Denis, "La Théologie du presbyterat de Trente à Vatican II," *Les Prêtres* (Paris: Cerf, 1968), 193 f. "It is by being a local church that a community enacts a liturgical prayer....This (church) must verify in itself the essential aspects of church (convocation, institution, communion)....But if the church is realized to a high degree in liturgical action, it is nonetheless not reduced to it. The church is also mission, kerygma, teaching, service, political critique and action." Y. Congar, "Reflexions sur l'assemblé liturgique," *La Maison-Dieu* 115 (1973): 8 ff.

36. "The principal roles in the Christian celebration manifest the very structure of the church. The functions in the assembly have two sides: on the one hand, they are (liturgical) functions; on the other, they reveal that which the 'ecclesia' is, its structure." P. Gy, "Ordres et fonctions dans l'assemblé liturgique," *Bulletin du comité des études* 52 (1968): 185.

37. H. Legrand, "The Presidency of the Eucharist according to the Ancient Tradition," *Worship* 53 (1979): 430.

38. *Summa theologiae* II–II, 183, 2 (citing Rom 12:4).

5. MINISTERS IN THE CHURCH

1. Michael Himes, "Making Priesthood Possible: Who Does What and Why?" *Church* 5 (1989): 7.

2. See J. Hainz, "Vom 'Volk Gottes' zum 'Leib Christi,'" *Journal*

of Biblical Theology 7 (1992): 145–64; J. Roloff, *Die Kirche im Neuen Testament* (Göttingen: Vandenhoeck und Ruprecht, 1993); H. Merklein, *Entstehung und Gestalt des paulinischen Leib-Christi-Gedenkens* (Freiburg: Herder, 1985).

3. "Orders is...a potestative whole. The nature of this is to be fully in one, but in others by participation. So it is in this case: for the fullness of the sacrament is one order, the priesthood, but in the others there is a participation of order...and so all orders are one sacrament." *In 4 Sent.*, d. 24, q. 2, a. 1. quest 3; see W. Croce, "Die niederen Weihen und ihre hierarchische Wertung," *Zeitschrift für katholische Theologie* 70 (1948): 257 ff.

4. *Denzinger-Schönmetzer* 1776.

5. *Denzinger-Schönmetzer* 1765. "...esse hierarchiam, divina ordinatione institutam, quae constat ex episcopis, presbyteris et ministris." *Denzinger-Schönmetzer* 1776.

6. *Denzinger-Schönmetzer* 1767; see Hans Küng, *The Church*, 418 ff.

7. E. Schillebeeckx, "The Catholic Understanding of Office," *Theological Studies* 30 (1969): 569. Yves Congar asks: "What does the usage of the expression 'divine right' signify in terms of ministers: their existence? the distinction between clergy and laity? the distinction between pope and bishop? Does not history oblige us to envisage the idea, proposed by some, of a 'divine right' submitted to historicity, and so, in a sense, 'reformable'...." "Ministères et structuration de l'église," *La Maison-Dieu* 102 (1970): 8.

8. K. Rahner, "Open Questions in Dogma Considered by the Institutional Church as Definitively Answered," *Journal of Ecumenical Studies* 15 (1978): 215; see "Reflections on the Concept of 'Jus Divinum' in Catholic Thought," *Theological Investigations* 5 (Baltimore: Helicon, 1966), 233 ff.

9. *Apostolic Constitutions*, 8, 1, Ante-Nicene Fathers 8 (New York: Scribners, 1926): 480.

10. Alexandre Faivre, *The Emergence of the Laity in the Early Church* (Mahwah, NJ: Paulist, 1990), 15 ff.; see, on the relationship of laity to liturgy ("the people's work"), Anscar Chupungco, *Introduction to the Liturgy. Handbook for Liturgical Studies* 1 (Collegeville: Liturgical Press, 1997).

11. Faivre, "The Laity in the First Centuries," *Lumen Vitae* 42 (1987): 132; see Richard Seagraves, *Pascentes cum disciplina* (Fribourg: Editions universitaires, 1993), 16 ff.

12. Faivre, "The Laity in the First Centuries," 132 f.

13. Faivre, *The Emergence*, 73; on Cyprian apparently excluding bishops from clergy and including acolytes in the clergy, see Seagraves, 18.

14. Origen, *On Jeremiah* (11:3), *Patrologia Latina* 13, 369, 370. Origen, commenting on Romans 16:1 writes: "This passage shows with apostolic authority that women too were designated for the church's ministry. Paul is commending and greatly praising Phoebe who had been installed in this office in the church at Cenchreae....This passage shows two things equally: first, as we have said, there were female ministers; secondly it was expected that those who had been of so much help and who had by their good service gone so far as to merit apostolic praise would be taken into the ministry." *Commentarium in Epistola ad Romanos* 10, *Patrologia Graeca* 14, 1278. On Origen's ecclesiology, see H. Vogt, *Das Kirchenverständnis des Origenes* (Cologne: Bohlau, 1974), and J. Chenevert, *L'Église dans le commentaire d'Origène sur le Cantique des Cantiques* (Brussels: Desclée de Brouwer, 1969). Faivre carefully takes his reader through the second and third centuries, through the theologies of Justin, Tertullian, Clement, Origen, and Cyprian: chapters 3, 4, 5 of Faivre, *The Emergence*. Of Justin Martyr, a "layman," Faivre writes that he "never lays claim in his writings to any institutional recognition or to any ministry in an attempt to justify his authority....In his view, it would be unthinkable for any Christian not to accept that the individual grace he has received from God is destined to be offered to and shared among the whole of humankind...the whole church must be missionary" (Faivre, 29). According to Origen, "all the church is the 'body of Christ' where 'there are various members' who are ourselves. Sometimes there are exceptional charismatic powers, like 'prophecy,' which for Origen means a discernment according to grace and understanding which helps the church as a whole or the individual soul in touch with the Spirit." P. Messié et al, Origène, *Homélies sur les Juges* (Paris: Cerf, 1993), 33, 36.

15. A. Faivre, *The Emergence of the Laity*, 15 f., 21 f.; I. de la Potterie, "The Origin and Basic Meaning of the Word 'Lay,'" in *The Christian Lives by the Spirit* (New York: Alba House, 1971), 267 ff. For a survey of conciliar and postconciliar documents and theologies on this topic, see Melvin Michalski, *The Relationship between the Universal Priesthood of the Baptized and the Ministerial Priesthood of the Ordained in Vatican II and in Subsequent Thelogy* (Lewiston: Mellen, 1996). On the similar linguistic meaning in the late Roman and medieval periods see Y. Congar, "Clercs et laïcs au point de vue de la culture au moyen age: 'Laicus = sans lettres,'" in *Studia mediaevalia et mariologica* (Rome: Antonianum, 1971), 309 ff.; E. Schillebeeckx, "La definition typologique du laïc chrétien selon Vatican II," *L'Église de Vatican II* 3 (Paris: Cerf, 1966), 1013 ff. For a survey of the word and its theology (but conceived apart from the expansion of lay ministry) see Giovanni Magnani, "Does the So-Called Theology of the Laity Possess a Theological Status?" in R. Latourelle,

Vatican II. Assessment and Perspectives 1 (Mahwah, NJ: Paulist, 1988), 568–633; and for a lengthy history of laity and lay ministry see Kenan Osborne, *Ministry: Lay Ministry in the Catholic Church–Its History and Theology* (Mahwah, NJ: Paulist, 1993).

16. The reference of a Catholic encyclopedia at the end of the last century is significant, for when one looks up "layperson," one finds the direction, "See 'Clergy'" [*Laie: siehe Klerus*], *Kirchenlexikon* (Freiburg: Herder,1891), 7, 1323.

17. Y. Congar, "Laïc et Laïcat," *Dictionnaire de Spiritualité* 9 (Paris: Beauchesne, 1976), 98.

18. G. Magnani, "Does the So-Called Theology of the Laity Possess a Theological Status?" 577, 585; see P. Guilmot, *Fin d'une Église cléricale? Le débat en France de 1945 à nos jours* (Paris: Cerf, 1969).

19. Y. Congar, *Ministères et communion ecclésiale* (Paris: Cerf, 1971), 9, 17, 19. Congar is citing his own *Lay People in the Church* (Westminster: Newman, 1967), xvi.

20. G. Magnani, "Does the So-Called Theology of the Laity Possess a Theological Status?" 593–603; Schillebeeckx, "A New Type of Layman," *The Mission of the Church* (New York: Crossroad, 1973), 121. The Flemish Dominican then offers an analysis of conciliar texts on the laity in light of subsequent progress: "We find on the one hand texts which speak in a more positive way about the layman than the constitution on the church and others which fall behind....The whole of the Second Vatican Council may in fact be regarded as a declericalization of the Catholic Church.... We may certainly say that the council did not unquestioningly take as its point of departure the laicity of the people of God, while conceding that the Christian laity could not dispense with the leadership and guidance of the hierarchy. Most of the fathers of the council had unconsciously to overcome a great deal of inner resistance before they could give lay people their rightful place in the church. The situation was precisely the opposite in the early church." *The Mission of the Church*, 125, 127; see Elissa Rinere, "Conciliar and Canonical Applications of Ministry to the Laity," *The Jurist* 47 (1987): 205–10; *The Term "Ministry" as Applied to the Laity in the Documents of Vatican II, Postconciliar Documents of the Apostolic See, and the 1983 Code of Canon Law* (Washington, Catholic University of America Press, 1986).

21. Remi Parent, *A Church of the Baptized. Overcoming Tension between the Clergy and the Laity* (Mahwah, NJ: Paulist, 1989), 7; a valuable analysis of how the Vatican II decree on priests implies "clerical reform" is Christian Duquoc, "Clerical Reform," and Hermann Pottmeyer, "A New Phase in the Reception of Vatican II: Twenty Years of Interpretation of the Council," in G. Alberigo, *The Reception of Vati-*

can II (Washington: Catholic University of America, 1987), 114–33, 297–308.

22. Y. Congar, "Laïc et Laïcat," 79.

23. The question of whether isolated communities without any ecclesial access over a long time can summon up a leader, a presbyter, to lead the community, that is, in sacrament as well as in word and assembly is not the place to begin a theology of the ministry. In a sense, too liberal and too ecclesiastical directions give similar answers. The one speaks of laity celebrating the Eucharist, but the leader of the Eucharist is a designated, full-time minister whose traditional name is bishop or presbyter; the second alters parish life by having a man or woman who is not a presbyter be the leader of the community but who is seriously constrained from offering the Eucharist and other sacraments.

24. Obviously a discussion of "essential distinction" cannot refer to the realm of metaphysics or to the realm of the human species (The ordained cannot be a second kind of a human being, a separate species on earth!); nor can it refer to a serious distinction within the reign of God or in terms of baptismal grace of the Spirit. That the *ministries* of bishop and reader are extensively and seriously different and, so, essentially different, is certainly true.

25. When a theology of ministry begins with Jesus' preaching the universality of the reign of God and its replacement of some directions of human religion, placing the Holy Spirit as the source of ministerial office through baptism and charism, it is very difficult to find arguments why half of the human race, women, should be excluded from public roles of the church.

26. Paul VI, *Ministeria quaedam, Ad pascendum,* in *The Rites of the Catholic Church* (New York: Pueblo, 1976), 726–42.

27. D. Power, *Gifts That Differ: Lay Ministries Established and Unestablished* (New York: Pueblo, 1980), 31 f.

28. *Ad Pascendum, The Rites* , 728.

29. D. Power, *Gifts That Differ*, 51 ff.

30. Ibid., 16 ff.

31. B. Sesbouë, *N'Ayez Pas Peur!* (Paris: Desclée de Brouwer, 1996), 130.

6. SOURCES OF MINISTRY

1. On various Protestant and Catholic theories from Harnack to Schnackenburg regarding charism and office, see Ulrich Brockhaus, *Charisma und Amt* (Wuppertal: Brockhaus, 1972), 1–94.

2. Hans Küng, *The Church* (New York: Sheed and Ward, 1967), 188. Küng, showing an affinity with the German tradition of tension between charism and office, seems not to find permanence or ordinary structure in the Pauline charismatic ministry. He contrasts it with a Jerusalemic ministry of special appointment. He has let projected conflict between Semitic and Hellenic churches, between structured diversity and free charism, disrupt his correct instinct that charism grounds ministry. Küng reads back into *episkopos* and *presbyteros* the postmedieval ecclesiology that he fears. There is no reason to suppose that the Spirit of Jesus was shy in the Semitic churches. Antioch and Jerusalem seem also to be filled with invocations of the Spirit upon people destined to ministry (Acts 2: 17), and the absence of the word *charism* does not mean that the theology of Spirit fashioning ministry through charism was unknown.

3. Bernard Cooke, *Ministry in Word and Sacrament* (Grand Rapids: Eerdmans, 1976), 198.

4. B. Cooke, *Ministry in Word and Sacrament*, 43–55; 197–212. Heribert Mühlen looks at the structures of the early church from the dialectic of desacralization/pneumaticization, calling attention to the replacement of honor by personal identity (*Entsakralisierung* [Paderborn: Schöningh, 1971], 259 ff.).

5. Y. Congar, *L'Église de Saint Augustin*, 110, 124, 253 ff., 271 ff.

6. Thomas Merton, *Seeds of Contemplation* (New York: New Directions, 1949), 26.

7. See Leonel Mitchell, *Baptismal Anointing* (Notre Dame: University of Notre Dame Press, 1978), 172 f.; Albert Vanhoye, *Old Testament Priests and the New Priest according to the New Testament* (Petersham: St. Bede's Publications, 1980), 243 ff., 286.

8. The theology and liturgical practice in the new rite of initiation raises questions about the relation of baptism and confirmation toward adult ministry; cf. A. Kavanagh, *The Shape of Baptism: The Rite of Christian Initiation* (New York: Pueblo, 1978).

9. Reported in Max Johnson, "Back Home to the Font: Eight Implications of a Baptismal Spirituality," *Worship*, 71 (1997): 499.

10. A. Kavanagh, *The Shape of Baptism: The Rite of Christian Initiation*, 25; see J. Guillet, "Baptism and the Spirit," in *Baptism in the New Testament. A Symposium* (Helicon: Baltimore, 1964), 63. It is interesting

how the rich writings of the liturgical and pastoral movements in Europe prior to Vatican II do not reach as far as the ministry of the baptized but speak of Exodus and the people of God, and of the Body of Christ endowed with holiness and vague charisms (see the essays by J. Giblet, Y. B. Tremel, and M. E. Boismard in *Baptism in the New Testament*, 161 ff.).

11. A. Kavanagh, "Unfinished and Unbegun Revisited: The Rite of Christian Initiation of Adults," in Max Johnson, ed., *Living Water, Feeling Spirit: Readings in Christian Initiation* (Collegeville: Liturgical Press, 1995), 270.

12. A. Kavanagh, "Unfinished and Unbegun Revisited," 269.

13. *The Shape of Baptism: The Rite of Christian Initiation*, 163–70. "We agree with Congar that ministries encourage the assembly and expansion of the community, and we should argue that this is helped by a diversification of the ministry....These gifts of the Spirit, all the more because they are different, permit the community to be truly the Body of Christ of which each of its functions does not exhaust its being....Christ served in multiple ways his Father and people. The unity of the faith like that of the church is enlarged to the extent that the fullness of Christ is progressive, but never totally recognized by Christians and by the world." Denise Lamarche, *Le baptême, une initiation?* (Paris: Cerf, 1984), 243.

14. Showing some influence from Pseudo-Dionysius, for whom diversity flows from unity, Aquinas wrote: "For the priestly power itself flows from the episcopal power....As the church is one, so must the Christian people be one. Therefore, for the specific congregation of one church, one bishop is called. He is head of that church" (*Summa contra Gentiles* 4, c. 76).

15. In 1896, Leo XIII wrote that bishops were not to be regarded as simple vicars of the pope, thus preparing the termination by Vatican II of a reduction of worldwide churches and bishops to be branches and ambassadors of the papacy ("*Satis cognitum*," *Acta Sanctae Sedis* 28 [Rome: Ex typographia polyglotta, 1895–6], 718 ff.). "To the bishop is fully committed the pastoral office in its normal form. He cannot therefore consider himself to be the mere recipient and executor of commands received from higher quarters. He has an independent duty and responsibility...(and) must strive to recognize for himself the scope of his task and the right moment for acting....to discover solutions which are not the mere application of universal norms. Only in this way can his diocese and the fulfillment of his office contribute to the good of the 'whole body' of the Church, for this Church is not a homogenous mass but an organic structure which possesses a real variety of members."

Karl Rahner, "Episcopacy in the Teaching of Vatican II," *Theological Investigations* 6 (Baltimore: Helicon, 1974), 362 f.

16. Herbert Vorgrimler sums up: "What is new in the perspective of Vatican II is, above all, its dynamic structure: basing itself on the sending of Jesus Christ in the Holy Spirit and upon the idea that people are given a share in this sending, ecclesial ministry is understood as a share in the threefold ministry of Jesus Christ in the service of his people. The sacrament of orders sees the ordination of the bishop as the primary and encompassing case of ordination, but the mutual relationship of the three ordinations are not gone into...and, if priests are subordinated to the bishop, still the source of their priesthood is not the office of bishop but only Jesus Christ alone." *Sakramenten-theologie* (Düsseldorf: Patmos, 1987), 290 f.

17. Cf. K. Hruby, "La notion d'ordination dans la tradition juive," *La Maison-Dieu* #102 (1970): 32 ff.; E. Lohse, *Die Ordination im Spätjudentum und im Neuen Testament* (Göttingen: Evangelische Verlagsanstalt, 1951); E. Kilmartin, "Ordination in Early Christianity against a Jewish Background," *Studia Liturgica* 13 (1979): 42 ff.; Hermann von Lips, "Die Ordination auf alt-jüdischem Hintergrund," *Glaube-Gemeinde-Amt Zum Verständnis der Ordination in den Pastoralbriefen* (Göttingen: Vandenhoeck und Ruprecht, 1979), 223–31; Georg Kretschmar, "Die Ordination im frühen Christentum," *Freiburger Zeitschrift für Philosophie und Theologie* 22 (1975): 35–69.

18. See Greshake, 53–60.

19. Y. Congar, *Ministère et communion ecclésiale* (Paris: Cerf, 1971), 21. "The older ecclesiology looked at the church as the united fellowship of all the faithful and saw there the validity of the sacraments conditioned by this unity of fellowship. The active consent of the people was expressed in prayer and was an indispensable element in celebration." S. Tromp, cited in Congar, *Lay People in the Church* (Westminster: Newman, 1965), 219.

20. Karl Rahner, *The Church and the Sacraments* (Freiburg: Herder, 1963), 105 f.

21. "Ministères, ordinations, clergé et peuple dans les 'Constitutions Apostoliques,'" in *Ordination et ministères* (Rome: Edizioni Liturgiche, 1995), 209.

22. See the writings of Rahner on the diaconate.

23. C. Renoux, "Liturgical Ministers at Jerusalem in the Fourth and Fifth Centuries," *Roles in the Liturgical Assembly* (New York: Pueblo, 1981), 221–25.

24. See C. Vogel, "Chirotonie et Chirosthenie," *Irenikon* 45 (1972): 7 ff., 201 ff.

25. Not in Rome, but in some churches the deaconess received a solemn, ordaining laying on of hands; see R. Gryson, *The Ministry of Women in the Early Church* (Collegeville: Liturgical Press, 1976), 109 ff.

26. R. H. Connolly, *Didascalia Apostolorum* (Oxford: Clarendon Press, 1929), 88 f.; cf. E. Braniste, "L'assemblée liturgique décrite dans les 'Constitutions Apostoliques'..."; B. Botte, "Peuple chrétien et hierarchie dans la tradition apostolique de S. Hippolyte," *Assemblée liturgique* (Rome: Edizioni liturgiche, 1977), 79 ff., 93 ff.

27. B. Botte, *Assemblée liturgique*, 79 f. Elsewhere Botte writes: "The bishop and the priest have nothing in common with the Roman *sacerdos*...nor do they have much in common with the priest of the Old Testament....In spite of the typology, the Christian priesthood is of another order: it is charismatic and spiritual....The episcopate, the priesthood and the diaconate appear less as ritual functions in the ancient documents than as charisms aimed at the upbuilding of the Church." "Holy Orders in the Ordination Prayers," *The Sacrament of Holy Orders* (Collegeville: Liturgical Press, 1962), 22.

28. Botte, "Holy Orders...," 81. For a detailed analysis of the development of the clergy and the distinction between ministries in the third century see Faivre; P.-M. Gy observes the diversity of ministry shown in early ordination ceremonies as well as the shift from the evangelical to the pastoral after the third century. "Ancient Ordination Prayers," *Studia Liturgica* 13 (1979): 82, 85.

29. David Power addresses succinctly and sagaciously the issue of eucharistic leadership coming from the community in times of necessity, and the confusion about a "lay" or "nonordained" leader: "On those odd occasions, therefore, which even history seems to attestify, when someone who has not received the laying on of hands presides at the Eucharist, the principle of sacramental efficacy applies in the same way as in baptism. But it is important to add immediately, that as in the case of baptism so in the case of the Eucharist the proper minister is the leader or president of the community of faith. This is not an arbitrary fittingness but one that goes with the sacramental structure of the whole ecclesial mystery. Were the position, indeed, to become such that one who had not received the laying on of hands were to assume the regular presidency of the Eucharist it could be asked whether it is any longer a case of a 'nonordained' person so presiding. *Ordination* is a broader notion than that of laying on of hands and there may be other, if unusual, forms of appointment to the office of leader and so to the sacramental roles that go with this office." "Basis for Official Ministry in the Church," *The Jurist* 41 (1981): 335; see Rahner, "Pastoral Min-

istries and Community Leadership," *Theological Investigations* 19 (New York: Crossroad, 1983), 80.

7. THE SPIRITUALITY OF MINISTRY

1. Alexandre Faivre, *The Emergence of the Laity in the Early Church* (Mahwah, NJ: Paulist, 1990), 9.

2. Y. Congar, *Esquisse du mystère de l'Église* (Paris: Cerf, 1941), 35–41, and others cited in B. Sesbouë, *N'Ayez Pas Peur!* (Paris: Desclée de Brouwer, 1996), 148 f.

3. J. Donahue, "'The Foolishness of God.' New Testament Foundations for a Spirituality of the Priesthood," *Worship* 66 (1992): 529; see Abraham Malherbe, *Paul and the Thessalonians: The Philosophic Tradition of Pastoral Care* (Philadelphia: Fortress, 1987).

4. Michael Buckley, "Ecclesial Mysticism in Ignatius Loyola," *Theological Studies* 56 (1995): 462 f.

5. Donald Cozzens, "Servant of the Servants of God," in *The Spirituality of the Diocesan Priest* (Collegeville: Liturgical Press, 1996), 4; see the characteristics selected by James Provost in the same volume, 38 ff. A similar work for religious is Paul J. Philibert, ed., *Living in the Meantime. Concerning the Transformation of Religious Life* (Mahwah, NJ: Paulist, 1994); for a pastoral theology of ministry that is also a spirituality, see James and Evelyn Whitehead, *Method in Ministry. Theological Reflection and Christian Ministry* (Kansas City: Sheed and Ward, 1995); see also valuable insights in William D. Perri, *A Radical Challenge for the Priesthood Today: From Trial to Transformation* (Mystic: Twenty-Third Publications, 1996).

6. Donald Cozzens, "Tenders of the Word," *The Spirituality of the Diocesan Priest*, 55.

7. Bishop Kenneth Untener, "Using the Wrong Measure?" *The Spirituality of the Diocesan Priest*, 25.

8. There are today what one might call imitation spiritualities. Although they have been recently founded, they do not indicate new directions for religious life or spirituality. They are shallow imitations of older traditions; ignorant of tradition and theology, they emerge as elitist groups bound together by the cult of the extraordinary. Upon close examination, we find that they characteristically lack both a spirituality grounded in the past and the capability to address the present. Their presence, which comes and goes in a few decades, does not indicate new directions for spirituality or ministry but is an avoidance of both.

9. R. McBrien, "The Ecclesiology of the Local Church," *Thought* 66 (1991): 365.

10. Ibid., 366.

11. R. McBrien, *Ministry* (San Francisco: Harper and Row, 1987), 62.

12. R. Gaillardetz, "In Service of Communion: A Trinitarian Foundation for Christian Ministry," *Worship* 67 (1993): 433; a rich collection of essays on spirituality in different kinds of ministries and different types of communities is Robert J. Wicks, ed., *Handbook of Spirituality for Ministers* (Mahwah, NJ: Paulist, 1995).

13. See T. O'Meara, "Spirituality," and "Grace in Life and Destiny," *Thomas Aquinas Theologian* (Notre Dame: University of Notre Dame Press, 1997), 80–81, 211–18.

14. Hauser, *L'Église*, 171.

15. Augustine, *De Libero Arbitrio* 1, xi, 22, in Aurelii Augustini *Opera, Corpus Christianorum, Series Latina* 29 (Turnhout: Brepols, 1970), 226.

16. St. Augustine, *On the Gospel of St. John, Nicene and Post-Nicene Fathers* 7, P. Schaff, ed., (Grand Rapids: Eerdmans, 1956), 257. See *Commentary on Matthew* (16:8), in Origen's *Werke, Die griechischen christlichen Schriftsteller* 40 (Leipzig: Hinrichs, 1899), 493.

17. *Summa theologiae* III, 21, 4.

18. *Summa theologiae* II–II, 183, 2, 3; I–II, 105.

19. See William Meissner, *The Kingdom Come. Psychoanalytic Perspectives on the Messiah and the Millennium* (Kansas City: Sheed and Ward, 1995).

20. There developed a first liturgical ceremony of entrance on the ladder of ecclesiastical orders: tonsure placed a man in the clerical state, wherein he had new obligations and rights without having any ministry. A cleric did not ipso facto act significantly for the Spirit or church, but nevertheless he existed in a novel form of being. Being had been separated from doing, manner of life from ministry. The liturgical and ecclesial reforms of Vatican II recognized this as superfluous and dubious. See D. Miller, "Lifestyle and Religious Commitment," *Religious Education* 76 (1981): 49 ff. Clothes are connected to modes of life (cf. Martha Bringemeier, *Priester- und Gelehrtenkleidung* [Münster: Rheinische-Westfälische Zeitschrift für Volkskunde, 1974]), and excessive concern with ritual or antique clothes indicates an avoidance of ministerial effort and a vocational misdirection, confusing church work with performance (see J. - C. Noonan, Jr., *The Church Visible. The Ceremonial Life and Protocol of the Roman Catholic Church* [New York: Amaranth, 1996]).

21. K. Rahner, "Priestly Existence," *Theological Investigations* 3 (Baltimore: Helicon, 1963), 257 ff.

CONCLUSION

1. See the report of the congress on the restoration of the diaconate for women printed in *Herder-Korrespondenz* 51 (1997): 248 ff.

2. K. Schatz, *Papal Primacy. From Its Origins to the Present* (Collegeville: Liturgical Press, 1996), 169 f.

INDEX OF NAMES

Albert of Lauingen (Albertus
    Magnus), 107
Ambrose, 81, 82
Anabaptists, 169
Aristotle (Aristotelian),
    151, 200
Augustine, 99, 152, 243

Balthasar, Hans Urs von, 286
Bañez, Domingo, 203
Baroque, 114–23, 233, 234,
    239, 281
Bellarmine, Robert, 140
Bernanos, Georges, 131
Bernard of Clairvaux, 101,
    103, 104
Botte, Bernard, 221, 294
Brown, Raymond, 273

Cajetan, Thomas de Vio,
    Cardinal, 267
Calvin, John (Calvinism),
    111–14, 169, 265
Campenhausen, Hans
    Freiherr von, 202
Catherine of Siena, 9, 81, 234
Catholic Action, 146, 282
Charles de Condren, 117

Claudel, Paul, 128
Clement of Alexandria, 70, 92,
    95, 174
Clement of Rome, 174
Columcille, 81
Conant, Kenneth J., 100
Congar, Yves, 10, 22, 28, 87,
    104, 155, 163, 180, 181,
    218, 231, 264, 266, 267,
    277–83, 286, 287, 293
Constantine, 175
Cooke, Bernard, 204
Counter-Reformation, The,
    114–23
Cozzens, Donald, 235
Cyprian, 93–96, 120, 175, 283

Dagens, Claude, 34
Dante Alighieri, 108
Day, Dorothy, 9, 252
Delorme, Jean, 77
Denis, Henri, 134
Diekmann, Godfrey, 210
Dominic Guzman (the Domini-
    cans), 104, 109, 110, 126, 252
Donahue, John, 233
Donovan, Daniel, 268
du Bourguet, Pierre, 90, 96

Emmeram, 101
Ephrem the Syrian, 82, 140
Eudes, Jean, 133
Eusebius, 81

Fahey, Michael, 266, 276
Faivre, Alexandre, 174, 177, 181
Fichte, Johann Gottlieb, 124
Francis de Sales, 115
Francis of Assisi (Franciscans), 104, 109, 110, 203
Francis Xavier, 81, 101, 115
Friedrich, Caspar David, 124

Gaillardetz, Richard, 238, 239
Gnilka, J., 273
Goppelt, Leonhard, 48
Görres, Joseph, 125
Gregory the Great, 99
Gregory VII, 99
Gregory XVI, 127
Guéranger, Prosper, 126
Gy, Pierre, 286, 294

Harnack, Adolf von, 202
Hauser, Hermann, 67, 242, 269
Heidegger, Martin, 43
Hermann, Ingo, 50
Hesburgh, Theodore, 282
Himes, Michael, 168
Hippolytus, 81, 92, 175, 221

Ignatius of Antioch, 81, 221
Ignatius Loyola (Jesuits), 30, 115, 121–23, 134, 234, 252
Innocent III, 81, 203

Jeanne Françoise de Chantal, 115
Jocists, 146
Justin Martyr, 44, 70, 91, 92, 95
Justinian, 175

Kandinsky, Wassily, 43
Kavanagh, Aidan, 51, 211
Kilian, 101
Klee, Paul, 43
Komonchak, Joseph, 261
Küng, Hans, 84, 204, 291

Lacordaire, Henri Dominique, 126
LaFont, Guy, 19, 270
Legrand, Hervé, 165, 264, 276, 283
Leo XIII, 130, 292
Lewis, C. S., 86
Louis de Montfort, 235
Luther, Martin, 111–14, 169

Magnani, Giovanni, 289
Maritain, Jacques, 131
Marmion, Columba, 235
Martin of Tours, 99
Mauriac, François, 131
McBrien, Richard, 16, 237, 238
McGinnis, Michael, 263
Meister Eckhart, 234, 267
Merton, Thomas, 131, 208
Metzger, Marchel, 219
Meyendorff, John, 278
Michalski, Melvin, 288
Möhler, Johann Adam, 125
Montalembert, Charles, 125

97350

Montanism, 203

Mühlen, Heribert, 291

Neri, Philip, 30

Nominalism, 248–49

Olier, Jean Jacques, 117

Origen, 93, 99, 175, 288

Osborne, Kenan, 289

Otto, Rudolf, 43

Paris, Gérard, 265

Patrick, Apostle of Ireland, 120

Paul VI, 33, 168, 192, 193

Paulinus of Nola, 99

Pierre de Berulle, 115, 117, 133

Pius IX, 126, 127

Pius XII, 130, 282

Pottmeyer, Hermann, 265

Power, David, 193, 194, 294

Pseudo-Dionysius, 99, 104–7, 112, 278–80

Rahner, Karl, 2, 145, 158–63, 170, 219, 239, 258, 263, 284, 285, 294

Reformation, Protestant, 111–14, 118, 120, 169, 170, 177, 215

Schatz, Klaus, 262

Schelling, Friedrich, 124

Schillebeeckx, Edward, 87, 163, 170, 181, 265, 270, 276, 289

Schlegel, Friedrich, 124

Semmelroth, Otto, 163

Sesbouë, Bernard, 195

Simon Magus, 243

Staudenmaier, Franz Anton, 125

Tauler, Johannes, 267

Teilhard de Chardin, Pierre, 81

Teresa of Avila, 30, 203

Tertullian, 92, 95, 152, 175

Thomas Aquinas, 2, 81, 107–11, 151, 154, 168, 169, 203, 205, 238–43, 248, 274, 279–81, 287, 292

Thomas of Ireland, 278

Thomas More, 101

Tillard, Jean-Pierre, 65

Tillich, Paul, 43

Trent, Council of, 169, 170

Untener, Kenneth, 235

Vatican I (Council), 126–29, 134

Vatican II (Council), 7, 8, 14–22, 87, 88, 129–35, 164, 172, 181, 183, 195, 210, 262

Vianney, Jean Baptiste Marie (Curé of Ars), 127–29

Zwinglians, 169